ORGANIZATIONAL BEHAVIOR
AND
MANAGEMENT

BY **Roxanne Helm-Stevens, Daniel Kipley,** AND **Ronald Jewe**

Azusa Pacific University

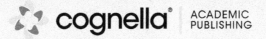

cognella® ACADEMIC PUBLISHING

Bassim Hamadeh, CEO and Publisher
Kassie Graves, Director of Acquisitions
Jamie Giganti, Senior Managing Editor
Jess Estrella, Senior Graphic Designer
Marissa Applegate, Senior Field Acquisitions Editor
Gem Rabanera, Project Editor
Elizabeth Rowe, Licensing Coordinator
Allie Kiekhofer, Associate Editor

Cover image copyright © Depositphotos/yanlev.

Printed in the United States of America

ISBN: 978-1-63189-847-1 (pbk) / 978-1-63189-848-8 (br)

 cognella® ACADEMIC PUBLISHING

CONTENTS *IN BRIEF*

SECTION 4:
MANAGING AND LEADING ORGANIZATIONAL PROCESSES 169

CONTENTS *EXTENDED*

ACKNOWLEDGMENTS

We would like to express our gratitude to the many people who saw us through the writing of this book; to all those who provided support, talked things over, read, wrote, and offered comments. In particular, we would like to thank Olivia Bartlett and Cassandra Threadgill, who provided invaluable support in the editing, proofreading, and design of this text.

INTRODUCTION TO ORGANIZATIONAL BEHAVIOR

1

INTRODUCTION TO ORGANIZATIONAL BEHAVIOR

CHAPTER LEARNING OBJECTIVES

After reading this chapter, you should have a good understanding of
- the definition of organizational behavior and why it influences the organization's effectiveness;
- the importance of studying organizational behavior and how this understanding will help you to respond to the events that take place at work;
- the three levels on which organizational behavior is examined;
- how the external environment has an influence on, and creates continual changes for, organizations; and
- the four main forces in the environment that pose the greatest threats and opportunities for organizations today.

"Effective leadership is putting first things first. Effective management is discipline, carrying it out."

- STEPHEN COVEY

Why do people behave in a certain way in an organizational environment? What factors affect job performance? How can managers make employees more committed to their job? How can employees interact with one another to increase organizational effectiveness? What style of leadership makes an effective manager? For decades individuals and organizations have studied the answers to these questions, hoping to find ways of increasing organizational performance.

Effectively managing the human resources of an organization is one of the most crucial responsibilities of a manager. Managers must consider human behavior, actions, and decisions, and how they relate to the organizational processes that are required to manage effectively. It is also vital to understand the effect of human behavior in the organizational setting on managerial decision making, and how understanding human behavior in an organizational setting is a fundamental requirement for all those who aspire to hold a management position. In this chapter, we introduce the meaning of organizational behavior and then explore its development, from its simple beginnings through its evolution to its current form—a complex and multidisciplinary field of study.

Figure 1.1. The Individual-Organizational Interface

WHAT IS ORGANIZATIONAL BEHAVIOR?

Organizational behavior (OB) is not the study of how organizations behave, but rather the study of individual behavior within an organizational setting. This includes the study of how individuals behave alone, as well as how individuals behave in groups.

The field of organizational behavior aims to gain a greater understanding of those factors that influence individual and group performance in an organizational setting, so that individuals and the groups and organizations to which they belong may become more efficient and effective.

In many ways, organizational behavior synthesizes several other fields of study. Perhaps the greatest contribution to organizational behavior comes from the field of organizational psychology. Organizational psychologists specifically study the behavior of people in organizational settings in order to better understand individual differences and motivation. Figure 1.1 illustrates the three levels of organizational behavior and their correlation. To fully understand organizational behavior, good managers should have knowledge of all three areas.

In order to fully understand the importance of studying organizational behavior, we must first define what an organization is. An **organization** is a collection of people who work together and coordinate their activities to meet a need or to pursue a common goal (or goals). Individual goals can be earning money, helping to promote a worthy cause, achieving a certain level of personal power, or enjoying a fulfilling work experience. But an organization also has goals, such as providing goods and services that customers want; making a profit for stockholders, managers, and employees; and being socially responsible and aware of its natural environment. A university, for example, is created to achieve the goal of providing a quality, affordable education for its students, while providing staff and faculty a secure and rewarding career.

WHAT IS THE IMPORTANCE OF ORGANIZATIONAL BEHAVIOR?

The importance of organizational behavior lies in understanding how individuals, groups, and organizational structures interact and affect one another. Organizational behavior studies examine communication patterns between individuals and groups, as well as the structure and culture of organizations. The study of organizational behavior can greatly clarify the factors that affect how managers manage, and such insights may generate solution-oriented policies and organizational change, causing leaders to implement rewards systems, new communication methods, or innovative management approaches.

Studying the ways that individuals and groups interact is often critical for handling challenges within an organization. Due to fear of change, employees may be reluctant to embrace a new piece of technology or a new method, thereby interfering with an organization's advancement efforts. The importance of organizational behavior in such a situation is highlighted by an effort to understand and effectively manage fear of change across the organization. Clearly an understanding of organizational behavior can play a major role in managerial work. However, to use the knowledge provided by this field most effectively, managers must understand the foundations of this field. To do so we must first examine the historical foundations.

EARLY CONTRIBUTORS TO THE MANAGEMENT FIELD

One of the first approaches to the study of management surfaced during the early 1900s. The **scientific management** era arose because of the need to increase productivity and efficiency. The emphasis then was on trying to find the best way to get the most work done by examining how the work process was actually accomplished. To do this, theorists studied the basic steps and motions, and determined the most efficient ways of doing them. Once the job was defined, workers could then be trained to do the job, and supervisors could be trained to best support and encourage workers to perform to the best of their abilities. Scientific management is based on four core principles:

1. Develop a "science" for each job that includes rules on motion, standard work tools, and proper work conditions.
2. Hire workers with the right skills and abilities for the job.
3. Train and motivate workers to do their jobs according to the science.
4. Support workers by planning and assisting their work using the job science.

Scientific management owes its roots to several major contributors, including Frederick Taylor, Henry Gantt, and Frank and Lillian Gilbreth.

Frederick Taylor is often called the "father of scientific management." Taylor believed that organizations should study tasks and then develop precise procedures to complete the tasks. This belief stemmed from his observations of how workers did their jobs, mostly in their own, seemingly haphazard way, and with little or no consistent supervision. As an example, in 1898, Taylor calculated how much iron from rail cars Bethlehem Steel plant workers could be unloading if they were using the correct movements, tools, and steps. The result was an amazing 47.5 tons per day, instead of the mere 12.5 tons each worker had been averaging. In addition, by redesigning the shovels the workers used, Taylor was able to increase efficiency and therefore decrease the number of people shoveling from 500 to 140. In 1909, Taylor published *The Principles of Scientific Management*, wherein he proposed that, by optimizing and simplifying workers' tasks, productivity would increase. Lastly, he developed an incentive system that paid workers more money for meeting the new standard. Productivity at Bethlehem Steel shot up overnight. As a result, many theorists followed Taylor's philosophy when developing their own principles of management. Today, companies like McDonald's still use some of the basic concepts that were introduced during the scientific management era in their efforts to increase efficiency.

The work of Frank and Lillian Gilbreth is often associated with that of Frederick Taylor. However, there were substantial philosophical differences between them. The stopwatch was the symbol of Taylorism—Taylor's primary concern was to reduce process times. The Gilbreth's primary concern was to increase the efficiency of the process by reducing the motions involved. The Gilbreths saw their approach as more interested and invested in a worker's welfare than Taylor's; the workers themselves often perceived Taylor's approach as primarily focused on increasing profit.

Frank and Lillian Gilbreth were a pioneering team in work and motion studies. In Frank's early career as an apprentice bricklayer, he was interested in standardization and method study. He watched bricklayers and saw that some workers were slow and inefficient, while others were very productive. He discovered that each bricklayer used a different set of motions to lay bricks. From his observations, Frank isolated the basic movements necessary to do the job and eliminated unnecessary motions. Workers using these movements raised their output from 1,000 to 2,700 bricks per day. This was the first **motion study** designed to isolate the best possible method of performing a given job. As a result, certain fields of work, such as medicine, have greatly improved in efficiency.

The **classical organizational** approach is unlike the scientific management approach, as it focuses on the total organization and the importance of the development of managerial principles, versus the productivity and study of the work methods of individuals. The classical organizational approach focuses on how a large number of workers and managers could be organized most effectively into an overall structure.

Contributors to this school of thought include Henri Fayol and Max Weber. These theorists studied the flow of information within an organization and emphasized the importance of understanding how an organization operated.

Henri Fayol is generally regarded as the pioneer of the classical administrative theory. Fayol was a French mining engineer who developed 14 principles of management based on his management experiences. Fayol's 14 principles cover a broad range of topics, but three common themes resonate throughout: organizational efficiency, how to manage people, and the use of appropriate managerial action. Principles such as planning, organizing, commanding, coordinating, and controlling are still the elements by which we study, analyze, and affect the management process today. The general principles provide today's managers with guidelines on how to supervise and manage (see Box 1.1).

BOX 1.1: FAYOL'S 14 PRINCIPLES OF MANAGEMENT

1. Division of work: Division of work and specialization produces more and better work with the same effort.
2. Authority and responsibility: Authority is the right to give orders and the power to exact obedience. A manager has official authority because of her position, as well as personal authority based on individual personality, intelligence, and experience. Authority creates responsibility.
3. Discipline: Obedience and respect within an organization are absolutely essential. Good discipline requires managers to apply sanctions whenever violation become apparent.
4. Unity of command: An employee should receive orders from only one superior.
5. Unity of direction: Organizational activities must have one central authority and one plan of action.
6. Subordination of individual interest to general interest: The interests of one employee or group of employees are subordinate to the interests and goals of the organization.
7. Remuneration of personnel: Salaries—the price of services rendered by employees—should be fair and provide satisfaction both to the employee and employer.
8. Centralization: The objective of centralization is the best utilization of personnel. The degree of centralization varies according to the dynamics of each organization.
9. Scalar chain: A chain of authority exists from the highest organizational authority to the lowest ranks.
10. Order: Organizational order for materials and personnel. The right materials and the right employees are necessary for each organizational function and activity.
11. Equity: In organizations, equity is a combination of kindliness and justice. Both equity and equality of treatment should be considered when dealing with employees.
12. Stability of tenure of personnel: To attain the maximum productivity of personnel, a stable work force is needed.
13. Initiative: Thinking out a plan and ensuring its success. Zeal, energy, and initiative are desired at all levels of the organizational ladder.
14. Esprit de corps: Teamwork or team spirit. Work teams and extensive face-to-face verbal communication encourages teamwork.

Max Weber is considered to be the father of **bureaucratic management**. Weber believed that organizations should be managed impersonally and that they should follow a formal organizational structure wherein specific rules are followed. This non-personal, objective form of organization was called a **bureaucracy**.

Weber believed that all bureaucracies have the following characteristics:

- A well-defined hierarchy: All positions within a bureaucracy are structured in a way that permits the higher positions to supervise and control the lower positions. This clear chain of command facilitates control and order throughout the organization.
- Division of labor and specialization: All responsibilities in an organization are specialized so that each employee has the necessary expertise to do a particular task.
- Rules and regulations: Standard operating procedures governing all organizational activities to provide certainty and facilitate coordination.
- Impersonal relationships between managers and employees: Managers maintain an impersonal relationship with employees so that favoritism and personal prejudice do not influence decisions.
- Competence: The basis for all decisions made in hiring, job assignments, and promotions. This fosters ability and merit as the primary characteristics of a bureaucratic organization.
- Records: Maintaining complete files regarding all of an organization's activities.

ORIGINS OF ORGANIZATIONAL BEHAVIOR

Both the scientific management and the classical organizational theory focused on efficiency, standardization, and rationality. The roles of the individuals and groups within the organization were either largely ignored, or given only a modicum of attention. However, a few theorists recognized the importance of individuals and the social process in organizations.

Robert Owens, a British industrialist, strove to better conditions for industrial workers. He improved working conditions, increased the minimum age for hiring children, introduced meals for employees, and shortened the workday.

Mary Parker Follett stressed the interactions of management with workers and the importance of an organization establishing common goals for its employees. She also stressed the importance and value of allowing employees to participate in the decision-making process—a concept quite ahead of its time. Follett looked at management and leadership holistically, foreshadowing today's modern systems approaches. Follett defined a leader as someone who sees the whole rather than the particular and was one of the first to integrate the idea of organizational conflict into management theory. Due to her pioneering work on organizational conflict, she is considered to be the "mother of conflict resolution." Much of what managers do today is based on the fundamentals that Follett established more than 80 years ago.

Unfortunately, both Follett and Owen's approaches to management–employee interaction were not widely accepted by practicing managers. Not until the mid-1930s did management's perception of the relationship between the individual and the workplace change significantly, largely due to a series of classical research studies known as the Hawthorne studies.

THE HAWTHORNE EFFECT

The Hawthorne Effect, also known as the observer effect, is a reactivity to being observed; individuals modify or change their behavior in response to being watched. The **Hawthorne studies** (1927) were a series of experiments that rigorously applied classical management theory only to reveal its shortcomings. The Hawthorne experiments consisted of two studies conducted at the Hawthorne Works of the Western Electric Company in Chicago from 1924 to 1932. The first study was conducted by a group of engineers seeking to determine the relationship of lighting levels to worker productivity.

What Elton Mayo found, however, was that work satisfaction depended to a large extent on the informal social pattern of the work group. Where norms of cooperation and higher output were established because of a feeling of importance, physical conditions or financial incentives had little motivational value. Mayo concluded that people naturally form work groups that can be used by management to benefit the organization. In short, he concluded that people's work performance is dependent on both social issues and job content.

The Bank Wiring Observation Room Experiment (1931–1932) was a major experiment conducted by Mayo and F. J. Roethlisberger, which focused on whether piecework incentives would increase productivity. Mayo and Roethlisberger supervised a group of nine women in a bank wiring room, giving the women special privileges such as the right to leave their workstations without permission, take rest periods, enjoy free lunches, and have variations in pay levels. Scientific management would have predicted that the women would work as hard as possible to maximize personal income. The researchers discovered that the group as a whole established an acceptable level of output for its members. Those individuals who failed to meet this level were dubbed "chiselers" and those who exceeded it by too much were branded "rate-busters." Hence, if a worker wanted to be accepted by the group, they could not produce too much or too little. The researchers also discovered that as a worker approached the "acceptable level" of daily output, their efforts decreased to prevent overproduction.

Mayo and Roethlisberger concluded that human relations and the social needs of workers are crucial aspects of business management. This principle of human motivation helped revolutionize theories and practices of management.

THE HUMAN RELATIONS MOVEMENT

The **Human Relations Movement** refers to the researchers of organizational development who studied the interactions of people in organizations. The ultimate objective of the approach is to enhance organizational success by building appropriate relationships with people. When management is able to stimulate high productivity and worker commitment to the organization and its goals, human relations are said to be effective. The ability of a manager to work with people in a way that enhances organizational success is called **human relations skills**.

Abraham Maslow, a practicing psychologist, developed one of the most widely recognized **need theories**. A need is defined as a physiological or psychological deficiency that a person wants to satisfy. His theory of human needs has three assumptions:

1. Human needs are never completely satisfied.
2. Human behavior is purposeful and is motivated by the need for satisfaction.
3. Needs can be classified according to a hierarchical structure of importance, from the lowest to highest.

Maslow broke down the needs hierarchy into five specific areas, from lowest to highest:

1. **Physiological needs**: Most basic of all human needs are in this category, such as food, water, and physical well-being. After the need is satisfied, however, it is no longer is a motivator.
2. **Safety needs**: These needs include basic security, stability, protection, and freedom from fear. A normal state exists for an individual to have all these needs generally satisfied. Otherwise, they become primary motivators.

3. **Social needs**: After the physical and safety needs are satisfied and are no longer motivators, the need for belonging, affection, and love emerges as a primary motivator.
4. **Esteem needs**: This is the first of the higher-order needs. An individual has the need for esteem in the eyes of others; need for respect, prestige, recognition, and self-esteem; and a personal sense of competence and mastery.
5. **Self-actualization needs**: This is the highest level of needs, the need for self-fulfillment, to grow and use abilities to their fullest and most creative extent.

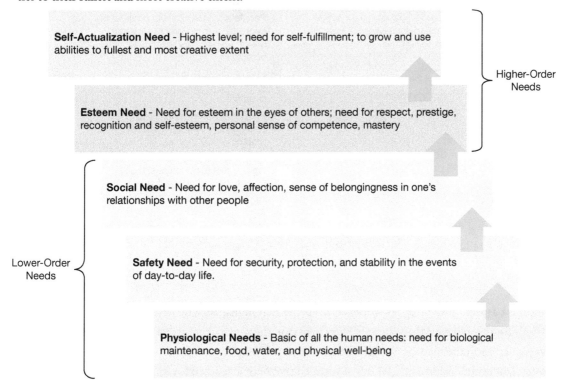

Figure 1.2. Maslow's Hierarchy of Human Needs

Maslow's hierarchy of needs theory helped managers better understand people's needs and help find ways to satisfy them through their work. Maslow's Hierarchy of Human Needs is illustrated in Figure 1.2.

Another prominent management theorist is **Douglas McGregor**. He was heavily influenced by both the Hawthorne studies and Maslow, and believed that two basic kinds of managers exist.

One type, the **Theory X manager,** has a negative view of employees and assumes that they generally dislike work, lack ambition, act irresponsibly, resist change, and are untrustworthy and incapable of assuming responsibility. The second type is the **Theory Y manager.** This group of managers assumes that employees are trustworthy and capable of assuming responsibility, and also have high levels of motivation, creativity, and are willing to work (Figure 1.3).

Theory X Assumptions	Theory Y Assumptions
• People do not like work and try to avoid it. • People do not like work, so managers have to control, direct, coerce, and threaten employees to work toward organizational goals. • People prefer to be directed, to avoid responsibility, to want security, they have little ambition	• People do not naturally dislike work; work is a natural part of their lives. • People are internally motivated to reach objectives to which they are committed. • People are committed to goals to the degree that they receive personal rewards when they reach their objectives. • People will seek and accept responsibility under favorable conditions. • People have the capacity to be innovative in solving organizational problems. • People are bright, but under most organizational conditions, their potentials are underutilized.

Figure 1.3. McGregor's Theory X and Theory Y Assumptions

An important aspect of McGregor's work was his belief that managers who hold either set of assumptions can create self-fulfilling prophecies; that, through their behavior, these managers create situations where subordinates act in ways that confirm the manager's original expectation.

The research of both Maslow and McGregor revealed that people worked for inner satisfaction and not materialistic reward, thus helping modern managers better understand the human component in organizations and how to appropriately work with it to enhance organizational success.

Additionally, a **Theory Z** proposed by Dr. William Ouchi, who disliked Theory X and Theory Y, focuses on long-term employment, job security, informal control, and the happiness and overall well-being of employees.

Ouchi argued that the following principles were key to business management success:

1. Strong company philosophy and culture: Employees need to believe in the work they're doing.
2. Long-term staff development and employment: When employment is long-term, programs for development are in place, and promotion is steady and measured, loyalty from team members will grow.
3. Consensus in decisions: Employees will be encouraged and expected to take part in important organizational decisions.
4. Generalist employees: Because employees will have that greater responsibility in making decisions, they should be "generalists" who try to understand as much as they can within the company. However, employees are still expected to have specialized responsibilities relevant to their position.
5. Concern for the happiness and well-being of workers: Measures and programs are put in place to help foster happiness and well-being.
6. Informal control with formalized measures: Employees are empowered to perform tasks the way they see fit, though there are still formalized measures in place to assess work quality and performance.

7. Individual responsibility: The organization recognizes the contributions of individuals within the context of the team as a whole.

In this kind of environment, people are treated as human beings and both organizational members and the organization itself are given an opportunity to develop to their fullest potential when there is an attempt to make work exciting and challenging.

RECENT ADVANCES IN MANAGEMENT SCIENCE

The **management science approach**, or operations research approach, was first developed during World War II to find solutions to warfare issues, such as which gun sight would best stop German attacks on the British mainland. The management science approach was also known at the quantitative approach because it used mathematical models to solve problems by analyzing a mix of variables, constraints, and costs to enable management to make optimal decisions. The management science approach combines rational thought with intuitive insight to resolve management concerns, such as cost, production, and service levels.

Management science is primarily concerned with exploring how a business can manage itself with the aim of maximizing productivity. Through adopting a system that allows integration of scientific thought, the managers and owners solve or prevent the range of problems and issues arising from managerial weaknesses, which can be one of the primary reasons that small firms are viewed as marginal or unprofitable businesses. The core function of the management science approach is to compare possible outcomes, and it dictates that scientists do the following:

1. Systematically observe the system behavior that must be explained to solve the problem.
2. Use these specific observations to construct a generalized model that is consistent with the specific observations, and from which consequences of changing the system can be predicted.
3. Use the model to determine how the system will behave under conditions that have not been observed but could be observed if the changes were made.
4. Test the model by performing an experiment on the actual system to see whether the effects of changes predicted using the model actually occur when the changes are made.

In short, a problem is encountered, it is systematically analyzed, an appropriate mathematical model is developed, computations are applied, and an optimal solution is identified. Consider the following two examples of the management science approach.

- An oil exploration company is concerned about future oil reserves in various parts of the world. *Quantitative solution*: Mathematical forecasting helps make future projections for reserve sizes and depletion rates that are useful in the planning process.
- A manufacturer wants to maximize profits for producing four different products on four different machines, each of which can be used for different periods of times and at different costs. *Quantitative solution*: Linear programming is used to determine how best to allocate production among different machines to maximize profits.

APPLICATION OF MANAGEMENT SCIENCE TODAY

Today, small-business owners and managers can use the management science approach to design specific measures that identify and evaluate the effectiveness of certain processes or decisions. For example, they can develop basic computer applications that can help predict and analyze optimal inventory levels, considering both the demand and costs. Managers use the techniques and tools of this quantitative approach to management to plan, organize, lead, and control operations within the workplace. For the company, the approach can result in increased production, industrial peace, and benefits of specialization.

THE CONTINGENCY APPROACH

The **contingency approach** to management can be summarized as an "it all depends" approach. In other words, the appropriate management action and approach depends on, or is contingent upon, a given set of circumstances. This approach emphasizes the "if-then" scenarios. Managers with a contingency view use a flexible approach, draw on a variety of theories and experiences, and evaluate many options as they solve problems.

Contingency management recognizes that there is no one best way to manage. In the contingency perspective, managers are faced with the task of determining which managerial approach is likely to be most effective in a given situation. For example, the approach used to manage a group of new student employees working in the university cafeteria would be very different from the approach used to manage a medical research team trying to find a cure for a disease. The main challenges in using the contingency approach are

1. perceiving organizational situations, as they actually exist;
2. choosing the management tactics best suited to those situations; and
3. competently implementing those tactics.

Contingency thinking avoids the classical "one best way" arguments and recognizes the need to understand situational differences and respond appropriately to them. It does not apply certain management principles to any situation. Contingency theory is recognition of the extreme importance of individual manager performance in any given situation; they must consider the realities of the specific situation before taking the appropriate action.

THE SYSTEMS APPROACH

The **systems approach** to management is based on the general systems theory proposed in the 1940s by biologist Ludwig von Bertalanffy. The main premise of the theory is that, to fully understand the operations of an entity, the entity must be viewed as a system. A **system** is a number of interdependent parts functioning as a whole for some purpose.

Each system executes its functions as a largely independent unit. For example, according to von Bertalanffy, in order to fully understand the operations of the human body, one must understand the workings of it interdependent parts (e.g., eyes, ears, heart, and brain).

In management, understanding how each functional area of the firm operates allows managers to steer the company in the direction it wishes to go. Each system must determine how best to reach those strategic goals to fulfill the mission of the leadership. A systems approach makes the assumption that each unit of the company operates at peak efficiency.

According to von Bertalanffy, there are two basic types of systems: open systems and closed systems.

An **open system** is continuously interacting with its environment. Von Bertalanffy uses a plant as an example of an open system, as the plant continuously interacts with its environment, influencing the plant's state of existence and determining whether the plant will have a future.

The open-system approach serves as a model of business activity. That is, business is a process of transforming inputs to outputs while realizing that inputs are taken from the external environment and outputs are placed into this same environment (Figure 1.4). The open system concept helps to explain why today's firms strive so hard to continually meet the needs of their customers.

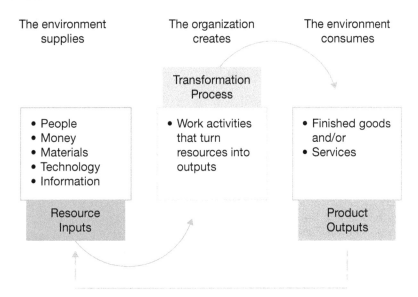

As open systems, organizations continually interact with their external environment to obtain resource inputs, transform those inputs through work activities into goods and services, and deliver finished products to their customers. Feedback from customers indicate how well they are doing.

Figure 1.4. Open System and External Environment

Kipley, D., Jewe, R., & Helm-Stevens, R., A Foundation in the Principles of Management, pp. 34. Copyright © 2015 by Cognella, Inc. Reprinted with permission.

A **closed system**, on the other hand, is not influenced by and does not interact with its environment. It is mostly mechanical and has predetermined motions or activities that must be performed regardless of the environment. A watch is an example of a closed system. Regardless of its environment, a watch's wheels, gears, and other parts must function in a predetermined way if the watch as a whole is to exist and serve its purpose.

A production line is an example of a closed system within an organization. The daily work that takes place on production or assembly lines can be insulated from outside factors, such as day-to-day meetings between upper-level executives, or information from other similar, competing production lines. Instead, workers on an assembly line are generally only responsible for completing their tasks on the line, depending on what type of line it is.

Companies use inputs such as labor, funds, technology, and materials to produce goods or to provide services, and they design their **subsystems** to attain these goals. Subsystems, either individually or collectively, support the work of the larger system. Figure 1.5 illustrates the importance of cooperation among organizational subsystems. For example, the operations and service management systems serve as a central point. They provide the integration among other subsystems, such as purchasing, accounting, sales, and information, all of which are essential to the work and success of the organization.

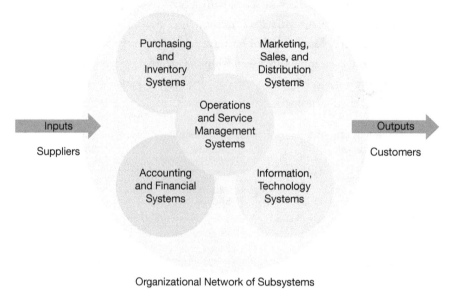

Organizational Network of Subsystems

Figure 1.5. Organizational Subsystems

Kipley, D., Jewe, R., & Helm-Stevens, R., A Foundation in the Principles of Management, pp. 35. Copyright © 2015 by Cognella, Inc. Reprinted with permission.

ORGANIZATIONAL BEHAVIOR AND MANAGEMENT

Organizational behavior and management are affected by multiple issues within an organization, from the type of work done, to the industry, to the rules and policies of the company. All of these elements work together to establish a culture within an organization and to provide direction and guidance for employees as they go about their day-to-day work.

Understanding organizational behavior (OB) and the use of the tools of OB is critically important to **managers**—those who direct and supervise the activities of others. Managers at all levels face the problems of understanding the behavior of their workers and responding appropriately (Box 1.2). A manager who understands how individuals, groups, and organizational characteristics interrelate, and the effect changing one or more of these factors, is more likely to increase **organizational effectiveness** (the ability of an organization to achieve its goals) than a manager who does not understand these concepts.

BOX 1.2: ORGANIZATIONAL BEHAVIOR EFFECTIVENESS TOOLS

- **SUPPORT** - A manager can work to raise an employee's self esteem or beliefs about his or her ability to accomplish a certain job in order to increase the employee's productivity or job satisfaction.
- **REWARD SYSTEM** - A manager can change the reward system to change employee's beliefs about the extent to which their rewards depend on their performance.
- **JOB DESIGN** - A manager can change the design of a person's job or the rules and procedures for doing the job to reduce costs, make the task more enjoyable, or make the task easier to perform.

The study of OB helps managers meet the challenge of improving organizational effectiveness by providing them with a set of tools that can help to improve the effectiveness of the individuals and groups.

Having a working knowledge of organizational behavior is not only important to managers, but to the employees at all levels of the organization, because it helps them to appreciate their work situation and how they should act to achieve their own goals, such as promotion or a pay raise.

LEVELS OF ANALYSIS IN ORGANIZATIONAL BEHAVIOR

People do not act in isolation. In order to understand the behavior within the organization it is necessary to analyze the multiple levels that exist within an organization; that is, workers influence their environment and are also influenced by their environment. There are three main levels that are examined in organizational behavior: the individual, the group, and the organization as a whole (Figure 1.6).

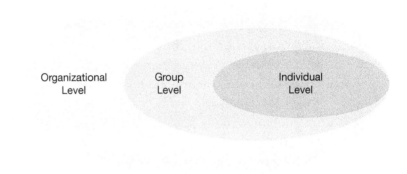

Figure 1.6. Levels of Analysis of Organizational Behavior

At the **individual level**, organizational behavior involves the study of learning, perception, creativity, motivation, personality, turnover, task performance, cooperative behavior, deviant behavior, ethics, and cognition. At this level of analysis, organizational behavior draws heavily upon psychology, engineering, and medicine.

At the **group level**, organizational behavior involves the study of **groups**, two or more people interacting to achieve their goal, and **teams**, groups in which members work together to achieve a common group goal, with resulting intra- and intergroup conflict and cohesion, leadership, power, norms, interpersonal communication, networks, and roles. A **virtual team** is a group whose members work together (via Skype, email, video conferencing, et cetera) on a common goal, but who may never meet in person. At the group level of analysis, organizational behavior draws upon the sociological and socio-psychological sciences.

Finally, there is the **organization level**. Organizational behavior involves the study of issues such as organizational culture, organizational structure, cultural diversity, inter-organizational cooperation and conflict, change, technology, and external environmental forces. At this level of analysis, organizational behavior draws upon anthropology and political science.

THE LEARNING ORGANIZATION

Changes in the external environment, such as an increasingly global marketplace, rapid technological advances, and growing pressure to do more with less, require managers to implement needed change as they build their organization.

A new approach to management is found in the **learning organization approach**, wherein all employees systematically participate in identifying and solving organizational problems to enable continuous change and improvement, increasing the organization's capacity to grow, learn, and achieve its purpose.

A learning organization promotes exchanges of information among employees, which creates a more knowledgeable workforce. Learning organizations exhibit flexibility, because employees accept and adapt to new ideas and changes through a shared vision.

Leadership in learning organizations requires something more than the traditional approach of setting goals, making decisions, and directing the troops. In learning organizations, managers learn to think in terms of "control with" rather than "control over" employees. They "control with" employees by building relationships based on shared visions and shaping the cultures of their organizations so that all can help achieve the same visions. A leader in this learning environment can help facilitate teamwork, initiate change, and expand the capacity of employees to shape their organization's future. Leaders who understand how the learning organization operates can help other leaders adapt to this organizational style.

Visionary leadership, a team-based structure, participative strategy, a strong and adaptive internal culture, empowered employees, and open information characterize the learning organization. Consultant **Peter Senge**, author of the popular book **The Fifth Discipline**, identifies the following ingredients of learning organizations:

- **Challenging of mental models**: Members routinely challenge the way business is done, setting aside of old ways of thinking.
- **Personal mastery**: Members are committed to gaining deeper self-awareness and the ability to remain open to others.
- **Systems thinking**: Every organizational member understands his or her own job and how the jobs fit together to provide final products to the customer.
- **Shared vision**: Members share the common purpose of the organization and a sincere commitment to accomplish said purpose.
- **Team learning**: Members work together, develop new solutions to new problems together, and apply solutions together to accomplish the plan of action.

The concept of the learning organization places high value on developing the ability to learn and then making that knowledge continuously available to all organizational members.

SUMMARY OF CHAPTER

1. Organizational behavior is the study of human behavior in organizational settings, the interface between human behavior and the organization, and the organization itself.
2. The study of organizational behavior is important because organizations have a powerful influence over our lives.
3. We learned that organizational behavior began to emerge as a scientific discipline as a result of the Hawthorne studies and contributors such as McGregor and Maslow who led the human relations movement that grew out of those studies.

DISCUSSION QUESTIONS

1. What reasons can you think of for the importance of studying organizational behavior?
2. It has been said that studying and understanding human behavior at work is the single most important requirement for a manager's success. Do you agree or disagree? Why?
3. Some have compared organizational behavior to the functional areas of an organization. In what ways is it different? How is it similar?

AM I MOTIVATED IN MY CLASSES?

INSTRUCTIONS

Indicate how often the following reasons for studying are true for you. Use the following scale:
1: Never | 2: Rarely | 3: Sometimes | 4: Often | 5: Always

1. I enjoy being praised for my work and grades by others.
2. I see my high scores and grades as a way to obtain status in the future.
3. I want to attend graduate school.
4. I don't want to be made fun of by my peers for my grades.
5. I want my friends to see my high scores and grades.
6. I want my professor to like me.
7. I want to have higher grades than my classmates.
8. I want to get good grades for myself, not for others.
9. I do not want to fail quizzes, exams, or finals.
10. I want a good job in the future.

SCORING KEY:

Count the number of 4s and 5s you indicated. This number will be between 0 and 10.

ANALYSIS:

First, it should be noted that there are no right or wrong goals when it comes to why you pursue certain grades in relation to your courses, nor is this a comprehensive list.

The importance of this assessment is to show that having clear goals will increase the chances that you will perform well. The number of 4s and 5s you have reveals how motivated you find yourself in your courses. There are no definitive cutoffs that determine if you are or are not motivated to succeed in your classes.

Few 4s and 5s reveal that you may not have strong motivations to succeed in your classes, and that your coursework may suffer as a result of this. You may want to reassess your course goals. A high number of 4s and 5s show that you have strong motivations for completing your coursework.

Originally adapted from T. Hayamizu and B. Weiner, "A Test of Dweck's Model of Achievement Goals as Related to Perceptions of Ability," Journal of Experimental Education, vol. 59, 1991, pp. 226-34.

Modified per C. Dupeyrat and E. V. Smith Jr., "Toward Establishing a Unified Metric for Performance and Learning Goal Orientations," Journal of Applied Measurement, vol. 2, no. 4, 2001, pp. 312-36

CHAPTER 1 REFERENCES

Carey, A. (1967). The Hawthorne studies: A radical criticism. *American Sociological Review*, 32, 403–416.

Demos, T. (2010, April 12). Motivate without spending millions. *Fortune*, April, 37–38.

Fayol, H. (1949). *General and industrial management.* London: Pittman & Sons.

Gillespie, R. (1991). *Manufacturing knowledge: A history of the Hawthorne experiments.* New York: Cambridge University Press

Greenwood, R. G., Bolton, A. A., & Greenwood, B. A. (1983). Hawthorne a half century later: Relay assembly participants remember. *Journal of Management*, 9(2), 217–231.

Hale, C. P. (1986). What do managers do? A critical review of the evidence. *Journal of Management Studies*, 23(*1*), 88–115.

Harrison, G.W. & List, J.A. (2004). Field experiments. *Journal of Economic Literature*, 42(4), 1009–1055.

Hart, C.W.M. (1943): The Hawthorne experiments. *The Canadian Journal of Economics and Political Science*, 9(2), 150–163.

Hill, L. A. (1992). *Becoming a manager: Mastery of a new identity.* Boston: Harvard Business School Press.

Hunsaker, P. L. (2005). *Management: A skills approach.* Upper Saddle River, NJ: Pearson Prentice Hall.

Huselid, M. A. (1995). The impact of human resource management practices on turnover, productivity, and corporate financial performance. *Academy of Management Journal*, *38(3)*, 635–672.

Huy, Q . (2001). In praise of middle managers. *Harvard Business Review*, September, 72–79.

Katz, R. L. (1974). Skills of an effective administrator. *Harvard Business Review*, September, 132–142.

Landy, F. J. (1997). Early influences on the development of industrial and organizational psychology. *Journal of Applied Psychology*, 82(4), 467–477.

Locke, E. A. (1982). The ideas of Frederick W. Taylor: An evaluation. *Academy of Management Review*, 7(1), 14–24.

Maslow, A. (1943). A theory of human motivation. *Psychological Review*, 50(4), 370–396.

Mayo, E. (1933). *The human problems of industrial civilization.* Cambridge, MA: Harvard University Press.

Mayo, E. (1949). *Hawthorne and the Western Electric Company, The Social Problems of an Industrial Civilization*, Routledge.

McCall Jr., M. W., & Lombardo, M. M. (1983). What makes a top executive? *Psychology Today*, 17(2), 26–31.

McDonald, D., & Smith, A. (1995). A proven connection: Performance management and business results. *Compensation and Benefits Review*, 27(6), 59.

McGregor, D. (1960). *The human side of enterprise.* New York: McGraw-Hill.

Mintzberg, H. (1973). *The nature of managerial work.* New York: Harper & Row.

Pfeffer, J. (1996). *The human equation: Building profits by putting people first.* Boston: Harvard Business School Press.

Pfeiffer, J., & Veiga, J. F. (1999). Putting people first for organizational success. *Academy of Management Executive*, *13*(2), 37–48.

Schmidt, F. L., & Hunter, J. E. (1992). Development of a causal model of process determining job performance. *Current Directions in Psychological Science*, 3(1), 89–92.

Stagner, R. (1969). Corporate decision making. *Journal of Applied Psychology, 53(1)*, 1–13.

Steckler, N., & Fondas, N. (1995). Building team leader effectiveness: A diagnostic tool. *Organizational Dynamics*, 23(3), 20–34.

Taylor, F. W. (1911). *Principles of scientific management.* New York: Harper.

Tully, S. (1995, February 20). What team leaders need to know. *Fortune*, 93.

Weber, M. (1921). *Theory of social and economic organization.* London: Oxford University Press.

Oglethorpe, R. What makes teams work? *Fast Company* (2000, November 1), 109.

Olson, R., Verley, J., Santos, L., Salas, C. (2004). What We Teach Students About the Hawthorne Studies, *The Industrial Organization Psychologist*, Volume 41(3), 23–39.

Parsons, H. M. (1992). Hawthorne: An early OBM experiment. *Journal of Organizational Behavior Management*, 12(1), 27–43.

Roethlisberger, F. J., & Dickson, W. J. (1939). *Management and the worker: An account of a research program conducted by the Western Electric Company, Hawthorne Works*, Chicago. Cambridge, MA: Harvard University Press

Wren, D. A., Bedeian, A. G., & Breeze, J. D. (2002). The foundations of Henri Fayol's administrative theory. *Management Decisions, 40(9)*, 906–918.

MANAGEMENT FUNCTIONS

CHAPTER LEARNING OBJECTIVES

After reading this chapter, you should have a good understanding of

- the four principle functions of management;
- the five kinds of managers, each with different jobs and responsibilities: top-level managers, middle-level managers, frontline managers, functional managers, and general managers;
- Mintzberg's three distinct roles of managers while performing their jobs: interpersonal, informational, and decisional;
- the key differences between managerial efficiency and managerial effectiveness as they relate to organizational performance; and
- the two widely accepted views on **management skills**: the classic view and the contemporary view.

"Good management consists in showing average people how to do the work of superior people."

- JOHN D. ROCKEFELLER

FOUR FUNCTIONS OF MANAGEMENT

Management has four principle functions or duties: planning, organizing, leading, and controlling an organization's human, financial, material, and other resources to increase effectiveness. Managers who are knowledgeable about organizational behavior are better positioned to improve their ability to perform these functions.

PLANNING

The first component in management is planning. **Planning** involves choosing tasks that must be performed to attain organizational goals, outlining how the tasks must be performed, and indicating when they should be performed. Planning actively focuses on attaining goals and is one of the best ways to improve performance. Planning encourages people to work harder for extended periods of time, with behaviors that are directly related to goal achievement. Planning is concerned with the success of the organization in the short term (profit making) as well as in the long term (strategic development). Research has proven that companies that plan effectively have larger profits and faster growth than companies that do not. Examples of types of plans for a new restaurant would most likely include a marketing plan, hiring plan, operational plan, and a sales plan.

ORGANIZING

The second function of management is getting prepared and getting organized. Managers are responsible for the organization of the company, which includes organizing the people as well as the resources. **Organizing** can be thought of as assigning the tasks developed in the planning stages to various individuals or groups within the organization. Organizing is creating a mechanism to put plans into action. People within the organization are given work assignments that contribute to the company's goals. Tasks are organized so that the output of each individual contributes to the success of departments, which, in turn, contributes to the success of divisions, which ultimately contributes to the success of the organization. An organization that is not organized indicates that management is critically unprepared to conduct successful business activities.

LEADING

The third management function is leading. Leading involves motivating, influencing, directing, or actuating, and is concerned primarily with people within the organization. Work under this function helps management control and supervise the actions of the staff. It also enables them to provide assistance to the employees by guiding them in the right direction to achieve the organization's goals. **Leading** can be defined as guiding the activities of organization members in the direction that helps the organization move towards the fulfillment of its goals. The overall purpose of leading is to increase productivity. Human-oriented work situations usually generate higher levels of production over the long term than do task-oriented work situations, because people find the latter type distasteful.

CONTROLLING

Controlling is the last of the four management functions. It includes establishing performance standards that are aligned to organizational objectives. Controlling also involves evaluation and reporting of job performance. The **controlling** function is an ongoing process that provides a means to check if the tasks assigned are being performed on time and according to the standards set by management. Managers play the following roles in controlling:

- Gather information that measures performance.
- Compare present performance to pre-established performance norms.
- Determine the next action plan and modifications for meeting the desired performance parameters.

In order to achieve organizational goals, managers are involved in daily activities that plan, organize, lead, and control the company's resources.

The four functions of management are integrally related and therefore cannot be separated in practice. To be effective, a manager must understand how the four functions are practiced together (Figure 2.1).

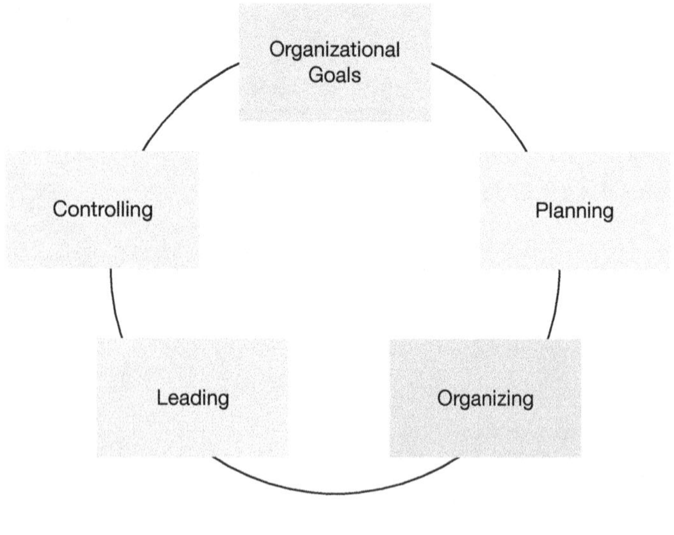

Figure 2.1. The Relationship of Management Functions

Organizing is founded on well–thought out plans developed during the planning process, and leading must be adapted to reflect both these plans and the organizational structure used to implement them. Controlling is necessary for possible modifications to the existing plans, organizational structure, or the motivation used to develop a more successful effort.

MANAGEMENT LEVELS AND TYPES

Although all managers take part in the same four functions of management, not all managerial jobs are the same. For example, the demands and requirements placed on Larry Page (the CEO of Google) are significantly different to those placed on the manager of a local Subway restaurant. There are five kinds of managers, each with different jobs and responsibilities: top-level managers, middle-level managers, frontline managers, functional managers, and general managers.

Top-level managers include boards of directors, presidents, vice presidents, CEOs, general managers, and senior managers. All of the important decisions are made at this level. Top-level managers are responsible for controlling and overseeing the entire organization. They do not direct the day-to-day activities of the firm, but rather develop goals, strategic plans, and company policies, and make decisions on the direction of the business. They are responsible for creating a context for change. Additionally, top-level managers play a significant role in the mobilization of outside resources and are accountable to the shareholders and general public. They are also responsible for framing policies for the business; creating a positive organizational culture through company values, strategies, and lessons; and closely monitoring their customers' needs, competitors' moves, and long-term business, economic, and social trends.

Mid-level managers are the intermediate management of a hierarchical organization, being subordinate to the top-level management, but above the lowest levels of operational staff. Mid-level managers consist of general managers, branch managers, and department managers. They are accountable to the top-level management for their department's function and dedicate more time to organizational and directional functions. Mid-level managerial roles include

- executing organizational plans in conformance with the company's policies and the objectives of the top management;
- communicating and discussing information and policies from top-level management with lower management; and
- inspiring and providing guidance to lower-level managers to better performance to achieve business objectives.

Mid-level managers may also communicate upward, by offering suggestions and feedback to top-level managers. Because mid-level managers are more involved in the day-to-day workings of a company, they may provide valuable information to top-level managers to help improve the organization's performance. Because mid-level managers work with both top-level managers and first-level managers, mid-level managers are expected to have excellent interpersonal skills to communicate, motivate, and mentor. Leadership skills are also important in delegating tasks to first-level managers.

Frontline managers hold positions like office manager, shift supervisor, section lead, foreman, or department manager. These managers are responsible for a work group to a higher level of management. They are normally in the lower layers of the management hierarchy and the employees who report to them do not themselves have any managerial or supervisory responsibility. Frontline management is the level of management that oversees a company's primary production activities and must generate efficient productivity and control costs. As such, they must have high technical skill. Furthermore, frontline managers are critical to a company's success and are also required to have high interpersonal skills, as they must encourage, motivate, monitor, and reward those employees who perform those essential production duties.

A **functional manager** is a person who has management authority over an organizational unit, such as a department within a business, company, or other organization. Most companies are grouped into areas of specialties, within which different functions of the organization occur (e.g., finance, marketing, research and development, engineering); functional management is the most common type of organizational management. Functional managers have ongoing responsibilities and are not often directly affiliated with project teams, other than ensuring that the organizational goals and objectives are aligned with the overall corporate strategy and vision.

General managers refer to any executive who has responsibility of the day-to-day operations of a business. General managers include owners and managers who head small business establishments, and whose overall responsibilities include managing both the revenue and cost elements of a company's income statement and the firm's marketing and sales functions. Frequently, general managers are responsible for effective planning, delegating, coordinating, staffing, organizing, and decision making, to attain desirable profit-making results for an organization.

Team leaders are a relatively new role in management that has resulted from companies shifting to more self-managed teams. A team leader is one who may not have any legitimate power over other members and, as such, has no authority to hire or fire workers. Typically, a team leader is appointed on either a permanent or rotating basis to represent the team to the next higher reporting level. Job duties of a team leader include making decisions in the absence of a consensus, resolving conflict between team members, facilitating team activities towards accomplishing organizational goals, and providing intellectual, emotional, and spiritual resources to the team. Team leaders also assist their team members to plan and schedule work, learn to solve problems, and work effectively with each other.

MANAGERIAL ROLES

Managers perform their four functions by assuming specific roles in the organization. A **role** is a set of behaviors or tasks a person is expected to perform because of the position they hold in a group or organization. Professor and author Henry Mintzberg shadowed five American CEOs for a week, analyzing their managerial activities. From his research he concluded that, although managers were engaged in planning, organizing, leading, and controlling, managers also fulfilled three main roles while performing their jobs: interpersonal, informational, and decisional roles. Within the three main roles, there are 10 sub-roles of management activities.

Interpersonal roles involve working and interacting with people and are very people intensive. In fact, some estimates of the amount of time that managers spend interacting with people face-to-face ranges from two-thirds to four-fifths of their entire workday. As such, if you prefer to work alone or have difficulty dealing with people, management may not be the career for which you are best suited. In the interpersonal role of management, managers perform three sub-roles:

1. **Figurehead:** As a figurehead of the company, the manager performs a number of routine duties of a legal or social nature, such as greeting company visitors, speaking at the openings of new facilities, or representing the company at community functions.
2. **Leader:** Mintzberg specifically defines the role of leader as one who is responsible for the motivation, training, and encouragement of subordinates to accomplish the organizational objectives.

3. **Liaison:** The manager in the liaison role networks by connecting people inside the company as well as externally. This role is not about dissemination of information, however, and is more about identifying the challenges and goals faced by others and connecting them with resources that will enable them to overcome obstacles or advance an agenda.

Informational roles are based on gathering and disseminating information through and with employees. Mintzberg's studies found that managers spend as much as 40% of their time communicating and acquiring information from others. Therefore, one might consider the manager's role to be an information processor, gathering information by scanning the business environment and listening to others, processing that information, and then disseminating it to others both inside and outside the organization. Mintzberg identified three sub-roles of the informational role:

1. **Monitor:** Monitoring involves actively seeking and obtaining a wide variety of information, both internal and external, to develop a thorough understanding of the organization and its environment.
2. **Disseminator:** Managers share information they have received from outsiders or from other subordinates with members of the organization. Some information is factual, while some information may involve management's interpretation and integration of other pertinent information in order to make managerial decisions.
3. **Spokesman:** In this role, managers share the information (plans, policies, results, et cetera) within and outside of the organization, and may also serve as experts on the organization's industry.

In order to make good, sound decisions, Mintzberg found that simply obtaining and sharing information with people inside and outside the organization was not sufficient. Managers must integrate the perspectives of others in order to make sound decisions. Mintzberg identified four sub-roles of the **decisional role:**

1. **Entrepreneur:** An entrepreneurial manager searches within both the organization and its environment, and initiates improvement projects to bring about change. They also supervise the design and improvement of certain projects.
2. **Disturbance handler:** These are responsible for corrective action when an organization faces important or unexpected disturbances.
3. **Resource allocator:** Resource allocators are responsible for the allocation of the organization's resources. They determine who will get what resources and how many resources will they get, and make or approve of all significant organizational decisions.
4. **Negotiator:** Negotiators are responsible for representing the organization at major negotiations, including schedules, projects, goals, outcomes, resources, and employee raises.

A manager's job is never static, and is always in movement. At any given time, a manager may be carrying out any combination of these roles to varying degrees.

MANAGERIAL SKILLS

Managerial skills are skills that are necessary to make business decisions and to reach the organization's goals by leading and working with people and utilizing other organizational resources within a company. Because management skills are so critical to the success of the organization, companies often focus on tactics that can be used to improve the skills of their managers. There are two widely accepted views on management skills: the classic view and the contemporary view.

The **classic view** on management is best illustrated by Robert Katz, a famous writer, manager, and consultant, who described three skills that are essential for administrative work. These are technical, human, and conceptual skills:

- **Human skills**: the ability to interact and motivate well with others. They involve working with people and groups building cooperation and communication. *Human skills are working with "people."*
- **Technical skills**: the knowledge and proficiency in the trade required to get a job done. Requires the ability to apply specialized knowledge and expertise to work-related techniques and procedures. *Technical skills are working with "things."*
- **Conceptual skills**: the ability to see the organization holistically and understand how the different parts of the company affect each other, and the skill to develop and implement ideas, concepts, and strategies. *Conceptual skills are working with "ideas."*

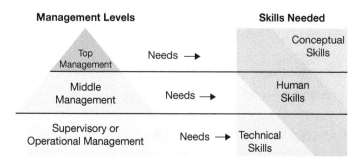

Figure 2.2. The Relationship Between Management Level and Managerial Skill: Classic View

Kipley, D., Jewe, R., & Helm-Stevens, R., A Foundation in the Principles of Management, pp. 16. Copyright © 2015 by Cognella, Inc. Reprinted with permission.

As a manager moves from a lower level of management to top-level management, the required mix of skills changes. At the lower levels (supervisor or operations manager) there is a high need for technical skills and human skills, with little need for conceptual skills. As managers progress to middle management, technical skills are less necessary, human skills are important, and now conceptual skills also become necessary. Finally, as top managers, both human skills and conceptual skills are critical. The relationship of the three management skills with management levels is illustrated in Figure 2.2.

The **contemporary view** is a more modern take on management skills. Although it is an extension of the classic view, the contemporary view has two unique differences: 1) the contemporary view defines the major activities that managers typically perform, and 2) the contemporary view lists the skills required to carry out those activities successfully.

The three basic types of major activities that modern managers typically perform are as follows:

1. **Task-related activities** are defined as the critical management-related activities, such as short-term planning, clarifying objectives of jobs in organizations, and monitoring operations and performance.
2. **People-related activities** are focused on managing people within the organization. Activities include providing support and encouragement to employees, providing recognition for achievements and contributions, developing skill and confidence of workers, consulting when making decisions, and empowering employees to solve problems.
3. **Change-related activities** are aimed at modifying organizational components, such as proposing new strategies and visions, encouraging innovation, and taking risks to promote needed change.

Because management skills are prerequisites for management success, managers should spend time defining the most formidable task they face and sharpen those skills that will help them become successful.

The following list provides seven important competencies that will increase the probability of managers successfully carrying out management activities.

BOX 2.1: SEVEN IMPORTANT MANAGER COMPETENCIES

To increase the probability of being successful, managers should be competent in the following skills.

4. Clarifying roles: assigning tasks and explaining job responsibilities, task objectives, and performance objectives.
5. Monitoring operations: checking on the progress and quality of the work, and evaluating individual and unit performance.
6. Short-term planning: how to use resources and personnel to accomplish a task efficiently, and to determine how to schedule and coordinate unit activities efficiently.
7. Consulting: checking with people before making decisions that affect them, encouraging participation in decision making, using ideas and suggestions of others.
8. Supporting: showing consideration for others, acting with empathy and support, providing encouragement when there is a difficult task.
9. Recognizing: providing recognition and acknowledgement of accomplishments, special contributions, and effective performance.
10. Developing: helping employees learn how to improve their skills, provide coaching, advice and opportunities for skills development.

MANAGING PROJECTS

Once a manager understands their role and their skills and understands what is required of them in order to make their company or their team thrive, they can start managing actual projects and there are some very important tools that can help them to organize and manage their projects as they go. One such tool is the Gantt chart.

Henry Gantt was an American engineer and famous management consultant who was best known for his planning methodology, the Gantt chart (Figure 2.3), a bar graph that measures planned and completed work along each stage of production. This methodology helped him realize major infrastructure projects, including the construction of the Hoover Dam. Gantt also developed the task and bonus system of wage payment and measurement instruments to provide an insight into worker efficiency and productivity.

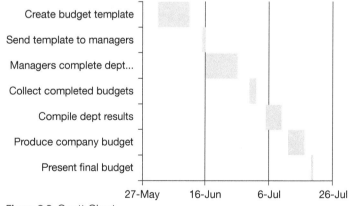

Figure 2.3. Gantt Chart

Frank and Lillian Gilbreth were a pioneering team in work and motion studies. In Frank's early career as an apprentice bricklayer, he was interested in standardization and method study. He watched bricklayers and saw that some workers were slow and inefficient, while others were very productive. He discovered that each bricklayer used a different set of motions to lay bricks. From his observations, Frank isolated the basic movements necessary to do the job and eliminated unnecessary motions. Workers using these movements raised their output from 1,000 to 2,700 bricks per day. This was the first **motion study** designed to isolate the best possible method of performing a given job. As a result, certain fields of work, such as medicine, have been greatly improved in efficiency.

EFFICIENCY VERSUS EFFECTIVENESS

Efficiency and effectiveness are very common terms found in business. However, most people are unclear on their meanings and occasionally mix them up. If you were to Google the definitions for both terms you'll find very similar definitions, which unfortunately only adds to the confusion. An easy way to remember the difference is to remember this sentence: "Being effective is about doing the right things, while being efficient is about doing things in the right manner."

Managerial effectiveness refers to management's use of organizational resources in meeting organizational goals. If organizations are using their resources to attain their goals, the managers are considered to be effective. However, managerial effectiveness is not simply measured as effective or not effective. The closer an organization comes to achieving its goals, the more effective the managers are considered. So managerial effectiveness is then on a continuum ranging from ineffective to effective. The effectiveness of a workforce has an enormous impact on the quality of a company's product or service, which often dictates a company's reputation and customer satisfaction.

Managerial efficiency is the proportion of total organizational resources that contribute to productivity during the manufacturing process. Efficient managers complete tasks in the least amount of time possible with the least amount of resources possible by utilizing certain timesaving strategies. Inefficient managers use or waste more resources during the production time. Similar to effectiveness, management efficiency is best described as being on a continuum, ranging from inefficient to efficient. For example, suppose a manager is attempting to communicate more efficiently. He can accomplish his goal by using email rather than sending letters to each employee. Efficiency and effectiveness are mutually exclusive. A manager who's efficient isn't always effective, and vice versa. Efficiency increases productivity and saves both time and money. In order to maximize organizational success, managers must be both effective *and* efficient (Figure 2.4).

Figure 2.4. The Combinations of Managerial Effectiveness and Efficiency

Kipley, D., Jewe, R., & Helm-Stevens, R., A Foundation in the Principles of Management, pp. 15. Copyright © 2015 by Cognella, Inc. Reprinted with permission.

SUMMARY OF CHAPTER

1. This chapter looked at the five kinds of manager, each with different jobs and responsibilities: top-level managers, middle-level managers, frontline managers, functional managers, and general managers.
2. In Henry Mintzberg's research on managers, he defined three distinct roles managers have while performing their jobs: interpersonal, informational, and decisional.
3. Within those three main roles there are 10 sub-roles of management activities.
4. There are differences between managerial efficiency and managerial effectiveness as they relate to organizational performance.
5. This chapter discussed the importance of management skills to the success of the organization and what tactics can be used to improve the skills of managers.
6. There are two widely accepted views on management skills: the classic view and the contemporary view.
7. There are seven important competencies that will increase the probability of managers becoming successful in carrying out management activities.

DISCUSSION QUESTIONS

1. Suppose you had to hire a new manager. One candidate has outstanding interpersonal skills but poor technical skills. The other candidate has the exact opposite mix of skills. Which would you hire? Why?
2. Some people believe that individuals working in an organization have the basic human right to satisfaction with their work and to the opportunity to grow and develop. Do you agree? Can you argue against this view?
3. What is the difference between efficiency and effectiveness? Which would a Gantt chart be used to improve?

AM I WILLING TO DELEGATE TASKS?

INSTRUCTIONS

Indicate how much you agree or disagree with the following statements. Respond depending on your work experience or what you know about your personal beliefs and yourself.

1: Strongly disagree | 2: Disagree | 3: No preference | 4: Agree | 5: Strongly agree

1. I don't see how delegation saves time. _1_
2. When a job isn't done right, even after I gave clear instructions, I get upset. _3_
3. My boss expects me to stay on top of all details of my job. _4_
4. I check over all work by my subordinates and fix their mistakes without telling them. _2_
5. I don't delegate because I am a perfectionist. _1_
6. I feel I can do jobs better than those I would be delegating them to. _3_
7. Whenever I delegate, the job doesn't get done right. _3_
8. Delegating means I lose control. _2_
9. I get criticized if those I delegate to do the job wrong, so I tend not to delegate. _2_
10. I work on things longer than I should. _3_
11. Even when I delegate, I end up doing the task anyway. _2_
12. I don't have the time to properly delegate tasks. _4_
13. My staff/team members do not have the same level of commitment as I do.
14. I feel that I cannot delegate, because those I delegate to do not have the experience needed.
15. I delegate the whole job and give up all control over it, only reviewing the final project.
16. When I delegate, I do not give away the tasks that are not routine.
17. My job would be less fun if I were to delegate tasks.
18. When I delegate, I give very detailed explanations of what needs to be done.

SCORING KEY:

To find your score, add up all your responses.

ANALYSIS:

Managers in modern times have to delegate tasks to have everything complete by their deadlines. However, many have difficulties doing so. Where does your willingness stack up?

A score of 18 to 35 reveals that your delegation skills are great and it comes easy to you. If you scored between 36 and 53 points, you are getting there in your delegation skills. A score of 54 to 71 reveals that your delegation skills could use some improvement. A score of 72 to 90 indicates that you may have ineffective delegation skills.

Adapted from: Robbins, S. P. (2009). III.A.2: How willing am I to delegate?, Self-assessment library (79-80). Upper Saddle River, NJ: Pearson Education Inc.

Originally adapted from: Klein, T. J. (May, 1982). How to improve delegation habits," Management Review. p. 59.

CHAPTER 2 REFERENCES

Carey, A. (1967). The Hawthorne studies: A radical criticism. *American Sociological Review*, 32(2), 403–416.

Chatfield, M. (1996). "Gantt, Henry Laurence (1861-1919)." *History of Accounting: An International Encyclopedia*, edited by Michael Chatfield and Richard Vangermeersch. New York: Garland Publishing.

Demos, T. (2010, April 10). Motivate without spending millions. *Fortune*, April, 37–38.

Fayol, H. (1949). *General and industrial management*. London: Pittman & Sons.

Gantt, H. L. (1903). "A graphical daily balance in manufacture," in: *Transactions of the American. Society of Mechanical Engineers*, 24, 1322-1336.

George, C. S. (1968). *The History of Management Thought*. Prentice Hall.

Gilbreth, F. Jr., Ernestine Gilbreth Carey, E. (1948). *Cheaper by the Dozen*. Thomas Y. Crowell Co.

Gilbreth, Frank Jr., 1950. *Belles on Their Toes*. Thomas Y. Crowell Co.

Hale, C. P. (1986). What do managers do? A critical review of the evidence. *Journal of Management Studies*, 23(*1*), 88–115.

Herrmann, J. W. (2005). *History of Decision-Making Tools for Production Scheduling*, Proceedings of the 2005 Multidisciplinary Conference on Scheduling: Theory and Applications, New York, July 18–21.

Hill, L. A. (1992). *Becoming a manager: Mastery of a new identity*. Boston: Harvard Business School Press.

Hunsaker, P. L. (2005). *Management: A skills approach*. Upper Saddle River, NJ: Pearson Prentice Hall.

Huselid, M. A. (1995). The impact of human resource management practices on turnover, productivity, and corporate financial performance. *Academy of Management Journal*, 38, 635–672.

Huy, Q. (2001). In praise of middle managers. *Harvard Business Review*, September, 72–79.

Katz, R. L. (1974). Skills of an effective administrator. *Harvard Business Review*, September, 132–142.

Landy, F. J. (1997). Early influences on the development of industrial and organizational psychology. *Journal of Applied Psychology*, 82(4), 467–477.

Locke, E. A. (1982). The ideas of Frederick W. Taylor: An evaluation. *Academy of Management Review*, 7(1), 14–24.

Maslow, A. (1943). A theory of human motivation. *Psychological Review*, 50(4), 370–396.

Mayo, E. (1933). *The human problems of industrial civilization*. Cambridge, MA: Harvard University Press.

McCall Jr., M. W., & Lombardo, M. M. (1983). What makes a top executive? *Psychology Today*, 17(2), 26–31.

McDonald, D., & Smith, A. (1995). A proven connection: Performance management and business results. *Compensation and Benefits Review, 27*(6), 59.

McGregor, D. (1960). *The human side of enterprise.* New York: McGraw-Hill.

Mintzberg, H. (1973). *The nature of managerial work.* New York: Harper & Row.

Mintzberg, H. (1990). The Design School: Reconsidering the basic premises of strategy formation, *Strategic Management Jour*nal, 11(3), 171–196.

Mintzberg, H., Ahlstrand, B., Lampel, J., (1998). *Strategy safari: A guided tour through the wilds of strategic management,* Free Press, New York.

Mintzberg, H. (2004). Managers, not MBAs: a hard look at the soft practice of managing and management development, Berrett-Koehler.

Pfeffer, J. (1996). *The human equation: Building profits by putting people first.* Boston: Harvard Business School Press.

Pfeiffer, J., & Veiga, J. F. (1999). Putting people first for organizational success. *Academy of Management Executive, 13*(2), 37–48.

Schmidt, F. L., & Hunter, J. E. (1992). Development of a causal model of process determining job performance. *Current Directions in Psychological Science,* 3(*1),* 89–92.

Stagner, R. (1969). Corporate decision making. *Journal of Applied Psychology, 53(1),* 1–13.

Steckler, N., & Fondas, N. (1995). Building team leader effectiveness: A diagnostic tool. *Organizational Dynamics,* 23(3), 20–34.

Taylor, F. W. (1911). *Principles of scientific management.* New York: Harper.

Tully, S. (1995, February 20). What team leaders need to know. *Fortune,* 93.

Weber, M. (1921). *Theory of social and economic organization.* London: Oxford University Press.

Oglethorpe, R. What makes teams work? *Fast Company* (2000, November 1), 109.

Wallace, C., Gantt, H. (1922). <u>*The Gantt chart, a working tool of management*</u>. New York, Ronald Press.

Wren, D. A., Bedeian, A. G., & Breeze, J. D. (2002). The foundations of Henri Fayol's administrative theory. *Management Decisions, 40(9),* 906–918.

UNDERSTANDING PEOPLE—PERSONALITY AND ABILITY

CHAPTER LEARNING OBJECTIVES

After reading this chapter, you should have a good understanding of

- the nature of personality and how it is determined by both nature and nurture;
- the Big Five personality traits and their implications for understanding behavior in organizations;
- other relevant personality traits and how they influence employees' behaviors in organizations;
- how to describe the different kinds of abilities that employees use to perform their jobs; and
- how organizations manage ability through selection, placement, and training.

"Every improvement, no matter how small, is valuable."

- AUBREY DANIELS

BEHAVIOR AND THE NATURE OF PERSONALITY

Have you ever asked yourself, "Why do people behave the way they do?" For example, why are the plans that they put into action producing the opposite results that were intended, or, why is the well-intended advice that is given to a friend met with so much resistance, retribution, and defensiveness? Equally deserving an explanation is our own behavior and how at times we are unable to understand our own actions. Why do we react differently at times when the circumstances are basically the same? Shouldn't we react the same in both instances? This chapter focuses on understanding what makes people think and act the way they do. Understanding why people behave as they do is the key to changing our own and others' behavior.

WHAT IS PERSONALITY?

While there are several definitions of personality, we will limit it to its most general and abstract meaning. **Personality** is a pattern of relatively enduring ways that a person thinks, feels, and behaves. The word personality is derived from the Greek *persona*, which means the "mask" or the "face" the individual displays to the world. One's personality can be described in a variety of ways. Some people are perfectionists—acting critical, impatient, demanding, and intense; others may be described as easygoing, relaxed, and fun to be around. Still others may seem gloomy, distant, and quiet. In each of these examples, we formulate a general description to try to explain the regularities or patterns we observe in people and what they are like in general, without referring to their specific feelings, thoughts, and behaviors in any given situation.

Personality is an important factor in accounting for why people feel, think, and behave, and can influence career choices, job satisfaction, stress, leadership, and job performance. A person's behavior is determined partly by their personality and partly by the norms and pressures of their situation. Understanding these elements helps to explain why employees act the way that they do in an organization.

NATURE VERSUS NURTURE: WHAT DETERMINES YOUR PERSONALITY?

The exact origins of personality elude any precise description. Given the multitude of influences that are implicated and the complexity with which they interact over time, there is little basis for believing that we will ever have an entirely satisfactory and complete account for how an individual comes to be the person they are. However, we can at least point to the major sources of influence as determinants of personality: nature and nurture.

Personality is partly determined by **nature**, or biological heritage. Every human child enters the world with a unique set of traits, both physical and non-physical, that will profoundly affect the direction that their personality development will take. Physical stature, facial attractiveness, gender, temperament, muscle composition, reflexes, energy level, and biological rhythms are factors that are completely or substantially influenced by your parents. Although specific genes for personality have not yet been identified, psychologists have studied monozygotic twins in an attempt to discover the extent to which personality is inherited.

Another view from psychologists is the **nurture** argument, wherein a person's environment or life experiences shape their personality. Nurture supporters argue that, if personality is determined by nature, then identical twins who grow up together in the same family and have the same permissive or strict parents, and share similar life experiences, should have the exact same personalities. However, research has shown this not to be the case. In fact, to further support their argument, they state that identical twins separated at birth and raised in different households, experiencing differing environmental influences, are more likely to have personalities that are similar to the siblings with whom they were raised instead of their twin.

In reality, both biological *and* environmental factors play important roles in determining our individual personalities, and it is therefore important for managers and other organizational members to take such knowledge into account in order to understand and predict how and why the people that they work with and manage feel, think, and act as they do in their organization (Figure 3.1).

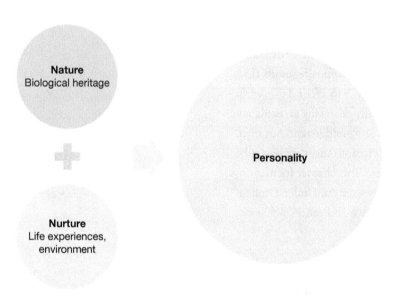

Figure 3.1. The Combinations of Nature and Nurture

PERSONALITY AND SITUATIONAL INFLUENCES

Personality has been shown to influence all aspects of a person's performance: general behavior, stress level, job satisfaction, and how they will react to different situations on the job. Not every personality is suited for every job. In some organizations, strong situational constraints and pressures, such as job requirements or strict rules and regulations, force people to behave in a certain way, regardless of their personality. Thus, it is important to recognize the individual personality traits within each individual employee and to pair employees with the duties that fit their personalities the best. Accomplishing this successfully will lead to increased productivity and job satisfaction, which will go a long way in helping any business to function more efficiently.

Characteristics of an individual's behavior—such as aggressiveness, submissiveness, shyness, laziness, ambitiousness, loyalty, or timidity—that occur frequently and in numerous situations are their **personality traits**. The more consistent the characteristic is over time and the more frequently it occurs in diverse situations, the more important that trait is in describing that individual.

As mentioned, personality will affect how a person does their job. For example, two university professors teaching courses in strategic management may teach the course quite differently based on their individual personalities. One professor who is less outgoing may teach concepts and theories directly from the text, whereas the second professor who has a flair for life may integrate those same theories with case studies using a hands-on approach. Both professors are following the curriculum, but their individual personalities affect how they do so.

A manager who understands the interaction between personality and situational factors can help employees perform at high levels and feel good about the work that they do (Figure 3.2). Employees at all levels benefit when they understand how their personalities interact with different situations, fostering good working relationships and promoting organizational effectiveness.

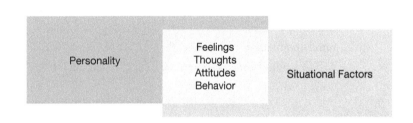

Figure 3.2. The Relationship Between Personality and Situation

THE MYERS–BRIGGS TYPE INDICATOR

The **Myers–Briggs Type Indicator (MBTI)** is the most widely used personality assessment tool in the world. It is a questionnaire designed to measure the psychological preferences of people based on how they usually feel or act in a particular situation. Based on their answers, individuals are classified as introvert (I) or extrovert (E), sensing (S) or intuitive (N), thinking (T) or feeling (F), and judging (J) or perceiving (P). Each classification is defined as follows.

Extrovert (E) or introvert (I). **Extroverts** derive their energy from others. They are typically outgoing, energetic, sociable, and assertive. They can be very demanding, liking being center stage and typically needing stimulation, or they become bored quite quickly. **Introverts**, on the other hand, derive their energy from time alone and do not like attention from a crowd. Introverts usually focus on their own internal dialogue, their own world in their mind. At times they can be quite oblivious to what is going on around them, and at other times quite observant. They are typically more quiet, reserved, and perceptive than their more outgoing counterparts and prefer to keep their ideas to themselves until they have fully thought them through.

Sensing (S) or intuitive (I). **Sensors** focus on what is immediate, practical, and real. They like logic and tend to pursue things in a clear sequence. At work, they pay attention to facts and solid data, and draw from their own direct experiences. Those who are **intuitive** may view sensors as frivolous or shortsighted. Those who are intuitive process data more deeply than sensors and are more likely to trust their subconscious, their "sixth sense," gut feel, or intuition. They are good at spotting patterns and taking a high-level "strategic" view, and tend to have a focus on the future. Sensors may see those who are intuitive as impractical, theoretical, and lacking determination.

Thinking (T) or feeling (F).   This category refers to how people make decisions. **Thinking** people are objective and make decisions based on facts. As such, their head rather than their heart rules them. Thinking people judge situations and others based on logic. **Feeling** people are more subjective and make decisions based on principles and values. They are ruled more by their heart than their head. Feeling people may judge situations and others based on feelings and extenuating circumstances.

Judging (J) or perceiving (P).   **Judging** does not mean "judgmental." Judging people like ordering, organization, and thinking sequentially. They like to have things planned and settled. Judging people seek closure. **Perceiving** people are flexible; they like to keep their options open and think freely. They like to act spontaneously and are adaptable. Perceivers like to keep things open-ended.

The MBTI classifications together describe 16 personality types, with every person identified with one of the items in each of the four groups. This personality assessment tool is widely used by many large organizations, including Apple, AT&T, GE, 3M, Citigroup, and even the U.S. Armed Forces.

Although it is popular, there is mixed evidence about the assessment's validity as a determinant of personality. One such issue is that the assessment absolutely types a person in either one or the other type. You are either categorized as an extrovert or an introvert; you can't be a combination of the two. Because the results tend to be unrelated to job performance, the tool should not be used as a selection test and, thus, the best application for the MBTI would be its use as a guide for increasing one's self-awareness.

THE BIG FIVE PERSONALITY MODEL

When you describe someone to other people, you may say things like, "He has a big personality," in order to convey that the person is fun loving, friendly, and outgoing. On the other hand, you may say, "He has no personality," meaning that the person is dreary, dimwitted, and boring. The truth is that there is no such thing as having no personality or, conversely, a lot of personality. Everyone has a different type of personality made up of hundreds of traits and combinations of traits and, thus, personality cannot be exactly measured in terms of size or dimension. Psychologists have identified thousands of personality traits and dimensions that differentiate one person from another.

The **Big Five Model** is one widely accepted model that has an impressive body of research supporting the theory that five basic dimensions underlie all others and encompass most of the significant variations in human personality. The following are the Big Five factors.

Openness to experience.   This dimension addresses a person's range of interests and fascination with novelty. Open people are intellectually curious, appreciative of art, and sensitive to beauty. They tend to be more aware of their feelings and tend to think and act in individualistic and nonconforming ways. People with low scores on openness to experience tend to have narrow, particular interests. They prefer the plain, straightforward, and the obvious to the complex, ambiguous, and subtle. They may regard the arts and sciences with suspicion, regarding these endeavors as obscure or of no practical use. Closed people prefer familiarity rather than novelty and tend to be more conservative and resistant to change.

Conscientiousness.   The conscientiousness dimension is a measure of reliability. Conscientiousness concerns the way in which we control, regulate, and direct our impulses. Impulses are not inherently bad; occasionally, time constraints require a snap decision, and acting on our first impulse can be an effective response. Also, in times of play rather than work, acting spontaneously and impulsively can be fun. Impulsive individuals may be seen as colorful, fun to be with, and unconventional.

Extroversion. The extroversion (positive affectivity) dimension captures our comfort level with relationships. Extroverts enjoy being with people, are full of energy, and often experience positive emotions. They tend to be enthusiastic, action-oriented individuals. In groups they tend to talk more, assert themselves, and draw attention to themselves. Introverts tend to be quieter, low-key, deliberate, and disengaged from the social world. Their lack of social involvement should not be interpreted as shyness or depression, however, as the introvert simply needs less stimulation than an extrovert and prefers to be alone.

Agreeableness. The agreeableness dimension refers to an individual's propensity to comply with others. Agreeable individuals value getting along with others, perhaps even at the cost of their own comfort. They are typically considerate, friendly, generous, helpful, and willing to compromise their interests with those of others. Agreeable people also have an optimistic view of human nature. They believe people are basically honest, decent, and trustworthy. People who score low on the agreeableness, however, are individuals that place their own self-interest above getting along with others. They are generally unconcerned with others' well-being, and therefore are unlikely to extend themselves for other people. Sometimes their skepticism about others' motives may cause them to appear suspicious, unfriendly, and uncooperative.

Neuroticism or emotional stability. The emotional stability dimension, or inversely, neuroticism, measures a person's ability to withstand stress. People high in neuroticism are emotionally reactive. They respond more emotionally to events that would not affect others so profoundly, and their reactions tend to be more intense. They are more likely to interpret ordinary situations as threatening, and minor frustrations as hopelessly difficult. Their negative emotional reactions tend to persist for unusually long periods of time, which means they may be often in a bad mood. These problems with their emotional regulation can diminish a neurotic person's ability to think clearly, make decisions, and cope effectively with stress. Conversely, individuals who score low in neuroticism are less easily upset and less emotionally reactive. They tend to be calm, emotionally stable, and free from the persistent negative feelings that affect those who score highly in neuroticism.

Most psychologists agree that the traits that make up a person's personality can be organized into a hierarchy. The Big Five Model of personality aligns the five general personality traits at the top of the trait hierarchy: extroversion, neuroticism, agreeableness, conscientiousness, and openness to experience (Figure 3.3).

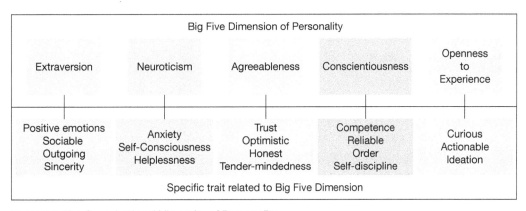

Figure 3.3. The Organizational Hierarchy of Personality

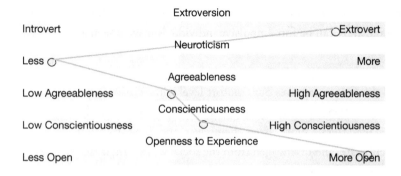

Figure 3.4. Big Five Personality Profile

Each of the traits, both specific and general dimension, are represented on a continuum wherein the person can be high, low, average, or anywhere in between on the scale. Figure 3.4 is an example of a Big Five personality profile for a person who is high on extroversion, low on neuroticism, average on agreeableness and conscientiousness, and more open to experience.

Research on the Big Five traits has shown that a relationship exists between these personality dimensions and job performance. Individuals who are dependable, reliable, careful, thorough, able to plan, organized, hardworking, persistent, and achievement-oriented tend to have higher job performance in most if not all occupations.

Certain traits have been shown to strongly relate to higher job performance. For example, highly conscientious people develop more job knowledge, exert greater effort, and have better performance. Interestingly, conscientious people also live longer because they take better care of themselves and engage in fewer risky behaviors like smoking, drinking, and drugs.

Those who score high on emotional stability are typically happier and more satisfied with their jobs than those who score low. Extroverts also tend to be happier with their jobs and tend to perform better in jobs that require significant interpersonal interaction, perhaps because they are more open to social situations with strangers, typically have more friends, and enjoy spending more time in social situations than introverts.

People who score high on openness to experience are usually more creative in the areas of science and art than those who score low. Because creativity is important in leadership, open people are also more likely to be effective leaders. Highly agreeable people are good in social settings and are typically liked better than disagreeable people, which explains why they tend to do better in interpersonally oriented jobs, such as customer service.

It is important to remember that there are no good or bad personalities, as all people are beautiful and unique in their own ways. Good managers, rather than considering one personality to be better or worse than another, need to recognize and respect individual differences and understand that unique personalities maybe best suited to different kinds of organizational jobs.

OTHER RELEVANT PERSONALITY TRAITS

In addition to the Myers–Briggs and the Big Five personality framework, there are several other more specific personality attributes that are powerful predictors of behavior in organizations. Among the most important are locus of control, self-monitoring, self-efficacy, authoritarianism, Machiavellianism, self-esteem, risk propensity, and Type A and Type B personalities.

Locus of control.   Are you one who feels that only your own actions and behaviors have an impact on what happens to you? Or, conversely, do you feel that fate, chance, luck, or other powerful people determine your fate? How you answer these questions may be an indicator of your locus of control. **Locus of control** is the extent to which people believe that their behavior has a real effect on what happens to them. "Externals," or individuals with an **external locus of control**, tend to believe that outside forces beyond their control are mainly responsible for their fate, and see little connection between their own actions and what happens to them. For example, an employee who fails to receive a promotion may attribute that failure to a politically motivated boss or just bad luck, rather than to their poor performance. "Internals," or individuals with an **internal locus of control**, believe that their own actions and behaviors have an impact on what happens to them. They feel that, so long as they work hard, they will succeed. They also may believe that people who fail do so because they lack ability or motivation.

Self-monitoring.   How would you react if your boss did not support your ideas at a meeting? Would you feel angry? Or pretend that you're not angry? Would you act as if you are happy with his actions? How you choose to use self-monitoring depends largely on the context, as well as the relationship that you have with your boss. **Self-monitoring** is the extent to which people try to control the way they present themselves to others. **High self-monitors** want their behavior to be socially acceptable and are attuned to any social cues that signal appropriate or inappropriate behavior. As such, they are likely to tailor their behavior to fit a given situation. High self-monitors perform well in jobs such as sales or consulting that require high interaction with different types of people. **Low self-monitors** are more likely to be frank with their response and say what they think is true or correct, without concern for how others will react to them. Low self-monitors may be well suited for providing organizational members with open, honest feedback and playing the devil's advocate in decision-making groups.

Self-efficacy.   Are you a person who is confident in your ability to complete a task or solve a problem? For example, if you believe that you are brilliant in math and that you can solve any algebra equation, you have high self-efficacy in math. Whether it is true that you're brilliant in math or not doesn't really matter—it only matters what you believe. **Self-efficacy** is that person's belief about their ability to perform a task. People with **high self-efficacy** believe that they can perform well on a specific task. Those with **low self-efficacy** tend to doubt their ability to perform a specific task. If your self-efficacy in an area is much lower than your ability, you will never challenge yourself or improve. If your self-efficacy in an area is much higher than your ability, you will set goals that are too high, fail, and possibly quit. The ideal self-efficacy is slightly above a person's ability: high enough to be challenging while still being realistic.

Authoritarianism.   Do you accept directives or orders from someone with more authority purely because the other person is your boss, or are you more likely to question things, express disagreement with the boss, and even refuse to carry out orders if they are for some reason objectionable? **Authoritarianism** describes the extent to which a person believes that power and status differences are appropriate within hierarchical social systems, such as an organization. **High authoritarians** may accept directives or orders from someone who is the boss. **Low authoritarians** are people who are more likely to question things and express disagreement with their leader. A highly authoritarian manager may be relatively autocratic and demanding, and highly authoritarian subordinates will be more likely to accept this behavior from their leader. Low authoritarian managers may allow subordinates a greater role in decision making, and less authoritarian subordinates will respond positively to this leadership style.

Machiavellianism.   Consider the following: Mitch is a young manager in Los Angeles. He has had four promotions in the past four years and makes no apologies for the aggressive tactics he has used to advance his career. Mitch says, "I will do what is necessary to get ahead." Mitch would properly be called Machiavellian. The personality characteristic of **Machiavellianism** is named after Niccolo Machiavelli, a 16th-century author famous for his book *The Prince*, in which how to gain power and control others is described. The term Machiavellianism is now used to describe behavior directed at gaining power and controlling the behavior of others. An individual high in Machiavellianism is pragmatic, maintains emotional distance, and believes the ends can justify the means. "High

Machs" manipulate more, win more, are persuaded less, persuade others more, and are more willing to lie to attain their personal goals. High Machs do well in jobs that require bargaining skills (such as labor negotiation) or jobs that offer rewards for winning (commissioned sales). Those who are low in Machiavellianism are more emotional, less willing to lie to succeed, highly value loyalty and friendship, and get little personal pleasure from manipulating people.

Self-esteem.   How do you feel when the grade you get on an exam is low? Or, how about the way your friends treat you? Or even still, the ups and downs in a romantic relationship? Your self-esteem is something more fundamental than the normal ups and downs associated with situational changes. For people with **high self-esteem**, normal ups and downs may lead to temporary fluctuations in how they feel about themselves, but only to a limited extent. In contrast, for people with poor or low self-esteem, normal ups and downs can drastically impact the way they see themselves. **Self-esteem** is the extent to which a person believes that he or she is a worthwhile and deserving individual. People with high self-esteem are more likely to seek higher-status jobs, set higher goals for themselves, be more confident in their ability to achieve higher levels of performance, and derive greater intrinsic satisfaction from their accomplishments. Those with **low self-esteem** may be content to remain in lower-level jobs, question their self-worth, are apprehensive about their ability to succeed in different endeavors, and focus more on extrinsic rewards. However, one must keep in mind that people with low self-esteem can be just as capable as those with high self-esteem, in spite of their self-doubts.

Risk propensity.   People differ in their willingness to take chances. **Risk propensity** is the degree to which a person is willing to take chances and to make risky decisions with a higher probability of failure, given that there is a worthwhile reward in the chance of success. Managers with **high risk propensity** may make more rapid decisions and use less information than managers with low risk propensity. They may lead the organization in new and different directions and be a catalyst for innovation or, on the other hand, might jeopardize the continued well-being of the organization if the risky decision proves to be a bad one. Managers with **low risk propensity** may lead the organization to stagnation and excessive conservatism, or might help the organization successfully navigate unpredictable and turbulent environmental shifts by maintaining calm and stability. Hence, the potential consequence of a manager's risk propensity depends heavily on the organizational environment.

Type A and Type B personalities.   Do you know people who are excessively competitive? Or perhaps they are always impatient, in a hurry, and are distressed by having to wait in lines? Chances are those people have a Type A personality. While the term Type A is used often, it's not always fully known what specific characteristics make up Type A personality, even among experts. For example, some people think the term applies to rude and impatient people. Others see workaholics as Type A. And still others may view competitiveness as the main characteristic. A person with **Type A behavior** (TAB) is aggressively involved in a chronic, incessant struggle to achieve more in less time and, if required to do so, against the opposing efforts of other things or people. According to research, the hallmark characteristics of TAB are

- walking or talking at a rapid pace;
- getting frustrated while waiting in line;
- feeling impatient with the rate at which most events take place
- attempting to accomplish more than one task at a time;
- find it difficult to cope with leisure time; and
- competitiveness.

A person with **Type B behavior** (TBB) is exactly the opposite. Type Bs never suffer from a sense of urgency with its accompanying impatience, and can relax without guilt. Some of the other characteristics include being more relaxed about time (they don't get overly stressed about being late), and not being easily angered. You probably know people who just seem to be relaxed, who don't get angry often, and seem to "kick back" or roll with the punches. Those people may be Type B.

ABILITY, APTITUDE, AND SKILLS

When examining individual differences and the way they affect the attitudes and behaviors of employees, it is important to consider the **abilities**, **aptitudes**, and **skills** that are unique to each employee. Ability is defined as an acquired or natural capacity or talent that enables an individual to perform a particular job or task successfully. Ability is an important factor in organizational behavior as it determines the level of performance an individual employee can achieve, as well as the cumulative effect of all of the employees in an organization. Hence, the cumulative organizational effectiveness depends on the performance levels of all of the employees, from the janitor to the CEO, in the organization.

There are two basic types of ability: cognitive ability and physical ability.

Cognitive abilities are brain-based skills that are needed to carry out any task, from the simplest to the most complex. They have more to do with the mechanisms of how we learn, remember, solve problems, and pay attention rather than with any actual knowledge. The most general dimension of cognitive ability is **general intelligence**, in which are eight specific types of cognitive ability (Figure 3.5) that reflect competence in different areas of mental functioning.

Researchers suggest that cognitive ability predicts job performance, as long as the ability in question is relied on in performing the particular job. For example, answering the telephone involves perception (hearing the ring tone), decision making (answering or not), motor skills (lifting the receiver), language skills (talking and understanding language), and social skills (interpreting tone of voice and interacting properly with another human being). However, numerical ability is unlikely to predict how well a writer or workout trainer will perform on the job.

To understand the relationship between cognitive ability and job performance, managers need to be able to identify the abilities required to effectively perform the task. Cognitive ability is also important to group and team effectiveness, as well as other things that determine performance. We shall discuss team effectiveness and performance in later chapters.

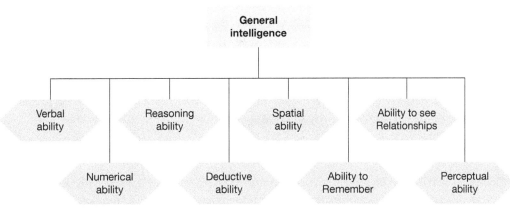

Figure 3.5. Types of Cognitive Ability

Table 3.1 is an example of each of the cognitive abilities and types of jobs in which the ability is important.

Table 3.1. Cognitive Abilities and Job Types

Ability	Description	Type of Jobs in Which Ability is Important
Verbal ability	Ability to understand and use written and spoken language	Professors, teachers, lawyers, writers, comedians
Numerical ability	Ability to solve mathmatical problems and numbers	Investment bankers, engineers, accountants
Reasoning ability	Ability to solve problems and understand the cause and effect by which different problems can be solved	Medical researchers, detectives, scientists, investigative reporters
Ability to see relationships	How things are related to each other and then apply this knowledge to other relationships and solutions	Consultants, travel agents. Anthropologists
Ability to remember	Ability to recall things ranging from simple associations to complex groups of statements or facts	Translators, salepeople, managers, researchers
Spatial ability	Ability to determine the location or arrangement of objects in relation to one's own position and to imagine how an object would appear if its position in space were altered	Air traffic controller, architects, clothing designers, astronauts
Perceptual ability	Ability to uncover visual patterns and see relationships within and across patterns	Professional photographers, airplane pilots, cruise and cargo ship captains, landscape designers

People obviously differ in cognitive abilities, but they also differ in physical abilities. We examine two types of physical skills: motor and physical. **Motor skills** are those abilities used to physically manipulate objects in an environment, whereas **physical skills** are a person's strength and fitness, including such abilities as static strength and stamina.

THE MANAGEMENT OF ABILITIES IN THE ORGANIZATION

As one can see, there are many types of abilities that people possess, and only a few abilities are likely to be important for job performance. For example, managerial work or work as a teacher requires cognitive ability but little physical ability, whereas a mechanic or a grocery store shelf stocker requires mainly physical ability. A heart surgeon requires both cognitive and physical abilities when performing a highly complicated and delicate surgery.

The importance for managers is to make sure employees have the necessary abilities they need to perform their jobs effectively. Managers have three fundamental ways to manage abilities within an organization to ensure that this alignment is successful: selection, placement, and training.

SELECTION

Selection first involves identifying the tasks that the employer wants the employee to accomplish and the abilities necessary to do them. Once these abilities are identified, managers then have to develop accurate measures for them. It is important that the tool selected for determining an applicant's abilities does indeed predict task performance. If it is not a good measure of the performance level required, there is no point in using it as a selection tool and it may be unethical to do so.

Once employees are selected and become part of an organization, managers must accurately match each employee to a job that will optimize their abilities. The process of placement is more involved than just assigning new employees to the appropriate positions, though. It also becomes crucial in horizontal moves or promotions within the organization.

TRAINING

Training is the process of enhancing the skills, capabilities, and knowledge of employees in preparation for doing a particular job. The training process molds the thinking of employees and leads to quality performance. It is continuous in nature. Training is crucial for organizational development and success, and is beneficial to both employers and employees of an organization. Extensive research has shown that job-appropriate training is effective in increasing employees' skills and abilities and, ultimately, their performance.

SUMMARY OF CHAPTER

1. Personality is the pattern of relatively enduring ways that a person feels, thinks, and behaves, and it is determined by both nature and nurture. Personality tends to be stable over time and, as such, managers should not expect to be able to change someone's personality, and should accept their employees' personalities as they are, learning to develop effective ways to deal with people.
2. The Big Five personality traits are extroversion, neuroticism, agreeableness, conscientiousness, and openness to experience.
3. Other personality traits that are relevant to organizational behavior include locus of control, self-monitoring, self-efficacy, authoritarianism, Machiavellianism, self-esteem, risk propensity, and Type A and B personalities.
4. In addition to having different personalities, employees also differ in their abilities, both cognitive and physical.
5. Cognitive abilities can be arranged hierarchically, with general intelligence at the top with specific types of abilities below. The specific abilities are verbal ability, numerical ability, reasoning ability, deductive ability, ability to see relationships, ability to remember, spatial ability, and perceptual ability.
6. Physical abilities include motor skills (the ability to manipulate objects in a given environment) and physical skills (fitness and strength).
7. Managers must realize the importance of selecting individuals who have the abilities necessary for the given task, placing employees in jobs that will optimize their abilities, and train employees to enhance their job performance.

DISCUSSION QUESTIONS

1. Why is it important to understand that both nature and nurture play a role in determining an employee's personality?
2. Do you think that it is good for an organization to be composed of individuals all with similar personalities? Why or why not?
3. Should organizations select or hire prospective employees on the basis of their personality traits? Why or why not?
4. Do certain personality traits make better team members? Team leaders?

WHAT MAKES UP
MY PERSONALITY?

INSTRUCTIONS

Indicate how true to your personality or preferences is each adjective that follows. For example, if the adjective is "Talkative" and you are more quiet than you are talkative, choose 2 (more false than true). Use the following scale:
1: False | 2: More false than true | 3: Somewhat true | 4: More true than False | 5: True

1. Talkative
2. Tense
3. Critical
4. Imaginative
5. Outgoing
6. Cooperative
7. Disorganized
8. Familiar
9. Dependable
10. Sociable
11. Adaptable to Change
12. Insecure
13. Enthusiastic
14. Goal-oriented
15. Trusting

SCORING KEY:

You will have five scores for this assessment. Total each group of scores, and be sure to reverse score those with an asterisk.
- Extroversion score: 1, 5, 10
- Agreeableness score: 3*, 6, 15
- Conscientiousness score: 7*, 9, 14

- Emotional stability score: 2*, 12*, 13
- Openness-to-experience score: 4, 8*, 11

ANALYSIS:

The Big Five, or the five-factor model, states that these five behaviors make up one's underlying personality. There are no definitive cut-offs of scores. However, a score of 3 to 6 can be considered low, 7 to 11, moderate, and 12 to 15 high. The higher the score, the more that factor affects your personality. An explanation of each follows.

- Extroversion: This considers the comfort one has with relationships. Extroverts (shown with a high score) tend to enjoy being around people, thrive on attention, and be assertive. Introverts are quieter and more reserved, and need alone time.
- Agreeableness: This looks at your tendency to comply with others. If you scored high, you value harmony, getting along with others, and compromise. Those who score low place self-interest above compromise.
- Conscientiousness: This looks at reliability. A highly conscientious person is dependable and regulates impulses. Someone who scores low on this factor is more spontaneous and can be seen as unconventional.
- Emotional stability: This looks at how you handle stress. If you score high, you have emotional stability—stress doesn't affect your emotions and you can remain calm. A low score indicates neuroticism—you are emotionally reactive and stress can take over your life.
- Openness-to-experience: This considers whether or not you enjoy novelty (new experiences). Those open to experience generally enjoy the arts and are more aware of their feelings. Those with lower scores prefer the conventional and familiar.

Adapted from: Robbins, S. P. (2009). 1.A.1: What's my basic personality? Self-assessment library (1–2). Upper Saddle River, NJ: Pearson Education Inc.

Original source: Based on John, O. P. (1990). The "Big Five" factor taxonomy: Dimensions of personality in the natural language and in questionnaires. In L. A. Pervin (Ed.), *Handbook of personality theory and research* (pp. 66–100). New York: Guilford Press; and Formy-Duval, D. L., Williams, J. E., Patterson, D. J., & Fogle, E. E. (1995). A "Big Five" scoring system for the item pool of the adjective check-list. *Journal of Personality Assessment, 65,* 59–76.

CHAPTER 3 REFERENCES

Baron, R. A. (1989). Personality and organizational conflict: Effects of the Type A behavior pattern and self-monitoring. *Organizational Behavior and Human Decision Processes, 44(2),* 281–297.

Barrick, M. R., & Mount, M. K. (1991). The Big Five personality dimensions and job performance: A meta-analysis. *Personnel Psychology, 44(1),* 1–26.

Burke, M. A., Brief, A. P., & George, J. M. (1993). The role of negative affectivity in understanding relationships between self-reports of stressors and strains: A comment on the applied psychology literature. *Journal of Applied Psychology, 78(3),* 402–412.

Carson, R. C. (1989). Personality. *Annual Review of Psychology, 40(1)*, 227–248.

Cetin, M.O. (2006) The relationship between job satisfaction, occupational and organizational commitment of academics. *The Journal of American Academy of Business*, Cambridge, 8(1), 78–88.

Coleman, D. F., Irving, G.P., & Cooper, C.L. (1999). Another look at the locus of control, organizational commitment relationship; it depends on the form of commitment. *Journal of Organizational Behaviour*, 20(6), 995–1001.

Digman, J. M. (1990). Personality structure: Emergence of the five-factor model. *Annual Review of Psychology, 41(February)*, 417–440.

Dunnette, M. D. (1976). Aptitudes, abilities, and skills. In M. D. Dunnette (Ed.), *Handbook of Industrial and Organizational Psychology* (pp. 473–520). Chicago: Rand McNally.

Fruyt, F., McCrae, R. R., Szirmak, A., Nagy, J. (2004). *The Five-Fctor Personality Inventory as a Measure of the Five-Factor Model*, Clinical Psychology, 11(3), 207–215.

George, J. M. (1992). The role of personality in organizational life: Issues and evidence. *Journal of Management, 18(2)*, 185–213.

George, J. M., & Zhou, J. (2001). When openness to experience and conscientiousness are related to creative behavior: An interactional approach. *Journal of Applied Psychology, 86(3)*, 513–524.

Ilies, R., & Judge, T. A. (2003). On the heritability of job satisfaction: The mediating role of personality. *Journal of Applied Psychology, 88(4)*, 750–759.

Kenrick, D. T., & Funder, D. C. (1988). Profiting from controversy: Lessons from the person-situation debate. *American Psychologist, 43(1)*, 23–34.

Lubinski, D., & Dawis, R. V. (1992). Aptitudes, skills, and proficiencies. In M. D. Dunnette and L. M. Hough (Eds.), *Handbook of Industrial and Organizational Psychology*, Vol. 3.

Locke, E.A. (1976). The nature and cause of job satisfaction. In M.D. Dunnette (Ed.) *Handbook of Industrial and organizational psychology*. Chicago: Rand McNally

McCrae, R. R., & Costa, P. T. (1987). Validation of the five-factor model of personality across instruments and observers. *Journal of Personality and Social Psychology, 52(1)*, 81–90.

McCrae, R. R., & Costa, P. T. (1992). Discriminant validity of NEO-PIR facet scales. *Educational and Psychological Measurement, 52(1)*, 229–237.

McCrae, R. R., & Costa, P. T. (1992). A gallery of risk takers. *BusinessWeek, Reinventing America*, 183.

Mowday, R. T., Porter, L. W., Steers, R. (1982). *Organizational linkages: The psychology of commitment, absenteeism, and turnover*. San Diego: Academic Press.

Rotter, J. B. (1966). Generalized expectancies for internal vs. external control of reinforcement. *Psychological Monograph, 80(1)*, 1–28.

Rowe, D. C. (1987). Resolving the person-situation debate: Invitation to an interdisciplinary dialogue. *American Psychologist, 42(3)*, 218–227.

Rotter, J. B. (1954). *Social learning and clinical psychology*. Englewood Cliffs, New Jersey: Prentice Hall.

Rotter, J. B. (1966). *Generalized expectancies for internal versus external control of reinforcement*. Psychological monographs 80 (Whale No. 609).

Rotter, J. B., Chance, J.E., Phares, E. J. (1972). Application of a social learning of personality, New York: Holt, Rinehart and Winston.

Sagie, A. (1998). Employee absenteeism, organizational commitment, and job satisfaction: Another look. Journal of Vocational Behaviour, 52(2),156–171.

Spector, P. (1982). Behavior in organizations as a function of employees' locus of control. *Psychological Bulletin, 91(3)*, 482–497.

Stahl, M. J. (1983). Achievement, power, and managerial motivation: Selecting managerial talent with the job choice exercise. *Personnel Psychology, 36(4)*, 775–789.

Tellegen, A., Lykken, D. T., Bouchard, T. J., et al. (1988). Personality similarity in twins reared apart and together. *Journal of Personality and Social Psychology, 54(6)*, 1031–1039.

Van den Berg, P. T., & Feij, J. A. (2003). Complex relationships among personality traits, job characteristics, and work behavior. *International Journal of Selection and Assessment, 11(4)*, 326–349.

INDIVIDUAL PROCESSES IN ORGANIZATIONS

2

FOUNDATIONS OF INDIVIDUAL BEHAVIOR

04

CHAPTER LEARNING OBJECTIVES

After reading this chapter, you should have a good understanding of

- the nature of people in organizations and the importance of understanding the psychological contract between an employee's contributions and the organizational performance to managers;
- psychological contracts and how they contribute to the organization and what the organization will provide the employee in return;
- the person–job fit and the extent to which the contributions made by the individual match the inducements offered by the organization;
- the complexity of individual attitudes, beliefs, and feelings as they relate to specific ideas, situations, and to other people;
- how organizations manage job satisfaction and organizational commitment;
- the basic perceptual process, including the danger of stereotyping in an organization; and
- the value of enhancing creativity in an organization, including how organizational citizenship makes a positive overall contribution to the organization.

"If you give somebody something for nothing, you make them good for nothing."

- AUBREY DANIELS

THE NATURE OF THE INDIVIDUAL– ORGANIZATION RELATIONSHIP

The relationship that exists between employees and organizations is similar to any contractual relationship in that each party has its own interest in mind, wanting more for itself while giving less to the other side. The downside to this type of arrangement is that employees are feeling less loyalty to their employers than workers have in recent times, and employers seem willing to trade employee loyalty for lower costs and greater flexibility.

Understanding how to deal with people in organizations and the various elements and characteristics that contribute to determining how and in what form they are willing to engage in behaviors that will benefit the organization is critical to managers.

This chapter examines the behavior of people in organizations and the basic nature of the individual–organizational relationship. Examining this relationship helps managers understand the nature of individual differences and it is these differences that play a crucial role in determining important workplace behaviors.

PSYCHOLOGICAL CONTRACTS

Whenever you buy a car, a house, or something that requires signing a contract that specifies the terms of the agreement, you have entered into a contract. A **psychological contract** is similar to a standard legal contract in some ways, but is less formal and not as well-defined. A psychological contract refers to the unwritten set of expectations of the employment relationship as distinct from the formal, codified employment contract. It is a person's overall set of expectations regarding what he or she will contribute to the organization and what the organization will provide in return. Taken together, the psychological contract and the employment contract define the employer–employee relationship.

The psychological contract develops and evolves constantly based on communication, or lack thereof, between the employee and the employer. Promises over promotion or salary increases, for example, may form part of the psychological contract. Figure 4.1 illustrates the essential nature of a psychological contract. The employee makes a set of contributions to the organization, such as effort, ability, and loyalty, and in return for these contributions, the organization provides incentives to the individual, such as pay, security, benefits, status, and career or promotion opportunities.

All organizations face the challenge of managing expectations so that they don't accidentally give employees the wrong perception of action that then doesn't materialize. Employees should also manage their expectations so that, for example, management doesn't see difficult situations or adverse personal circumstances that affect productivity as deviant.

Fairness is a significant part of the psychological contract, bound up in **equity theory**—employees need to perceive that they're being treated fairly to sustain a healthy psychological contract. Perceived inequity of the psychological contract may initiate a change and can severely damage the relationship between employer and employee, leading to disengagements, reduced productivity, and, in some cases, workplace nonconformity.

THE PERSON–JOB FIT THEORY

One effective way to manage psychological contracts is by managing the person–job fit (PJ). The **person–job fit theory** is a match between an employee's abilities, needs, and values, and the organizational demands, rewards, and values. Person–job fit theory centers around the idea that every organization and every individual has specific and different personality traits. The more similar the traits between the person and the organization, the higher the probability of workplace productivity and employee satisfaction.

Achieving the optimal personality fit will also decrease turnover rates, stress, absenteeism, and poor job satisfaction. However, it is important to realize that optimal person–job

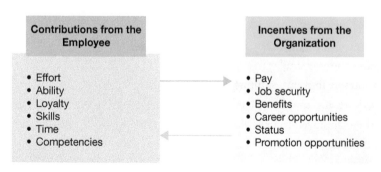

Figure 4.1. The Psychological Contract

fit is seldom achieved, as hiring procedures are imperfect, estimating employee skill levels is difficult, and assessing attitudes and personalities is complicated.

Finally, both the employee and the organization will change over time. An employee who initially finds a new job stimulating and exciting may consider the same job boring and monotonous a few years later, and the organization may change by adopting new technology that may require an entirely new skillset from its employees.

INDIVIDUAL DIFFERENCES

Individual differences, simply put, are personal attributes that vary from one person to another. We all know that we are different from each other in many ways, such as our physical aspects, our likes, dislikes, interests, values, and psychological makeup. Those aspects make us unique and define our personalities.

It is important for managers to understand the specific differences that characterize a given person. Determining this, of course, depends on other factors and circumstances. One person may be dissatisfied, withdrawn, and negative in one job setting but is satisfied, outgoing, and positive in another. Working conditions, coworkers, and leadership are just a few of the factors that affect how a person performs and feels about a job. Hence, whenever a manager attempts to assess or account for individual differences among their employees, they must also consider the situation in which the behavior occurs.

Given the importance of establishing effective psychological contracts with their employees and achieving optimal fits between employees and their jobs, managers are confronted with the major challenge of attempting to understand both the individual differences and the contributions made in relation to any organizational inducements.

ATTITUDES IN ORGANIZATIONS

An important determinant of employee behavior in an organization is their attitude. **Attitudes** are sets of complex beliefs and feelings that people have about specific ideas, people, or situations. Attitudes are important because they are the mechanisms through which most people express their feelings. Attitudes influence a person's action and response to challenges, incentives and rewards. For example, if an employee says that she is underpaid by the organization, she is reflecting a **feeling** about her pay. "I like working on this project" and "I do not like working after office hours" are some other examples of attitudes because they express a person's general feeling, either favorable or unfavorable, toward something.

Typically, attitudes have been considered along with two other elements—beliefs and behaviors. **Beliefs** represent what we have learned or come to know through experience. As such, they are either true or represent what we think is true. For example, thinking that working on a challenging project would bring recognition in the organization or that working after office hours would affect health and personal life is a *belief*. **Behaviors**, on the other hand, represent the actions we take with regard to a particular object or entity. For example, whether one completes the project successfully or leaves the office at six in the evening is their *behavior*.

In the simplest case, attitudes, beliefs, and behaviors could be easily related. For example, a dislike of nuclear power plants would be associated with negative beliefs about them, such as believing that they are dangerous and often run in an irresponsible manner, and negatively oriented behaviors toward them, such as signing a petition to stop construction of a nuclear power plant.

Attitudes are usually stable natures to behave toward objects in a certain way and consist of three basic components: affect, cognition, and intention.

Affect.   The emotion component involves the person's feelings toward something, whether they are positive, neutral, or negative, about an object, idea, or person. For example, most people react to words such as "love," "hate," "sex," and "war" in a manner that reflects their feelings about what those words convey to them. You may like one of your professors, dislike another, and be indifferent towards a third. If the professor you dislike is one teaching an elective, you may not be particularly concerned. However, if the professor is teaching a course in your major, your affective reaction may be one of anxiety.

Cognition.   The information component is the knowledge or beliefs a person presumes to have about an object. For example, a manager may believe that it is necessary for an employee to have two weeks of training on new office software, when in reality, the average employee is able to operate the software after only one week. The information that the manager is using is the key to his attitude about the amount of training that is necessary. Cognitions are based on perceptions of truth and reality, and perceptions that agree with reality to a varying degree.

Intention.   This is the behavior component—intentions guide a person's behavior toward an object. Returning to the previous example, the manager may assign two weeks of software training to all of his new employees as a response to the information used for his decision making.

COGNITIVE DISSONANCE

In order to explain cognitive dissonance, we must first look at what cognition is. **Cognition** is bits of knowledge that can pertain to any variety of thoughts, values, facts, or emotions. People have countless cognitions in their head. For example, liking frozen yogurt is cognition. Also, identifying as a man is cognition. Some cognition is even related—for instance, "I have a sweet tooth" and "I like ice cream." These cognitions are consonant or congruent, meaning that they are related and that one follows from the other. Sometimes we have cognitions that are related, but do not follow from one another. In fact, they may be opposites—for instance, using the previous example, "I like frozen yogurt," but also, "I am trying to lose weight." These two thoughts are problematic—if you eat frozen yogurt, then you may gain weight, and if you really want to lose weight then you cannot eat frozen yogurt. These types of cognitions are referred to as dissonant.

The basic idea behind **cognitive dissonance** theory is that when two sets of cognitions or perceptions are contradictory or **incongruent**, a person experiences a level of conflict and anxiety.

Cognitive dissonance affects people in a variety of ways. We frequently encounter situations in which our attitudes conflict with each other or with our behaviors. Dissonance reduction is the way we deal with these feelings of discomfort and tension. In organizational settings, an employee who may consider leaving the organization may wonder why they continue to stay and work hard. As a result of this dissonance, they may realize that the company really isn't so bad after all. Conversely, they may realize that they may have no immediate options elsewhere or, perhaps, they think that they will leave at some point in the future.

ATTITUDE CHANGE

Unlike personality attributes, attitudes are not stable. For example, learning new information about a person may change your attitude toward them. A manager may have a negative attitude toward an employee because of her lack of work experience. However, after working with her for a while, the manager realizes that the person is actually very talented and, subsequently, develops a more positive attitude toward the employee.

Similarly, if the object of an attitude changes, a person's attitude toward that object may also change. For example, let's say that employees feel that they are underpaid and, as a result, have a negative attitude toward management. A big salary increase may cause these attitudes to become more positive.

Attitudes can also change when the object becomes less important or less relevant to the person. For example, suppose an employee has a negative attitude about his company's retirement plan. When he receives a sizable inheritance from his uncle, his attitude toward his retirement may become more moderate simply because he no longer has to worry about it.

Finally, while some attitudes change easily, deeply rooted attitudes that have a long history are far more resistant to change. For example, Frank Lorenzo, the former Eastern Airlines executive, developed a reputation in the industry as being anti-union and for cutting employee benefits and wages. As a result, employees throughout the industry came to dislike and distrust him. When he took over Eastern Airlines, the employees had such a strong attitude of distrust they could never agree to cooperate with any of his programs or ideas. When Eastern Airlines finally went bankrupt, many employees, even after losing their jobs, cheered.

JOB SATISFACTION

What was the best job that you have ever had? What made that job so good? Was it the people that you worked with? Was the job interesting to you—providing training, variety, independence, and control?

Research has proven that there is a strong correlation between how well people enjoy the social context of their work and how satisfied they are with their work. **Job satisfaction** is those attitudes that reflect the extent for which people find gratification or fulfillment in their work. The first aspect that comes to mind when we think about causes for job satisfaction is the reward a person gets while doing their job. A satisfied employee tends to be absent less often, to make positive contributions to the organization, and to stay with the organization longer. Dissatisfied employees may be absent more often, may experience stress on the job that is disruptive to coworkers, and are less productive.

You may have noticed that people often mention pay as a determinant of job satisfaction. This is somewhat true. However, this mainly applies to people who are poor or live in poor countries. Once an individual reaches a level of comfortable living (in the United States that happens at about $40,000 a year, depending on the region and family size), the relationship between pay and job satisfaction disappears. In fact, research has shown that people making $80,000 a year are, on average, no happier with their jobs than those who earn $40,000. Thus, money has proven to be a motivator, but what motivates us is not necessarily what make us happy.

WHAT IS JOB SATISFACTION?
Job satisfaction is composed of several factors, including mentally challenging work, equitable rewards, supportive working conditions, and supportive colleagues. Commitment to and involvement with the organization and the actual job are also factors.

Mentally challenging work. Are there opportunities to use skills and abilities with a variety of tasks, some freedom, and constant feedback? Jobs with too little challenge are deemed boring and frustrating, and can produce feelings of failure.

Equitable rewards. Employees want to work in a system that is perceived as just and fair. Are your promotions and pay systems policies meeting their requirements? While not everyone seeks a paycheck as the sole reward, the key is linking pay to satisfaction, which does not mean the salary paid but the perception of fairness. If these policies are perceived as just and fair, there is likely to be greater job satisfaction.

Supportive working conditions. The working environment is very important in terms of safety, health, and wellness. Physical comfort, location heating, noise, and professionalism are all important contributors. Ensuring that your environment is complying with all legislation and listening to employee complaints is important here.

Supportive colleagues. For many employees, the opportunity for social interaction with friendly coworkers and supervisors adds greatly to the dimension of job satisfaction. The supervisor's role is a major determinant of satisfaction because of the direct impact this role plays with the employee. Whether there is praise, good listening skills, positive role modeling, or a fair attitude, the supervisor will affect the satisfaction level.

Job involvement. Employees with a high level of involvement strongly identify with and care about the kind of work they do. The person identifies closely with their job title and the perceived value of their individual performance and contribution to the organization.

Organizational commitment. Some employees identify strongly with the employing organization. Perhaps it is the mission, vision, or value system of the organization. However, an interesting development can occur: while the employee may be dissatisfied with his or her particular job, the employee may view this as a "temporary" condition, due to high satisfaction with the organization as a whole, and remain loyal. Though, when dissatisfaction spreads to the organization itself, the employee is more likely to resign.

IMPACT OF SATISFIED AND DISSATISFIED WORKERS

It is logical to assume that satisfied workers will be more productive and helpful, and that dissatisfied workers will be the opposite, but what exactly happens when employees like their job, and when they dislike their job? One model to help us understand the consequences of dissatisfaction is the **exit, voice, loyalty, neglect framework**. The framework's four responses differ along two dimensions: constructive/destructive and active/passive. The four responses are as follows:

1. **Exit:** The exit response directs behavior toward leaving the organization, including looking for a new position, as well as resigning.
2. **Voice:** The voice response includes actively and constructively attempting to improve conditions, including suggesting improvements, discussing problems with superiors, and undertaking some form of union activity.
3. **Loyalty:** The loyalty response means passively but optimistically waiting for conditions to improve, including speaking up for the organization in the face of external criticism and trusting the organization and its management to "do the right thing."
4. **Neglect:** The final response is the neglect response, which passively allows conditions to worsen and includes chronic absenteeism or lateness, reduced efforts, and increased error rates.

Voice and loyalty encompass our constructive behavior, allowing us to tolerate unpleasant situations or revive satisfactory working conditions. Exit and neglect behaviors affect performance variables such as productivity, absenteeism, and turnover. This framework also helps us understand the situations we might find with unionized workers, for which there is often low job satisfaction but also a low turnover rate. Members often express dissatisfaction through the grievance procedure or formal contract negotiation. This **voice** response allows them to continue in their jobs while convincing themselves they are acting to improve the situation.

SATISFACTION AND PERFORMANCE

How important is a satisfied worker? In a 2010 study conducted by James Harter and colleagues, they found that lower job satisfaction among workers foreshadowed a poorer bottom-line performance of the company. One Gallup study estimated the cost of American workers' disengagement to be a staggering $300 billion in lost productivity per year. When employees are dissatisfied, they are more absent, produce less, or the quality of their output suffers.

The concept that job satisfaction leads to better performance is supported by Vroom's (1964) work that is based on the notion that performance is natural product of satisfying the needs of employees. Research has shown that satisfied workers have a profound impact on creativity, productivity, commitment, and collegiality.

Managers can help ensure that people are happily engaged at work. Doing so isn't expensive. Workers' well-being depends in large part on their managers' ability and willingness to facilitate their accomplishments by removing obstacles, providing help, and acknowledging strong effort.

ORGANIZATIONAL CITIZENSHIP BEHAVIOR

Have you ever been asked by your manager to help a new employee learn a new task or skill during your lunch hour or after work, and you have done so willingly? If so, you have positive organizational citizenship behavior. **Organizational citizenship behavior** (OCB) is defined as behavior that goes beyond the basic requirements of the job, is to a large extent discretionary, and is of benefit to the organization. Job satisfaction is a major determinant of an employee's OCB. Satisfied employees are more likely to talk positively about the organization, help others, and go beyond the normal expectations in their job. Lack or loss of OCB is a good indicator of a dissatisfied employee, and often a precursor to the employee exiting the firm.

SATISFACTION AND ABSENTEEISM

Absenteeism is a natural part of having human employees. Illness or injury, care of a loved one, jury duty, and vacations are normal and valid reasons that employees miss work. When organizational culture, job responsibilities, working conditions, or compensation fall below what employees expect, job satisfaction plummets. Subsequently, absenteeism rates will climb, often disguised as sick days or medical leave, although invalid absences also rise. Studies indicate that no matter the industry or organizational structure, when job satisfaction among employees drops, absenteeism consistently rises for that organization.

JOB SATISFACTION AND TURNOVER

It is well documented that losing an employee is a very expensive occurrence. There is a recruiting cost, interviewing, reference checking, testing, orientation cost, transitional time required to train the new employee, and more. There is also the cost of losing experience. Your clients lose their contacts and employees lose co-workers, both of which result in productivity loss. So why do employees leave? Most HR managers would say that people leave because of the following reasons:

- there are better opportunities elsewhere;
- it is difficult to work here;
- never fit in;
- can't get ahead; and
- poor management.

Surprisingly, however, a recent study of 1,100 employees who were identified as "at risk" of leaving for another job listed the following five reasons, in order of importance, as their main concerns:

1. Workload
2. Insufficient support from management
3. Concerns about the future
4. Lack of challenge
5. Insufficient recognition

The relationship between job satisfaction and turnover is stronger than between satisfaction and absenteeism. The satisfaction–turnover relationship is also affected by alternative job prospects. If an employee is presented with an unsolicited job offer, job dissatisfaction is less predictive of turnover because the employee is more likely leaving because of the lure of the other job, rather than the unattractiveness of the current job. Job dissatisfaction is also more likely to result in turnover when employment opportunities are abundant, because employees perceive it is easy to move; and if employees feel that they have high human capital (high level of education, high skill set and abilities), job dissatisfaction is more likely to translate into turnover because they have, or perceive, many available alternatives.

JOB DISSATISFACTION AND ANTAGONISTIC BEHAVIOR

Job dissatisfaction and antagonistic behavior with co-workers are precursors to multiple behaviors that are undesirable to organizations. Substance abuse, theft of company property, tardiness, and attempt at unionization are all behaviors of a broad syndrome researchers call **deviant behavior in the workplace**. If employees don't like their work environment, they will express their dissatisfaction through some creative, outward action, often looking for ways to "get even" with the company. These actions are not always easily forecastable. One worker may quit and another may spend time surfing the Internet or even taking office supplies home for personal use. Because these types of behaviors are quite creative, controlling only one behavior leaves the main cause of the problem unresolved. Hence, to effectively control the undesirable consequences of job dissatisfaction, managers should address the source of the problem, the dissatisfaction itself, rather than trying to control the different responses.

ORGANIZATIONAL COMMITMENT

Why are some people emotionally committed to an organization? Some are committed to their jobs because they love what they do, or because their goals align with those of the company. Others might stay because they fear what they could lose if they leave. Still others might stay because they feel obligated to the company, or to their manager.

Clearly, some of these types of commitment can have a negative effect on a person's well-being, self-respect, and job satisfaction. So, how can an organization avoid this but still help team members feel committed to your organization in a positive way?

Organizational commitment reflects an individual's identification with and attachment to the organization. Highly committed employees may see themselves as a true member of the team, often referring to the organization in personal terms, such as, "We have excellent customer service." In contrast, less committed employees are more likely to see themselves in less personal terms, such as, "They don't pay their employees very well," to express more dissatisfaction about things, and not act as a long-term member of the organization.

There are three common components that explain how employees feel about the organization where they work: affective commitment, continuance commitment, and normative commitment.

AFFECTIVE COMMITMENT

If you're enjoying your work, you're likely to feel good, and be satisfied with your job. In turn, this increased job satisfaction is likely to add to your feeling of affective commitment. Affection for your job occurs when you feel a strong emotional attachment to your organization, and to the work that you do. You'll most likely identify with the organization's goals and values, and genuinely want to be there.

CONTINUANCE COMMITMENT

This type of commitment occurs when you weigh up the pros and cons of leaving your organization. You may feel that you need to stay at your company because the loss you'd experience by leaving is greater than the benefit you think you might gain in a new role. These perceived losses could be monetary (you lose salary and benefits), professional (you might lose seniority or role-related skills that you've spent years acquiring), or social (you lose friendships or allies). The severity of these losses often increases with age and experience. You're more likely to experience continuance commitment if you're in an established, successful role, or if you've had several promotions within the organization.

NORMATIVE COMMITMENT

This type of commitment occurs when you feel a sense of obligation to your organization, even if you're unhappy in your role or if you want to pursue better opportunities. You feel that you should stay with your organization because it's the right thing to do. This sense of obligation can stem from several factors. You might feel that you should remain with your organization because it has invested money or time in your training or, perhaps, it provided a reward in advance, such as paying for your college tuition. This obligation can also result from your upbringing. For instance, your family might have stressed that you should stay loyal to your organization.

PERCEPTIONS IN ORGANIZATIONS

Another important element of workplace behavior is perception. **Perception** is the set of processes by which an individual becomes aware of and interprets information about the environment. People often assume that reality is objective—we all see and therefore perceive the same things in the same way. Unfortunately, that is not the case. For example, if we were to ask all of the students at Azusa Pacific University and Cal Poly Pomona to describe the most recent basketball game between the two schools, most likely we would hear two conflicting stories. These conflicting stories are primarily based on the perceptions of those fans. Even though they saw the same game, they interpreted the game in contrasting ways.

Since perception is key in a variety of workplace behaviors, managers should understand the basic perceptual process. In perception we receive information in many forms, from spoken words to visual images of movement and forms; we then assimilate the various types of incoming information for the purpose of interpreting it. Perception actually consists of two distinct processes: **selective perception** and **stereotyping** that are particularly relevant to managers (Figure 4.2).

EVALUATING OTHERS

We use a number of shortcuts when we evaluate others, but although they are frequently valuable in allowing us to make accurate perceptions rapidly, they are not foolproof and can get us into trouble. Understanding these shortcuts can help you recognize when they can result in significant distortions.

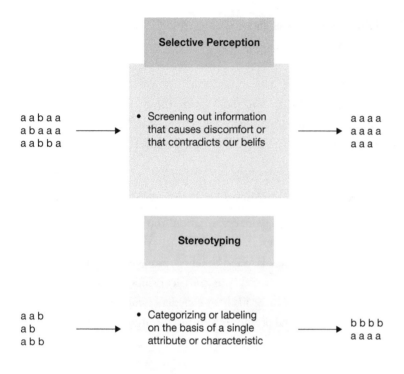

Figure 4.2. The Basic Perceptual Processes

Selective Perception

a a b a a
a b a a a
a a b b a

• Screening out information that causes discomfort or that contradicts our belifs

a a a a
a a a a
a a a

Stereotyping

a a b
a b
a b b

• Categorizing or labeling on the basis of a single attribute or characteristic

b b b b
a a a a

Halo effect.   The halo effect occurs when our general, overall impression of a person influences or distorts how we feel and think about their character. Essentially, your overall impression of a person impacts your evaluations of that person's specific traits. For example, an employee may be considered high performing and always meeting deadlines even though their work is full of mistakes and is usually late. Because of the halo effect, the employee will not receive the feedback necessary to improve performance or the specific dimensions in question. Halo effects can also be negative, though. A manager who has a negative impression of an employee may mistakenly perceive that employee as uncooperative and lazy. The halo effect may also include the **physical attractiveness stereotype** and the **"what is beautiful is good" principle**. At the most basic level, this bias refers to the habitual tendency of people to rate attractive individuals more favorably for their personality traits or characteristics than those who are less attractive.

Contrast effect.   This is a form of bias that results from the perceptions one has of the target person, which become distorted by the perceiver's perception of others in the same situation. For example, a professor's perception of a student whose performance is average is likely to be less favorable if that student is a member of a group of very high-performing students than if that student were in a group of average-performing students. As well, the perception of an average job applicant is more favorable by an interviewer if two or three below-average applicants preceded him or her.

Primacy effect.   This is the tendency for the first items presented in a series to be remembered better or more easily, or for them to be more influential than those presented later in the series. If you hear a long list of words, it is more likely that you will remember the words you heard first (at the beginning of the list) than words that occurred in the middle. Primacy effects are common problems in interviews, as interviewers decide in the first few minutes of an interview whether a job candidate is a good prospect and then spend the rest of the interview confirming their initial judgment by selectively paying attention to information consistent with that judgment, and discounting or ignoring inconsistent information. An interviewer who falls victim to the primacy effect may turn down qualified candidates who fail to perform well in the first minute or two of an interview because they are nervous.

Similar-to-me effect.   It is a fact of life that people tend to like others similar to themselves. In fact, research has clearly shown that interviewers and supervisors have an unconscious tendency to favor people who are physically and professionally similar to them. Job interviewers tend to favor candidates who are like them and mentors often select protégés that are similar to them. For example, similar-to-me effects may lead male CEOs to groom as their successors men like themselves, and thus not perceive a woman as a viable successor. This is one of the factors that holds women and minorities back in the working world. The similar-to-me bias is especially important to overcome today given the increasing diversity in organizational membership. In a workforce that includes many women, members of minority groups, and increasing numbers of people with disabilities, managers and subordinates have more frequent contact with people unlike themselves. When evaluating others who are different, people must try to be as objective as possible and avoid the similar-to-me trap.

Harshness, leniency, and average tendency bias.   These sets of biases occur when a supervisor rates a subordinate's performance. Some may tend to be overly harsh, whereas others are overly lenient, and still others rate everyone the same. All of these tendencies are problematic for two reasons. First, the supervisor does not correctly perceive the variations in the performance of his or her subordinates. As a result, high performers do not receive appropriate recognition and rewards for their superior accomplishments, and low performers do not receive the constructive feedback they need to improve their performance. Secondly, it makes it difficult to evaluate and compare the performance of subordinates who have different supervisors. A subordinate who has received relatively poor ratings from a harsh supervisor may be just as accomplished as a subordinate who has received average or high ratings from a lenient one. Evaluations biased in this manner can result in faulty decision making about pay raises and promotions. These biases can also operate in the classroom setting, where one professor gives mostly As in a course in which another professor gives mainly Cs as a class average. Students in the first professor's class may be content, whereas students in the other professor's class are likely to feel they are not being treated fairly.

Knowledge-of-predictor bias.   This bias occurs when a manager or even a professor knows a person's standing on a predictor of performance, and this information biases their perception of that person. For example, if a professor knows that a student has scored highly on some predictor of academic performance, such as the SAT or the GMAT, this knowledge may lead the professor to perceive the student more positively than he or she deserves. This bias could also work to the disadvantage of a student who scored poorly on the predictor.

Self-fulfilling prophecy.   Sometimes, knowledge-of-predictor bias results in a self-fulfilling prophecy. A classic demonstration of this bias was performed in a classroom setting in the 1960s. At the beginning of the school year, teachers were told that a few of their students were potential "late bloomers" who, given the proper encouragement, should excel. In fact, these students had been randomly selected from the class rosters and were no different from their peers. Later on in the school year, however, the late bloomers were indeed doing better and had even improved their scores on standardized IQ tests compared to their earlier performance and the performance of the other children in the class. What was responsible for the change? The teachers in the study probably gave the late bloomers more attention, encouragement, and feedback, and had higher expectations of them all, which resulted in their improved performance. The teachers may have also looked more at these students and made encouraging body gestures toward them. In this way, knowledge of a predictor (albeit a false predictor) resulted in behavior changes that caused the predictions to become true. Another example occurs often in the workplace during the job interview; once interviewers have made an initial judgment about a candidate, they tend to look for evidence to support their conclusion. If they like you, they tend to interpret your responses more favorably than if their initial reaction is less favorable. This bias can also occur even before you enter the room. If you are an interviewer's top candidate, he or she will look for actions and responses on your part that tend to

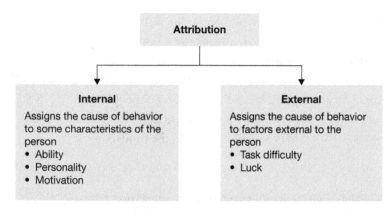

Figure 4.3. Types of Attributions

ATTRIBUTION THEORY

When we are around people, we try to explain why they behave in certain ways. Our perception and judgment of a person's actions will be significantly influenced by the assumptions we make about that person's internal state. **Attribution theory** suggests that we attribute causes to behavior based on our observations of certain internal or external characteristics of that behavior. **Internally** caused behaviors are those we believe to be under the personal control of the individual. **Externally** caused behavior is what we imagine the situation forced the individual to do. If you are late for class, you might attribute that to partying into the late hours and then oversleeping, which is an internal attribution. However, if you missed class because you were involved in heavy traffic due to an accident on the freeway, then you are making an external attribution. Figure 4.3 illustrates the types of attributions.

Our determination of internal or external depends largely on three factors: distinctiveness, consensus, and consistency (Figure 4.4).

Distinctiveness. Distinctiveness refers to the extent to which a specific action engaged in by an individual is unusual or uncommon for that particular individual. The judgment of whether an action is **high in distinctiveness**, that is, uncommon for the individual who engaged, or **low in distinctiveness**, that is, common for the individual, depends on knowledge of that individual's past behavior. For example, a student who arrives late for class is also one who other students say often blows off his group commitments. Such information is referred to as distinctiveness information.

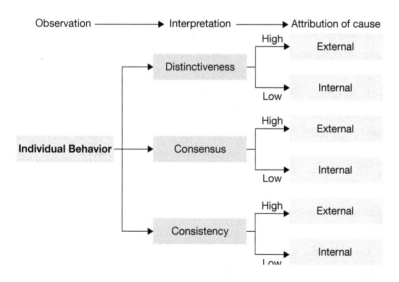

Figure 4.4. The Attribution Theory

Consensus. If everyone who faces a similar situation responds in the same way, we can say the behavior shows consensus. As in our previous example, our tardy student meets this criterion if other students who took the same route to school were also late. From an attribution perspective, if consensus were high, you would probably give an external attribution to the student's tardiness. However, if other students who took the same route made it to class on time, you would attribute his lateness to an internal cause.

Consistency. Consistency refers to the observation of a person's actions over time. Does the person respond in the same manner over a given period of time? Coming to class 10 minutes late is not perceived in the same way for a student who has never been late the entire semester as it is for a student who is late for class two or three times a week. The more consistent the behavior, the more we are inclined to attribute it to internal causes.

Research has shown that errors or biases distort attributions. When we make judgments about the behavior of other people, we tend to underestimate the influence of external factors and overestimate the influences of internal or personal factors. This is called the **fundamental attribution error** and can explain why a sales manager is prone to attribute the poor performance of her sales agent to laziness rather than to the innovative product line introduced by a competitor.

Self-serving bias occurs when individuals and organizations tend to attribute their own success to internal factors such as ability and effort, while placing the blame for failure on external factors such as bad luck or unproductive co-workers. For example, when good things happen to your spouse, people are more likely to attribute those causes to internal factors, whereas if something bad happens to your spouse, people are likely to attribute that to external causes. The **actor–observer bias** is the tendency to attribute the behavior of others to internal causes and to attribute one's own behavior to external causes. We tend to consider other people's behavior to be relatively stable from situation to situation because it is due to their very nature, but we consider our own behavior to vary from situation to situation.

UNDERSTANDING OURSELVES

As we have seen, we often form biases when attempting to understand the behavior of others; this dilemma also exists when we try to gain insight into our own behaviors. There are five major ways that we delude ourselves: unrealistic optimism, self-serving bias, omniscience, omnipotence, and the process of adaptation.

Unrealistic optimism.   Have you ever encountered someone, perhaps a friend or relative, who may be very smart and yet act quite foolish? Unrealistic optimism is the tendency for people to believe that they are so smart they can do whatever they want and not worry about the consequences. In short, people with this type of bias hold an inflated and erroneous view of themselves.

Self-serving bias.   Also known as egocentrism, self-serving bias describes people who are motivated to maintain a favorable view of themselves, even if it means deluding themselves. In short, people give themselves more credit than others are willing to give them.

Omniscience.   Perhaps you have heard your professors say, "The more educated I became, the more I realized how little I knew." Omniscience in people is the opposite. Omniscience occurs when people believe they know everything and lack awareness of what they do not know. In short, they are unaware of their own limitations.

Omnipotence.   Omnipotence is closely related to the illusion of invulnerability. It is the faulty belief that someone is all-powerful and can get away with whatever actions they might engage in, no matter how inappropriate or irresponsible they may be.

The process of adaptation.   How people adapt to both good and bad news is severely underestimated. People immediately begin a rationalization process when they receive bad news, such as rejection by an employer or a breakup with a boyfriend or girlfriend. When it comes to good news, people underestimate how much they will adapt to the good news. Often, people take good news for granted, such as a promotion.

Understanding others and ourselves is one of the most important aspects of management. As discussed, management makes constant judgments of people and continually tries to predict the behavior of others in an effort to maximize organizational value and effectiveness; but prediction is a highly complex task. As a general rule, predictions of another person can be improved the more information we have about that person. Additionally, the more similar the assessment technique is to the actual task performed, the more accurate our prediction will be.

SUMMARY OF CHAPTER

1. Understanding how to deal with people in organizations and the various elements and characteristics that contribute to determining how and in what form they are willing to engage in behaviors that benefit the organization is critical to managers.
2. A psychological contract is similar to a legal contract, but less formal, as it refers to the unwritten set of expectations of the employment relationship between employer and employee.
3. The person–job fit theory matches an employee's abilities, needs, and values, and the organizational demands, rewards, and values.
4. We know that we are all different. Individual differences are those personal attributes that vary from one person to another, such as our likes, dislikes, interests, values, and psychological makeup.
5. Attitudes are sets of complex beliefs and feelings that we have about specific ideas, and consist of three basic components: affect, cognition, and intention.
6. Cognitive dissonance theory is when two sets of cognitions or perceptions are contradictory, creating experiences of anxiety and conflict within the individual.
7. Job satisfaction is composed of several factors, including mentally challenging work, equitable rewards, supportive working conditions, and supportive colleagues.
8. Organizational citizenship behavior is that behavior that goes above and beyond the basic requirements of the job, is to a large extent discretionary, and is of the benefit to the organization.

DISCUSSION QUESTIONS

1. The attribution theory suggests that we attribute causes to behavior based on our observations. Explain the two characteristics of that behavior.
2. Sometimes people describe an individual as having "no personality." What is wrong with this statement? What does this statement actually mean?
3. Explain fundamental attribution, actor–observer, and self-serving bias. Provide an example for each.
4. Explain the five major ways that we delude ourselves when trying to understand our own behavior.

DOES MY JOB MOTIVATE ME?

INSTRUCTIONS

Use the following questions to describe either your current job, or any past work experience or internship you have had. Choose a number from 1 to 7, whichever describes it best.

1. Is there a lot of variety in your job? Are you using a multitude of skills and doing different types of assignments?

1	2	3	4	5	6	7
Very little			Moderate			Very much

2. Does your job involve you doing a "whole" piece of work? Does it have an obvious beginning and end, or do you only do a small part of it?

1	2	3	4	5	6	7
I only do small part			I do a moderate piece of the work			I do the whole piece of work

3. How important is your job? Do you believe it directly affects others' lives or well-being?

1	2	3	4	5	6	7
Not very significant; Does not affects others			Moderately significant		Highly significant; affects others	

4. How much autonomy is there in your job? Do you get to make decisions on how things should be done?

1	2	3	4	5	6	7
Very little			Moderate			Very much

5. Does the work itself provide feedback, separate from your supervisor or co-workers?

1	2	3	4	5	6	7
Very little			Moderately			Very much

SCORING KEY:

Insert your responses into the following formula to find your score.

MPS = (Skill variety (Ques. #1) + Task identity (#2) + Task significance (#3)) × Autonomy (#4) × Feedback (#5)

ANALYSIS:

This assessment looks at the Job Characteristics Model. Your score should range between 1 and 343. The average is 128. The higher your score is, the more motivation potential your job has. This can lead to high performance levels and satisfaction. It also reduces absenteeism and turnover.

Adapted from: Robbins, S. P. (2009). I.C.8: What's my job's motivating potential?, Self-assessment library (33-34). Upper Saddle River, NJ: Pearson Education Inc.

Original Source: J.R. Hackman and G.R. Oldham, Work Redesign (Reading, MA: Addison- Wesley, 1980), pp. 277-79.

CHAPTER 4 REFERENCES

Allen, N. J., Meyer, J. P. (1990). The Measurement and Antecedents of Affective, Continuance and Normative Commitment to the Organization, *Journal of Occupational Psychology*, 63(4), 1–18.

Breckler, S. J. (1984). Empirical validation of affect, behavior, and cognition as distinct components of attitude. *Journal of Personality and Social Psychology*, 47(6),1191–1205.

Elizu, D., Borg, I., Hunt, R., Beck, I. M., (1991). The Structure of Work Values: A Cross-Cultural Comparison, *Journal of Organizational Behavior*, 12(1,), 21–38

Diefendorff, J. M., Brown, D. J., Kamin, A. M., & Lord, R. G. (2002). Examining the roles of job involvement and work centrality in predicting organizational citizenship behaviors and job performance. *Journal of Organizational Behavior*, 23(1), 93–108.

Festinger, L. (1957). *A theory of cognitive dissonance.* Stanford, CA: Stanford University Press.

Feinstein, A. H., Vondrasek, D. (2001). A Study of Relation- ships between Job Satisfaction and Organizational Commitment among Restaurant Employees, *Journal of Hospitality, Tourism, and Leisure Science*, 1(4), 1–20.

Freeman, R. B. (1978). Job satisfaction as an economic variable. *American Economic Review*, 62(2), 135–141.

Gaertner, S. (1999). Structural Determinants of Job Satisfaction and Organizational Commitment in Turnover Models, *Human Resource Management Review*, 9(4), 479–493.

Griffith, J. (2001). Do satisfied employees satisfy customer? Support-services staff morale and satisfaction among public school administrators, students, and parents. *Journal of Applied Social Psychology*, 31(8), 1627–1658.

Gong, Y., Law, K. S., Chang, S., & Xin, K. R. (2009). Human resources management and firm performance: The differential role of managerial affective and continuance commitment. *Journal of Applied Psychology*, 94(1), 263–275.

Harrison, D. A., Newman, D. A., & Roth, P. L. (2006). How important are job attitudes? Meta-analytic comparisons of integrative behavioral outcomes and times sequences. *Academy of Management Journal*, 49(2), 305–325.

Holland, K. (2007, January 28). Inside the minds of your employees. *The New York Times*, p. B1.

Jernigan, I.E., Beggs J. M., Kohut, G F. (2002). Dimensions of Work Satisfaction as Predictors of Commitment Type, *Journal of Managerial Psychology*, 17(7), 564–579.

Judge, T. A., Thoresen, C. J., Bono, J. E., & Patton, G. K. (2001). The job satisfaction–job performance relationship: A qualitative and quantitative review. *Psychological Bulletin*, 127(3), 376–407.

Konovsky, M. A., & Organ, D. W. (1996). Dispositional and contextual determinants of organizational citizenship behavior. *Journal of Organizational Behavior*, 17(3), 253–266.

Koys, D. J. (2001). The effects of employee satisfaction, organizational citizenship behavior, and turnover on organizational effectiveness: A unit-level, longitudinal study. *Personnel Psychology*, 54(1), 101–114.

Lambert, S. J. (2006). Both art and science: Employing organizational documentation in workplace-based research. In M. Pitt-Catsouphes, E. E. Kossek, & S. Sweet (Eds.), *The work and family handbook: Multidisciplinary perspectives, methods, and approaches* (pp. 503–525). Mahwah, NJ: Lawrence Erlbaum & Associates.

Lee, K., & Allen, N. J. (2002). Organizational citizenship behavior and workplace deviance: The role of affect and cognitions. *Journal of Applied Psychology*, 87(1), 131–142.

Lockwood, N. R. (2007). *Leveraging employee engagement for competitive advantage.* Alexandria, VA: Society for Human Resource Management.

Luchak, A. A., & Gellatly, I. R. (2007). A comparison of linear and nonlinear relations between organizational commitment and work outcomes. *Journal of Applied Psychology*, 92(3), 786–793.

Macey, W. H., & Schneider, B. (2008). The meaning of employee engagement. *Industrial and Organizational Psychology*, 1(1), 3–30.

Martin, T. N., Hafer, J. C., (1995). The Multiplicative Interaction Effects of Job Involvement and Organizational Commitment on the Turnover Intentions of Full-Time and Part-Time Employees, *Journal of Vocational Behavior*, 46(3), 310–331.

McClurg, L. N. (1999). Organizational Commitment in the Temporary-Help Service Industry," *Journal of Applied Management Studies*, 8(1), 5–26.

Morrow, P. C. (1993). *The Theory and Measurement of Work Commitment*, JAI Press, Greenwich.

Moynihan, D. P., & Pandey, S. K. (2007). Finding workable levers over work motivation: Comparing job satisfaction, job involvement, and organizational commitment. *Administration & Society*, 39(7), 803–832.

Saks, A. (2008). The meaning and bleeding of employee engagement: How muddy is the water? *Industrial and Organizational Psychology*, 1(1), 40–43.

Spector, E. (1997). *Job satisfaction: Application, assessment, causes, and consequences.* Thousand Oaks, CA: Sage.

Vance, R. J. (2006). *Employee engagement and commitment.* Alexandria, VA: Society for Human Resource Management.

Vroom, V. H. (1964). Work and motivation. San Francisco, CA: Jossey-Bass.

Vroom, V. H., Deci, E. L., (1983). Management and Motivation, Penguin (first published 1970)

Wright, T. A., & Bonett, D. G. (2002). The moderating effects of employee tenure on the relation between organizational commitment and job performance: A meta-analysis. *Journal of Applied Psychology, 87*(6), 1183–1190.

MOTIVATION, GOAL SETTING

CHAPTER LEARNING OBJECTIVES

After reading this chapter, you should have a good understanding of

- why motivation is of importance in organizations;
- the difference between intrinsic and extrinsic motivation;
- motivation from the needs theory;
- why expectancy, valence, and instrumentality are of importance for work motivation;
- why equity and inequity are so important in motivation;
- the different motivational theories and approaches; and
- the methods for enhancing motivation in organizations.

"Our greatest weakness lies in giving up. The most certain way to succeed is always to try just one more time."

- THOMAS A. EDISON

MOTIVATION AND WORK BEHAVIOR

Motivation is the process of arousing and sustaining goal-directed behavior. Put simply, it is literally the desire to do things. Motivation theories attempt to explain and predict observable behavior and may be classified as internal, process, or external theories. Motivation is one of the most complex topics in organizational behavior because of the vast number of variables that affect motivation.

This chapter provides an overview of the need-based theory, equity theory, expectancy theory, and the organizational justice theory of motivation, as well as a framework for enhancing motivation in organizations. Each theory addresses different questions about motivation in organizations and the relationships between inputs, performance, and outcomes (Figure 5.1). Keep in mind that each theory has its own merits and delimitations, hence there is no single "best theory."

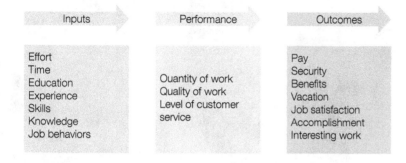

Figure 5.1. The Motivation Equation

NEED-BASED THEORIES OF MOTIVATION

Need-based perspectives represent the starting point for most contemporary thought on motivation. The basic premise of need-based theories and models is that humans are motivated primarily by deficiencies in one or more important needs or need categories. Need theorists have attempted to identify and categorize the needs that are most important to people.

MASLOW'S HIERARCHY OF NEEDS

The hierarchy of needs, developed by psychologist Abraham Maslow in the 1940s, is the best-known need theory. Influenced by the human relations school, Maslow argued that human beings are "wanting" animals: they have innate motivations to satisfy a given set of needs. Furthermore, Maslow believed that these needs are arranged in a hierarchy of importance, with the most basic needs at the foundation of the hierarchy.

Figure 5.2 shows Maslow's hierarchy of needs. The three sets of needs at the bottom of the hierarchy are called "deficiency needs" because they must be satisfied for the individual to be fundamentally comfortable. The top two sets of needs are termed "growth needs" because they focus on personal growth and development.

The most basic needs in the hierarchy are **physiological** needs, which include the need for food, water, and air. Next in the hierarchy are **security** needs, which include things that offer safety and security, such as adequate housing and clothing, and freedom from worry and anxiety. The third level in the hierarchy, **belongingness** needs, is primarily concerned with social needs, such as the need for love and affection, and the need to be accepted by peers. The fourth level, **esteem** needs, encompasses two slightly different kinds of needs: the need for a positive self-image and self-respect, and the need to be respected by others. At the top of the hierarchy are the **self-actualization** needs. These involve a person realizing his or her full potential and becoming all that he or she can be.

Maslow believed that each need level must be satisfied before the level above it can become important. Thus, once physiological needs have been satisfied, their importance diminishes, and security needs emerge as the primary sources of motivation. This escalation up the hierarchy continues until the self-actualization needs become the primary motivators.

In most businesses, physiological needs are probably the easiest to evaluate and to meet. Adequate wages, bathroom facilities, ventilation, comfortable temperatures, and working conditions are measures taken to satisfy this most basic level of needs. Security needs in organizations can be satisfied by such things as job continuity, a grievance system, and an adequate insurance and retirement system. Most employees' belongingness needs are satisfied by family ties and group relationships both inside and outside the

Figure 5.2. Maslow's Hierarchy of Needs

Griffin, R.W. & Moorhead, G., "Maslow's Hierarchy of Needs," Organizational Behavior, pp. 93. Copyright © 2004 by American Psychological Association.

organization. In the workplace, people usually develop friendships that provide a basis for social interaction and can play a major role in satisfying social needs. Managers can help satisfy these needs by fostering a sense of group identity and interaction among employees. At the same time, managers can be sensitive to the probable effects on employees of family problems or lack of acceptance by coworkers. Esteem needs in the workplace are met at least partially by job titles, choice offices, merit pay increases, awards, and other forms of recognition. Of course, to be sources of long-term motivation, tangible rewards such as these must be distributed equitably and be based on performance.

Self-actualization needs are perhaps the hardest to understand and the most difficult to satisfy. For example, it is difficult to assess how many people completely meet their full potential. In most cases, people who are doing well on Maslow's hierarchy will have satisfied their esteem needs and will be moving toward self-actualization. Working toward self-actualization, rather than actually achieving it, may be the ultimate motivation for most people. In recent years, there has been a pronounced trend toward people leaving well-paying but less fulfilling jobs to take lower-paying but more fulfilling jobs, such as nursing and teaching. This might indicate that they are actively working toward self-actualization.

Maslow's needs hierarchy makes a certain amount of intuitive sense and, because it was the first motivation theory to become popular, it is also one of the best known among practicing managers. However, the theory's primary contribution seems to lie in providing a general framework for categorizing needs.

ERG THEORY

Clayton Alderfer, a psychologist, developed a new model, the **ERG theory of motivation**, to explain motivation after seeing Maslow's hierarchy and deciding that Maslow's model poorly reflected the true complexity of human motivation.

In his theory, Alderfer compressed Maslow's hierarchy of needs from five to three: existence, relatedness, and growth (ERG; Figure 5.3).

First, there are the existence needs. At this level, put simply, there are the things that we need to exist. Thus, safety and physiological needs from Maslow's hierarchy are both included at this level. Second, there are the relatedness needs, where we fulfill our need for satisfying interpersonal relationships. This level relates to Maslow's social needs and to the external part of self-esteem needs. Lastly, there is the growth needs level. Here, we experience personal growth and development by doing work that is of high quality and is meaningful. This equates to the internal part of Maslow's self-esteem needs and to his self-actualization needs.

While Alderfer maintains that there is a general order for pursuing needs, he also claims that this order is not nearly as fixed as it is in Maslow's hierarchy. Even though existence needs will generally have a higher priority than relatedness and growth needs, priorities change depending on the person and the situation.

ERG theory differs from Maslow's theory in three key ways:

- People can be motivated by needs from more than one level at once. There is not a strict progression from one level to the next.

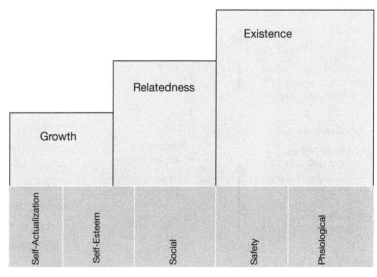

Figure 5.3. ERG Theory Versus Maslow's Hierarchy of Needs

- The importance of the needs will vary for each person as circumstances change. A person's priorities will change with age, time, and depending on the situation.
- It includes a concept called the **frustration-regression** element. Essentially, if needs remain unsatisfied at the higher levels, a person will become frustrated and return to pursuing lower-level needs again.

HERZBERG'S DUAL STRUCTURE THEORY

Frederick Herzberg and his associates developed the dual-structure or two-factor theory in the late 1950s and early 1960s. Herzberg began by interviewing approximately two hundred accountants and engineers in Pittsburgh. He asked them to recall times when they felt especially satisfied and motivated by their jobs and times when they felt particularly dissatisfied and unmotivated. He then asked them to describe what caused the good and bad feelings. To his surprise, Herzberg found that entirely different sets of factors were associated with the two kinds of feelings about work. For example, a person who indicated "low pay" as a source of dissatisfaction would not necessarily identify "high pay" as a source of satisfaction and motivation. Instead, people associated entirely different causes, such as recognition or achievement, with satisfaction and motivation. The findings led Herzberg to conclude that the prevailing thinking about satisfaction and motivation was incorrect. Herzberg had reasoned that one set of factors should influence movement back and forth along the continuum, but because his research had identified differential influences from two different sets of factors, Herzberg argued then that two different dimensions must be involved. Thus, he saw motivation as a dual-structured phenomenon (Figure 5.4).

In the dual-structure concept, there is one dimension ranging from satisfaction to no satisfaction and another ranging from dissatisfaction to no dissatisfaction. The two dimensions must presumably be associated with the two sets of factors identified in the initial interviews. Thus, this theory proposed, employees might be either satisfied or not satisfied and, at the same time, dissatisfied or not dissatisfied.

Motivation factors such as achievement and recognition were often cited by people as primary causes of satisfaction and motivation. When present in a job, these factors apparently could cause satisfaction and motivation. When they were absent, the result was feelings of no satisfaction rather than dissatisfaction.

The other set of factors, **hygiene factors**, came out in response to the questions about dissatisfaction and lack of motivation. The respondents suggested that pay, job security, supervisors, and working conditions, if seen as inadequate, could lead to feelings of dissatisfaction. When these factors were considered acceptable, however, the person still was not necessarily satisfied. Rather, he or she was simply not dissatisfied.

To use the dual-structure theory in the workplace, Herzberg recommended a two-stage process. First, the manager should try to eliminate situations that cause dissatisfaction, which Herzberg assumed to be the more basic of the two dimensions. Unlike many other theorists, Herzberg described explicitly how managers could apply his theory. In particular, he developed and described a technique called "job enrichment" for structuring employee tasks. Herzberg tailored this technique to his key motivation factors. This unusual attention to application may explain the widespread popularity of the dual-structure theory among practicing managers.

Figure 5.4. Herzberg's Dual Structure Theory
Source: Adapted from Schermerhorn (2013).

ACHIEVEMENT, AFFILIATION, AND POWER

Maslow's theory of needs identified the basic needs that all humans have and listed them order of their importance: physiological, safety, social, esteem, and self-actualization. Building on Maslow's work, David McClelland identified three motivators and described them in his 1961 book *The Achieving Society.* McClelland's **human motivation theory** states that every person has one of three main driving motivators: the need for achievement, affiliation, and power (Figure 5.5). These motivators are not inherent, however. Rather, we develop them through our culture and life experiences. According to McClelland, these motivators are learned and largely dependent on our culture and life experiences, regardless of our gender or age.

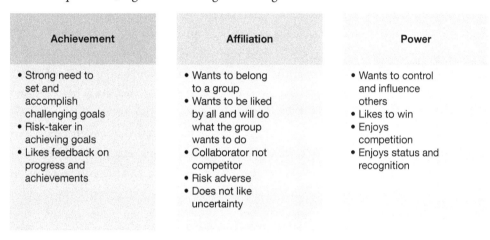

Figure 5.5. McClelland's Needs Theory Characteristics

The need for achievement (nAch).   Individuals with a **high need for achievement** require challenging, but not impossible tasks. They thrive on overcoming difficult problems or situations, so make sure you keep them engaged this way. People motivated by achievement work very effectively either alone or with other high achievers, but require frequent feedback—they need to know what they are doing right and wrong so that they can improve. Managers and entrepreneurs are especially likely to have a high need for achievement. McClelland found that, 10 years after graduation, undergraduates who had shown to have a high need for achievement were more likely to be found in entrepreneurial occupations.

The need for affiliation (nAff).   A person with a **high need of affiliation** is concerned with establishing and maintaining good relations with other people. They want to belong to groups and create connections with others. This might include joining office organizations, making friends with coworkers, and trying to create a sense of belonging within the company. Individuals with a high need of affiliation work best in a group environment, so try to integrate them with a team (as opposed to working alone) whenever possible. The downside of high need affiliates is that they are driven by their desire for everyone to get along. As such, they can also be demanding, clingy, and have a low tolerance for dissent, making it difficult for them to provide negative feedback. A **low need of affiliation** can be part of a more independent personality. People who do not feel a strong desire to affiliate with others may be viewed as loners, and could have difficulty finding support.

The need for power (nPow).   Individuals with a **high need for power** have a strong desire to exert emotional and behavioral control or influence over others. These people work best when they're in charge and are often found in managerial or leadership positions, which requires one person to exert influence over others. Because they enjoy competition, they do well with goal-oriented projects or tasks and may be more effective as leaders than those with a low need for power. Individuals with a high need for power may be very effective in negotiations or in situations in which another party must be convinced of an idea or goal.

THE NEED FOR ACHIEVEMENT

The **need for achievement** is most frequently associated with the work of David McClelland. This need arises from an individual's desire to accomplish a goal or task more effectively than they have in the past. Individuals who have a high need for achievement tend to set moderately difficult goals and to make moderately risky decisions. High-need achievers also want immediate, specific feedback on their performance. They want to know how well they did something as quickly after finishing it as possible. For this reason, high-need achievers frequently take jobs in sales, where they get almost immediate feedback from customers, and avoid jobs in areas such as research and development, where tangible progress is slower and feedback comes at longer intervals. Preoccupation with work is another characteristic of high-need achievers. They think about it on their way to the workplace, during lunch, and at home. They find it difficult to put their work aside, and they become frustrated when they must stop working on a partly completed project. Finally, high-need achievers tend to assume personal responsibility for getting things done. They often volunteer for extra duties and find it difficult to delegate part of a job to someone else. Accordingly, they derive a feeling of accomplishment when they have done more work than their peers without the assistance of others. High-need achievers tend to do well as individual entrepreneurs with little or no group reinforcement. Steve Jobs, the cofounder of Apple, and Bill Gates, the cofounder of Microsoft, are both recognized as being high-need achievers. Their need for achievement was the desire to accomplish a task or goal more effectively than it was done in the past.

Although high-need achievers tend to be successful, they often do not achieve top management posts. The most common explanation is that, although high need for achievement helps these people advance quickly through the ranks, the traits associated with the need often conflict with the requirements of high-level management positions. Because of the amount of work they are expected to do, top executives must be able to delegate tasks to others. In addition, they seldom receive immediate feedback, and they often must make decisions that are either more or less risky than those with which a high-need achiever would be comfortable.

THE NEED FOR AFFILIATION

Individuals also experience the need for affiliation or the need for human companionship. Researchers recognize several ways that people with a high need for affiliation differ from those with a lower need. Individuals with a high need tend to want reassurance and approval from others and usually are genuinely concerned about others' feelings. They are likely to act and think as they believe others want them to, especially those with whom they strongly identify and desire friendship.

As one might expect, people with a strong need for affiliation most often work in jobs with a lot of interpersonal contact, such as sales and teaching positions. A recent Gallup survey suggests that people who have at least one good friend at work are much more likely to be highly engaged with their work and to indicate higher levels of job satisfaction.

Another individual need is the need for power or the desire to control one's environment, including financial, material, informational, and human resources. People vary greatly along this dimension. Some individuals spend much time and energy seeking power, while others avoid power if at all possible.

People with a high need for power can be successful managers if three conditions are met. First, they must seek power for the betterment of the organization rather than for their own interests. Second, they must have a fairly low need for affiliation because fulfilling a personal need for power may alienate others in the workplace. Third, they need plenty of self-control to curb their desire for power when it threatens to interfere with effective organizational or interpersonal relationships.

COGNITIVE THEORIES OF MOTIVATION

EQUITY THEORY

The **equity theory of motivation** is based on the relatively simple premise that people in organizations want to be treated fairly. The theory defines equity as the belief that we are being treated fairly in relation to others, and inequity as the belief that we are being treated unfairly compared with others. Equity theory is just one of several theoretical formulations derived from social comparison processes that involve evaluating our own situation in terms of others' situations.

People in organizations form perceptions of the equity of their treatment through a four-step process. First, they evaluate how they are being treated by the firm. Second, they form a perception of how a "comparison-other" is being treated. The **comparison-other** might be a person in the same work group, someone in another part of the organization, or even a composite of several people scattered throughout the organization. Third, they compare their own circumstances with those of the comparison-other and then use this comparison as the basis for forming an impression of either equity or inequity. Fourth, depending on the strength of this feeling, the person may choose to pursue one or more of the alternatives discussed in the next section.

Equity theory describes the equity comparison process in terms of an input-to-outcome ratio. **Inputs** are an individual's contributions to the organization, including such factors as education, experience, effort, and loyalty. **Outcomes** are what the person receives in return, such as pay, recognition, social relationships, intrinsic rewards, and such similar things. In effect, this part of the equity process is a personal assessment of one's psychological contract. If the two sides of this psychological equation are comparable, the person experiences a feeling of equity and, if the two sides do not balance, a feeling of inequity results.

Figure 5.6 summarizes the results of an equity comparison. If a person feels equitably treated, they are generally motivated to maintain the status quo. For example, they will continue to provide the same level of input to the organization as long as their outcomes do not change and the ratio of inputs and outcomes of the comparison-other do not change.

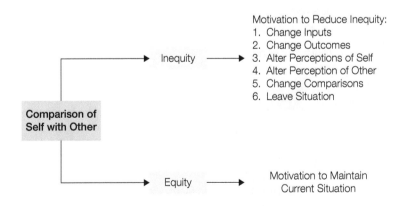

Figure 5.6. Responses to Equity and Inequity
Source: Adapted from Griffin and Moorhead (2014).

Though, a person who is experiencing inequity is motivated to reduce it. The greater the inequity, the stronger the level of motivation.

People may use one of six common methods to reduce inequity:

1. We may change our own inputs. Thus, we may put more or less effort into the job, depending on which way the inequity lies, as a way to alter our ratio. If we believe we are being underpaid, for example, we may decide not to work as hard.

2. We may change our own outcomes. We might, for example, demand a pay raise, seek additional avenues for growth and development, or even resort to stealing as a way to "get more" from the organization. We also might alter our perceptions of the value of our current outcomes, perhaps by deciding that our present level of job security is greater and more valuable than we originally thought.

3. We may alter our perceptions of ourselves and our behavior. After perceiving an inequity, for example, we may change our original self-assessment and decide that we are really contributing less, but receiving more than we originally believed. For example, we might decide that we are not really working as many hours as we had first thought, admitting, perhaps, that some of our time spent in the office is really just socializing and not actually contributing to the organization.

4. We may alter our perception of the comparison-other's inputs or outcomes. After all, much of our assessment of other people is based on perceptions, and perceptions can be changed. For example, if we feel under-rewarded, we may decide that our comparison-other is working more hours than we originally believed, say by coming in on weekends and taking work home at night.

5. We may change the object of comparison. We may conclude, for instance, that the current comparison-other is the boss's personal favorite, is unusually lucky, or has special skills and abilities. A different person would, thus, provide a more valid basis for comparison. We might change comparison-others fairly often.

6. We may simply leave the situation. That is, we might decide that the only way to feel better about things is to be in a different situation altogether. Transferring to another department or seeking a new job may be the only way to reduce the inequity.

EXPECTANCY THEORY

The basic premise of **expectancy theory** is that motivation depends on how much we want something and how likely we think we are to get it. Victor Vroom is generally credited with first applying the theory to motivation in the workplace. The theory attempts to determine how individuals choose among alternative behaviors.

In order for an employee to be motivated to perform desired behaviors and to perform them at a high level, the following conditions are necessary:

1. **Valence** must be high: The employee wants outcomes the organization has to offer.
2. **Instrumentality** must be high: The employee perceives that he or she must perform the desired behaviors at a high level to obtain these outcomes.
3. **Expectancy** must be high: The employee thinks that trying hard will lead to performance at a high level.

If just one of the three factors is zero, motivation will be zero.

Figure 5.7 summarizes the basic expectancy model. The model's general components are effort (expectancy), performance (instrumentality), and outcomes (valence). Expectancy theory emphasizes the linkages among these elements, which are described in terms of expectancies and valences.

| Expectancy must be high. Employees must perceive that if they try hard, they can perform at a high level | Instrumentality must be high. Employees must perceive that if they perform at a high level, they will receive certain outcomes | Valence must be high. Employees must desire or want the outcomes they will receive if they perform at a high level |

| Effort | Instrumentality | Outcomes |

Figure 5.7. Vroom's Expectancy Theory

Effort-to-performance (expectancy). This is a person's perception of the probability that effort will lead to successful performance. If we believe our effort will lead to higher performance, this expectancy is very strong, perhaps approaching a probability of 1.0, where 1.0 equals absolute certainty that the outcome will occur. If we believe our performance will be the same no matter how much effort we make, our expectancy is very low, perhaps as low as 0, meaning that there is no probability that the outcome will occur. A person who thinks there is a moderate relationship between effort and subsequent performance, the normal circumstance, has an expectancy somewhere between 1.0 and 0.

Performance-to-outcome (instrumentality). This is a person's perception of the probability that performance will lead to certain other outcomes. If a person thinks a high performer is certain to get a pay raise, this expectancy is closer to 1.0. At the other extreme, a person who believes raises are entirely independent of performance has an expectancy closer to 0. Finally, if a person thinks performance has some bearing on the prospects for a pay raise, his or her expectancy is somewhere in between 1.0 and 0.

In a work setting, several performance-to-outcome expectancies are relevant because several outcomes might logically result from performance. Each outcome, then, has its own expectancy. For example, New England Patriots quarterback Tom Brady may believe that, if he plays aggressively all the time, he has a great chance of leading his team to the playoffs. Playing aggressively may win him individual honors like the Most Valuable Player award, but he may also experience more physical trauma and throw more interceptions.

Outcome (Valence). Outcome is anything that might potentially result from performance. High-level performance conceivably might produce such outcomes as a pay raise, a promotion, recognition from the boss, fatigue, stress, or less time to rest, among others. The **valence** of an outcome is the relative attractiveness or unattractiveness, the value of that outcome to the person. Pay raises, promotions, and recognition might all have positive valences, whereas fatigue, stress, and less time to rest might all have negative valences. The strength of outcome valences varies from person to person. Work-related stress may be a significant negative factor for one person but only a slight annoyance to another. Similarly, a pay increase may have a strong positive valence for someone desperately in need of money, a slight positive valence for someone interested mostly in getting a promotion, or for someone in an unfavorable tax position, even a negative valence.

The basic expectancy framework suggests that three conditions must be met before motivated behavior occurs:

1. The effort-to-performance expectancy must be well above zero. That is, the worker must reasonably expect that exerting effort will produce high levels of performance.
2. The performance-to-outcome expectancies must be well above zero. Thus, the person must believe that performance will realistically result in valued outcomes.
3. The sum of all the valences for the potential outcomes relevant to the person must be positive. One or more valences may be negative as long as the positives outweigh the negatives. For example, stress and fatigue may have moderately negative valences, but if pay, promotion, and recognition have very high positive valences, the overall valence of the set of outcomes associated with performance will still be positive. Conceptually, the valences of all relevant outcomes and the corresponding pattern of expectancies are assumed to interact in an almost mathematical fashion to determine a person's level of motivation. Most people do assess likelihoods of and preferences for various consequences of behavior, but they seldom approach them in such a calculating manner.

ORGANIZATIONAL JUSTICE THEORY

Organizational justice refers to an employee's perception of their organization's overall fairness. Organizational justice does not refer to a single worker per se, but rather describes a group of theories that focus on the nature, determinants, and consequences of organizational justice. This theory addresses the question of motivation by considering if the processes used to assess inputs and performance and the distributive outcomes are perceived to be fair. Additionally, it considers whether the employees are treated with dignity and respect, and whether the managers provide adequate feedback on their decisions and the procedures used to arrive at them.

The **organizational justice theory** proposes that employees will not be motivated to contribute their inputs unless they perceive fair procedures will be used to distribute outcomes in the organization and that they will be treated fairly by managers.

When these procedures are perceived to be unfair and employees feel unfairly treated, motivation suffers, because all of the relationship inputs are weakened: assessing the inputs, determining the performance, and ultimately distributing the outcomes.

TYPES OF ORGANIZATIONAL JUSTICE

There are four types of organizational justice theory that we will examine: distributive justice, procedural justice, interpersonal justice, and informational justice.

Distributive justice.   This type deals with the employees' concerns of the fairness of outcomes they receive, such as pay, promotions, and desirable working conditions and assignments. One of the biggest reasons for issues with employee productivity or morale is that employees feel their company lacks fairness.

For example, Mitch has worked for an international skateboard manufacturer for over a year. He has just found out that he will be receiving only a 1% raise in pay this year (outcome). Mitch does not feel that this is a fair outcome given the amount of time and effort he has invested (inputs) into the company during this period (performance). One approach to providing a sense of equal distributive justice is by educating, communicating, and enacting fair employment practices with all of the employees.

Procedural justice.   Another type of organizational justice, procedural justice is concerned with how employees view the fairness of the process of how outcomes are decided. Employees are going to be more motivated to perform at a high level when they perceive that the procedures used to make decisions about the distribution of outcomes are fair.

For example, Paul has issues with how the warehousing department provides overtime to their employees. He feels that they lack procedural justice because they do not provide enough advance notice nor seek input from employees for the scheduling of shifts.

Paul is more likely to perceive that procedural justice is high when he is able to have input on the procedures used to determine the distribution of outcomes. Procedural justice is also likely to be high when employees perceive that the procedures are used consistently across employees (e.g., all employees with the same job have their performance appraised through the same process), accurate information is relied on (e.g., quantitative data free of errors), and procedures are unbiased (e.g., no personal likes or dislikes enter into the decision process). Finally, employees who have the option to appeal judgments and decisions that have been made and who know that the procedures used adhere to the organization's code of ethics will promote procedural justice.

Interpersonal justice. Interpersonal justice focuses on the perceived fairness of the interpersonal treatment employees receive from the distributors of outcomes (typically managers). Interpersonal justice is an important area of manager's focus, as this justice theory deals with how courteous, polite, respectful, and refraining from improper remarks or comments the manager is with the employee when providing feedback on outcomes.

Informational justice. This is the perception that the employee has about the manager's extent in explaining their decisions and the procedures used to arrive at them. For example, managers can explain to employees how they assess inputs, including time, effort, education, and previous work experience, how they appraise performance, and how they decide to distribute outcomes.

When managers provide a full description of the procedures they use to distribute outcomes in an honest, forthright, thorough, and timely manner, perceptions of informational justice are likely to be high.

LEARNING THEORY

Learning is another important component in employee motivation. In any organization, employees quickly learn which behaviors are rewarded and which are ignored or punished. Thus, learning plays a critical role in maintaining motivated behavior. Learning is a relatively permanent change in behavior or behavioral potential that results from direct or indirect experience.

Classical conditioning. Developed by Ivan Pavlov, classical conditioning is a simple form of learning in which a conditioned response is linked with an unconditioned stimulus. In organizations, however, only simple behaviors and responses can be learned in this manner. For example, suppose an employee receives very bad news one day from his boss. It's possible that the employee could come to associate, say, the color of the boss's suit that day with bad news. Thus, the next time the boss wears that same suit to the office, the employee may experience dread and foreboding. Learning theorists soon recognized that, although classical conditioning offered some interesting insights into the learning process, it was inadequate as an explanation of human learning. Because of the shortcomings of classical conditioning, theorists eventually moved on to other approaches that seemed more useful in explaining the processes associated with complex learning.

Although it is not tied to a single theory or model, contemporary learning theory generally views learning as a cognitive process. That is, it assumes that people are conscious, active participants in how they learn. First, the cognitive view suggests that people draw on their experiences and use past learning as a basis for their present behavior. These experiences represent knowledge or cognitions. For example, an employee faced with a choice of job assignments will use previous experiences in deciding which one to accept. Second, people make choices about their behavior. The employee recognizes that she has two alternatives and chooses one. Third, people recognize the consequences of their choices. Thus, when the employee finds the job assignment rewarding and fulfilling, she will recognize that the choice was a good one and will understand why. Finally, people evaluate those consequences and add them to prior learning, which affects future choices. Faced with the same job choices next year, the employee will probably be motivated to choose the same one.

Learning reinforcement theory.   Also known as operant conditioning, this theory is generally associated with the work of B. F. Skinner. In its simplest form, reinforcement theory suggests that behavior is a function of its consequences. Behavior that results in pleasant consequences is more likely to be repeated and behavior that results in unpleasant consequences is less likely to be repeated. Reinforcement theory also suggests that, in any given situation, people explore a variety of possible behaviors. Future behavioral choices are affected by the consequences of earlier behaviors. Cognitions, as already noted, also play an important role. Therefore, rather than assuming the mechanical stimulus-response linkage suggested by the traditional classical view of learning, contemporary theorists believe that people consciously explore different behaviors and systematically choose those that result in the most desirable outcomes. The consequences of behavior are called reinforcement. Managers can use various kinds of reinforcement to affect employee behavior.

There are four basic forms of reinforcement: positive reinforcement, avoidance, extinction, and punishment (Table 5.1).

Table 5.1. Forms of Reinforcement

Positive reinforcement	A reward or other desirable consequence that a person receives after exhibiting behavior
Negative reinforcement (avoidance)	The opportunity to avoid or escape from an unpleasant circumstance after exhibiting behavior
Extinction	Decreases the frequency of behavior by eliminating a reward or desirable consequence that follows that behavior
Punishment	An unpleasant or aversive consequence that results from behavior

Positive Reinforcement.   Positive reinforcement is a reward or other desirable consequence that follows behavior. Providing positive reinforcement after a particular behavior motivates employees to maintain or increase the frequency of that behavior. A compliment from the boss after an employee has completed a difficult job, and a salary increase following a worker's period of high performance are examples of positive reinforcement.

Avoidance.   Also known as **negative reinforcement**, avoidance is another means of increasing the frequency of desirable behavior. Rather than receiving a reward following a desirable behavior, the person is given the opportunity to avoid an unpleasant consequence. For example, suppose that a boss habitually criticizes employees who dress casually. To avoid criticism, an employee may routinely dress to suit the supervisor's tastes. The employee is thus motivated to engage in desirable behavior to avoid an unpleasant, or aversive, consequence.

Extinction.   Extinction decreases the frequency of behavior, especially behavior that was previously rewarded.

If rewards are withdrawn for behaviors that were previously reinforced, the behaviors will probably become less frequent and eventually die out. For example, a manager with a small staff may encourage frequent visits from subordinates as a way of keeping in touch with what is going on. Positive reinforcement might include cordial conversation, attention to subordinates' concerns, and encouragement to come in again soon. As the staff grows, however, the manager may find that such unstructured conversations make it difficult to get her own job done. She then might begin to brush off casual conversation and reward only to-the-point business conversations. Withdrawing the rewards for casual chatting will probably extinguish that behavior. We should note that if managers, inadvertently or otherwise, stop rewarding valuable behaviors such as good performance, those behaviors also may become extinct.

Punishment.   This is an unpleasant, or aversive, consequence of a behavior. Examples of punishment are verbal or written reprimands, pay cuts, loss of privileges, layoffs, and termination. Many experts question the value of punishment and believe that managers use it too often or use it inappropriately. In some situations, however, punishment may be an appropriate tool for altering behavior. Many instances of life's unpleasantness teach us what to do by means of punishment. Furthermore, certain types of undesirable behavior may have far-reaching negative effects if they go unpunished. For instance, an employee who sexually harasses a coworker, a clerk who steals money from the petty cash account, and an executive who engages in illegal stock transactions all deserve punishment.

BEHAVIORAL THEORIES OF MOTIVATION

A goal is what an individual is trying to accomplish through his or her behavior and actions. Goal setting theory focuses on how to motivate employees to contribute inputs to their jobs. The theory also stresses the importance of ensuring their inputs result in acceptable job performance levels.

GOAL SETTING THEORY

Edwin Locke and Gary Latham, leaders in goal setting theory and research, suggest that the goals employees try to attain at work have a major impact on their levels of motivation and performance.

Goal setting is a very useful method of enhancing employee performance. From a motivational perspective, a goal is a meaningful objective. Goals are used for two purposes in most organizations. First, they provide a useful framework for managing motivation. Managers and employees can set goals for themselves and then work towards them. Thus, if the organization's overall goal is to increase sales by 10%, a manager can use individual goals to help attain that organizational goal. Second, goals are an effective control device. Comparing people's short-term performances with their goals can be an effective way to monitor the organization's longer-term performance.

LOCKE AND LATHAM'S FIVE PRINCIPLES

According to Locke and Latham, there are five goal-setting principles that can improve the chances of success.

1. **Clarity:** When goals are clear, you know what you're trying to achieve. You can also measure results accurately, and you know which behaviors to reward.
2. **Challenge:** People are often motivated by challenging goals; however, it is important not to set a goal that is so challenging it can't be achieved.
3. **Commitment:** To be effective, you must understand and agree to the goals; you will be more likely to buy into to a goal if you have been involved in setting it.

4. **Feedback:** In addition to selecting the right goals, you should also listen to feedback, so that you can gauge how well you are progressing. Feedback gives you the opportunity to clarify people's expectations and adjust the difficulty of their goals. Keep in mind that feedback doesn't have to come from other people. You can check how well you're doing by simply measuring your own progress.
5. **Task complexity:** Take special care to ensure that work doesn't become too overwhelming when goals or assignments are highly complex. People who work in complicated and demanding roles can often push themselves too hard if they don't take account of the complexity of the task.

A person who achieves a goal will be proud of having done so, whereas a person who fails to achieve a goal will feel personal disappointment and perhaps even shame. People's degree of pride or disappointment is affected by their self-efficacy, the extent to which they feel that they can still meet their goals even if they failed to do so in the past.

The research of Edwin Locke and his associates most clearly established the utility of goal setting theory in a motivational context. Locke's goal setting theory of motivation assumes that behavior is a result of conscious goals and intentions. Therefore, by setting goals for people in the organization, a manager should be able to influence their behavior. Given this premise, the challenge is to develop a thorough understanding of the processes by which people set their goals, and then work to reach them.

Goal difficulty is the extent to which a goal is challenging and requires effort. If people work to achieve goals, it is reasonable to assume that they will work harder to achieve more difficult goals. But a goal must not be so difficult that it is unattainable. Reinforcement also fosters motivation to achieve difficult goals. A person who is rewarded for achieving a difficult goal will be more inclined to strive toward the next difficult goal than will someone who received no reward for reaching the first goal.

Goal specificity is the clarity and precision of the goal. A goal of "increasing productivity" is not very specific, whereas a goal of "increasing productivity by 3% in the next six months" is quite specific. Some goals, such as those involving costs, output, profitability, and growth, can easily be stated in clear and precise terms. Other goals, such as improving employee job satisfaction and morale, company image and reputation, ethical behavior, and social responsibility, are much harder to state in specific terms. Like goal difficulty, goal specificity has been shown to be consistently related to performance.

INTRINSIC AND EXTRINSIC MOTIVATION

INTRINSIC MOTIVATION

Intrinsically motivated work behavior is behavior performed for its own sake, in which the source of motivation actually comes from performing the behavior itself. Employees that have intrinsic work values want challenging assignments, the opportunity to make important contributions to their work and organization, and the opportunity to reach their full potential at work.

For example, Mitch, a college business student, worked as an unpaid intern in a Chinese manufacturing company during his summer. Learning and having the opportunity to develop new skills on the job was an important source of intrinsic motivation.

EXTRINSIC MOTIVATION

Extrinsically motivated work behavior is behavior performed to acquire material or social rewards or to avoid punishment. The behavior is performed not for its own sake but, rather, for its consequences—positive, negative, or punishment reinforcers can be used to generate extrinsically motivated behavior. Examples of extrinsic motivators are pay, praise, and status. Employees with extrinsic work values desire some of the consequences of working, such as earning money, having status in the community, creating social contacts, and having time off from work for family and leisure.

An employee can be extrinsically motivated, intrinsically motivated, or both. When employees are primarily extrinsically motivated and doing the work itself is not a source of motivation, it critically important for an organization and its managers to make a clear connection between the behaviors the organization wants employees to perform and the outcomes or rewards employees want.

MOTIVATION AND WORK DESIGN

Work design is an important method managers can use to enhance employee performance. When work design is addressed at the individual level, it is most commonly referred to as **job design**, and it can be defined as how organizations define and structure jobs. Properly designed jobs can have a positive impact on the motivation, performance, and job satisfaction of those who perform them. On the other hand, poorly designed jobs can impair motivation, performance, and job satisfaction (Table 5.2).

Table 5.2. Top 10 Ways to Destroy Motivation at Work.

Treat employees like children.

Make rules for the many because of the behavior of a few.

Focus on mistakes and errors no matter how trivial they are in comparison with successes.

Apply policies unfairly and inequalitably.

Stomp on employee initiative and ideas.

Tell employees that they're empowered but then review and retain veto power over the smallest decisions.

Hold meetings, coaching sessions, and performance reviews in which the manager does the majority of the talking.

Violate employee confidentiality by sharing information inappropriately.

Measure aspects of work for employee review that the employee can't control.

Set unattainable goals and penalize employees for not meeting them.

Susan M. Heathfield, "Top 10 Ways to Destory Motivation at Work," About.com. Copyright © 2014 by About.com.

The first widespread model of how individual work should be designed is **job specialization**. For example, a worker who applies safety decals to a piece of equipment as that equipment moves down an assembly line is performing a specialized job. On the surface, job specialization appears to be a rational and efficient way to structure jobs. The jobs in many factories, for instance, are highly specialized and are often designed to maximize productivity. In practice, however, performing those jobs can cause problems, foremost among them the extreme monotony of highly specialized tasks. Managers began to recognize that, although job specialization might lead to efficiency, if carried too far, it could have a number of negative consequences.

Job rotation and job enlargement seemed promising, but eventually disappointed managers seeking to counter the ill effects of extreme specialization. They failed partly because they were intuitive, narrow approaches rather than fully developed, theory-driven methods. Consequently, a new, more complex approach to task design, **job enrichment**, was developed based on the dual-structure theory of motivation. That theory contends that employees can be motivated by positive job-related experiences such as feelings of achievement, responsibility, and recognition. To achieve these, job enrichment relies on vertical job loading, not only adding more tasks to a job, as in horizontal loading, but also giving the employee more control over those tasks.

Employee involvement in their work can also play an important role in motivation. Involvement is most often enhanced through what are called **participative management and empowerment**. In most cases, managers who use these techniques are attempting to enhance employee motivation. In a sense, participation and empowerment are extensions of job design, because each fundamentally alters how employees in an organization perform their jobs. Participation occurs when employees have a voice in decisions about their own work. **Empowerment** is the process of enabling workers to set their own work goals, make decisions, and solve problems within their spheres of responsibility and authority.

Beyond the actual redesigning of jobs and the use of employee involvement, many organizations today are experimenting with a variety of **flexible work arrangements**. These arrangements are generally intended to enhance employee motivation and performance by giving workers more flexibility in how and when they work. Among the more popular flexible work arrangements are variable work schedules, flexible work schedules, extended work schedules, job sharing, and telecommuting.

SUMMARY OF CHAPTER

1. Motivation starts with a need. People search for ways to satisfy their needs and then behave accordingly.
2. According to Maslow, human needs are arranged in a hierarchy of importance, from physiological to security to belongingness to esteem and then to self-actualization.
3. In Herzberg's dual-structure theory, satisfaction and dissatisfaction are two distinct dimensions, instead of opposite ends of the same dimension. Motivation factors are presumed to affect satisfaction and hygiene factors are presumed to affect dissatisfaction. Other important individual needs include the needs for achievement, affiliation, and power.
4. The equity theory of motivation assumes that people want to be treated fairly. People compare their own input-to-outcome ratio in the organization with the ratio of a comparison-other. If they feel their treatment has been inequitable, they take steps to reduce the inequity.
5. Expectancy theory follows from the assumption that people are motivated to work toward a goal if they want it and think that they have a reasonable chance of achieving it.
6. Various kinds of reinforcement provided according to different schedules can increase or decrease motivated behavior. Organizations can use learning and reinforcement principles to enhance employee motivation and performance by effective measurement of performance and the provision of rewards to employees after they perform at a high level.
7. The goal setting theory of motivation suggests that appropriate goal difficulty, specificity, acceptance, and commitment will result in higher levels of motivated performance. Rewards for achieving goals in the form of money, indirect compensation or benefits, perquisites, awards, and incentives can be effective motivators.
8. Managers seek to enhance employee performance by capitalizing on the potential for motivated behavior to improve performance. Methods often used to translate motivation into performance include work design, job enrichment, participation and empowerment, alternative work arrangements, performance management, goal setting, and rewards.
9. Employee involvement using participative management and empowerment can help improve employee motivation in many business settings.
10. Flexible work arrangements are commonly used today to enhance motivated job performance.

DISCUSSION QUESTIONS

1. Why might a person who is very highly motivated be a poor work performer? Why might a person who has very low motivation be a high work performer?
2. Is inequity always dysfunctional for an organization? Why or why not?
3. Why might employees perceive "fair procedures" to actually be unfair to some employees?

WHAT MOTIVATES ME MOST?

INSTRUCTIONS

Think about the job you hope to obtain in the future. Indicate how important each of the items are to you, based on the following scale.

1: Not important | 2: Somewhat important | 3: Important | 4: More important | 5: Very important

1. Obtaining growth of skill set and knowledge
2. Acceptable pay rate
3. Cooperation between coworkers
4. Ability to think and act independently within the work environment
5. Raises in pay on a regular basis
6. Feeling like part of the group
7. Having a sense of self-esteem
8. Having a fringe-benefit plan in place
9. Ability to obtain personal growth and development of self
10. Creating and maintaining friendships with coworkers
11. Not fearing physical harm or injury
12. Honesty among coworkers

SCORING KEY:

This score will include three sections. To find these scores, add up your totals for each of the following groups:

    1, 4, 7, 9 for growth needs
    3, 6, 10, 12 for relatedness needs
    2, 5, 8, 11 for existence needs

ANALYSIS:

The three needs—growth, relatedness, and existence—come from the ERG theory. The theory says that everyone has each of the needs; only their importance varies. The more important a need is to you, the higher the score for it will be. Low scores in a need mean that it is either not as important to you, or that it can be considered already well-satisfied. Interestingly, it is noted that college students generally see growth needs as being the most important to them.

Adapted from: Robbins, S. P. (2009). I.C.1: What motivates me? Self-assessment library (21-22). Upper Saddle River, NJ: Pearson Education Inc.

Original source: The Free Press, from Existence, Relatedness, and Growth: Human Needs in Organizational Setting, by C.P. Alderfer. Copyright c 1972 by The Free Press.

CHAPTER 5 REFERENCES

Baltes, B. B., Briggs, T. E., Huff, J. W., Wright, J. A., & Neuman, G. A. (1999). Flexible and compressed work-week schedules: A meta-analysis of their effects on work-related criteria. *Journal of Applied Psychology, 84*(4), 496–513.

Bratton, J., Gold, J. (2007). *Human Resource Management: Theory and Practice*, 4th Edition, Palgrave-MacMillian. Basingstroke.

Cotton, J. L. (1993). *Employee involvement: Methods for Improving Performance and Work Attitudes.* Newbury Park, CA: Sage.

Datta, K., Guthrie, J. P., & Wright, P. M. (2005). Human resource management and labor productivity: Does industry matter? *Academy of Management Journal, 48*(1), 135–145.

Easterby, M., Thorp, R., Lowe, A. (2008). *Management Research*, 3rd Edition, New York, NY: Sage.

Fegley, S., Schramm, J., Phil, M., Escen, E., Williams, S., Frincke, J. (2008). Society for Human Resource Management, *2008 Employee Benefits. Alexandria, VA: SHRM.*

Grant, M., Campbell, E. M., Chen, G., Cottone, K., Lapedis, D., & Lee, K. (2007). Impact and the art of motivation maintenance: The effects of contact with beneficiaries on persistence behavior. *Organizational Behavior and Human Decision Processes, 103(1),* 53–67.

Griffin, R. W., & Moorhead, G. (2014). *Organizational behavior* (11th ed.). Mason:OH: South-Western Cengage.

Hackman, J. R., & Oldman, G. R. (1976). Motivation through the design of work: Test of a theory. *Organizational Behavior and Human Performance*, 16, 250–279.

Hackman, J. R., & Oldman, G. R. (1980). *Work design.* Reading, MA: Addison-Wesley.

Heathfield, S. M. (2014). Top ten ways to destroy motivation at work. *About.com. Human Resources.* Retrieved from: http://humanresources.about.com/od/motivation/a/how-organizations-destroy-motivation.htm

Henry, T. (1999, September 30). States to tie teacher pay to results. *USA Today*, p. 1A.

Herzberg, F., Mausner, B., Synderman, B. (1959). *The Motivation to Work*, Wiley, New York.

Huws, U. (1999). Wired in the country. *People Management*, November, 46–47.

Kossek, E., Lautsch, B. A., & Eaton, S. C. (2006). Telecommuting, control, and boundary management: Correlates of policy use and practice, job control, and work-family effectiveness. *Journal of Vocational Behavior, 68*(2), 347–367.

Locke, E. A., Latham, G. P. New Directions in Goal-Setting Theory, Current Directions in Psychological Science, 15(5), 265–268.

Maslow, A. H. (1943). A theory of human motivation. *Psychological Review, 50(4)*, 374–396.

Miller, K. L., & Monge, P. R. (1986). Participation, satisfaction, and productivity: A meta-analytic review. *Academy of Management Journal*, 29(4), 727–753.

Pritchard, R. D., Harrell, M. M., DiazGrandos, D., & Guzman, M. J. (2008). The productivity measurement and enhancement system: A meta-analysis. *Journal of Applied Psychology*, 93(3), 540–567.

Schermerhorn, J. (2013). *Principles of management* (12th ed.). Hoboken, NY: Wiley.

Zwilling, M. (2012). Eight ways leaders can motivate employees beyond money. *Forbes Magazine*. January. Retrieved from: http://www.forbes.com/sites/martinzwilling/2012/01/10/8-ways-leaders-can-motivate-employees-beyond-money/#48d3c0ee74dd

JOB DESIGN, EMPLOYEE INVOLVEMENT, ALTERNATIVE WORK ARRANGEMENTS, AND VARIABLE PAY PROGRAMS

CHAPTER LEARNING OBJECTIVES

After reading this chapter, you should have a good understanding of
- the job characteristics model and the way it motivates by changing the work environment;
- the main ways jobs can be redesigned;
- employee involvement measures and how they can motivate employees; and
- the different types of variable-pay programs available to employees.

"Success in most things is achieved at the margin. The little extra things done day after day soon add up to extraordinary achievement."

- ANONYMOUS

JOB DESIGN

Job design, a critical and key component of organizational design, is defined as the number, kind, and variety of tasks performed by an individual employee. Particularly, job design examines how the characteristics of skill variety and autonomy affect the employee. Job design, also referred to as work design, is equally concerned with aligning the job specifications to organizational requirements as how the job affects the social and personal requirements of the worker. In principle, the goal of job design is to improve quality, employee motivation, and job satisfaction and, thereby, reduce problems caused by low employee morale, such as absenteeism and turnover.

Increasing job satisfaction and performance has become increasingly important as organizations face environmental challenges such as globalization and the economic crises. Managers must be alert and proactive in both decreasing job dissatisfaction and increasing employee morale. By eliminating workplace dissatisfaction caused by conditions like low wages, poor working environment, and increasing workplace satisfaction by providing opportunities for growth, promotion, and recognizing employee achievements, organizations will begin to see an increase in worker morale and productivity.

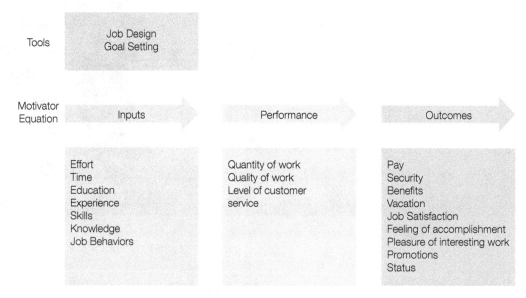

Figure 6.1. Job Design/Motivation

In general, managers try to design jobs in order to motivate employees to perform well, enjoy their work, and receive the outcomes they deserve. Job design also influences the motivation of employees and their input level (Figure 6.1). When employees are motivated to contribute, to work harder, more efficiently, and more creatively, and to perform their jobs more effectively, organizational effectiveness increases.

JOB CHARACTERISTICS MODEL

The **job characteristic model** developed by Hackman and Oldman (1976) is a contemporary job design theory. Similar to job rotation, job enlargement, and job enrichment, the job characteristic model (JCM) attempts to overcome the deficiencies of job specialization. Building upon the traditional job design methods, the JCM model provides a comprehensive approach to job design intended to influence employees in three psychological states: experiencing meaning in their work (employees must view their work as being important), understanding their contributions (employees must know who they are performing for in their jobs), and feeling responsible for outcomes (employees must feel personally responsible for their work). Hackman and Oldman propose that these three critical psychological states are necessary for employees to find internal motivation. Hence, the central concern of the job characteristics theory is motivation that comes from the job itself, instead of motivation that comes from external or outside rewards, such as a raise.

The JCM provides a framework for job design, utilizing five core job characteristics intended to positively influence workers' intrinsic motivation: skill variety, task identity, task significance, autonomy, and feedback (Figure 6.2).

1. **Skill variety:** The dimension of skill variety encompasses the different skills or activities needed for the job. The more variety in an employee's work, the less likely the employee is to experience boredom and the more likely the employee is to be satisfied at work.
2. **Task identity:** The dimension of task identity measures individual portions of tasks and the portions required to complete the entire task or assignment. The more an employee is involved in the entire activity (from start to finish), the more likely the employee is to be satisfied at work.

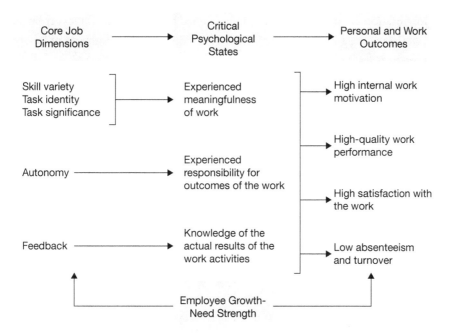

Figure 6.2. Job Characteristics Model

3. **Task significance:** The importance of the task significance dimension is an examination of the job's influence and impact. The more an employee feels that they are making a contribution and making a difference, the more likely the employee is to be satisfied at work.

4. **Autonomy:** The dimension of autonomy looks at the amount of individual choice and discretion allowed an employee. The more an employee is involved in the decisions surrounding their job, instead of being issued commands, the more likely the employee is to be satisfied at work.

5. **Feedback:** The feedback dimension brings about a need for continuous measurement and communication of information regarding performance and the impact of their work. The more communication an employee receives about their performance and the impact of their work on the organization, department, or customer, the more likely the employee is to be interested in their work and satisfied at work.

HOW CAN JOBS BE RE-DESIGNED?

There is strong evidence to support the presence of the JCM concept. Variety, identity, significance, autonomy, and feedback all do generate higher and more satisfying job performance. Take a moment and think about your job. Do you have the opportunity to work on different tasks, or is your day the same routine? Are you able to work independently or is a supervisor or co-worker continually reviewing your work? After answering these questions, what do you think it says about your job's motivating potential? In the following sections we will look at some ways to put JCM into practice to make some jobs more motivating.

Historically, there have been three major approaches to job design, each of these methods attempting to overcome the disadvantages of specialized work:

1. Job rotation
2. Job enlargement
3. Job enrichment

Job rotation. Job rotation is a method of job redesign aimed at motivating employees by introducing variety into an employee's workday. The goal of job rotation is to overcome the disadvantages of job specialization, such as monotony and boredom.

For example, a company practicing job rotation will implement processes and timetables to transfer workers through different jobs or tasks. Job rotation has several key advantages. By introducing more variety and the opportunity for employees to use different skills, the company gains a multi-skilled worker, employee attitudes and job satisfaction improves, and workplace productivity generally increases. Yet, organizations can still gain the economic benefits produced by job specialization.

Job enlargement. This method of job redesign is aimed at motivating employees by increasing the number of different tasks assigned to an employee. Similar to job rotation, the goal of job enlargement is to overcome the disadvantages of job specialization. Unlike job rotation, the employee does not transfer to different jobs but instead takes responsibility for more tasks. The goal of job enlargement is to introduce variety into the employee's tasks. The advantage of job enlargement is that employees experience a reduction in monotony and boredom. However, the disadvantage with job enlargement is that the employee may see the variety as more work. In order to execute job enlargement successfully, companies must ensure that employees have sufficient time to complete all assigned duties.

Job rotation and job enlargement seemed promising, but eventually disappointed managers who sought to counter the ill effects of extreme specialization. They failed partly because they were intuitive, narrow approaches rather than fully developed, theory-driven methods. Consequently, a new, more complex approach to task design, job enrichment, was developed.

Job enrichment. Job enrichment is based on the dual-structure theory of motivation. That theory contends that employees can be motivated by positive job-related experiences such as feelings of achievement, responsibility, and recognition. To achieve these, job enrichment relies on vertical job loading, not only adding more tasks to a job, as in horizontal loading, but also giving the employee more control over those tasks.

Job enrichment is aimed at motivating employees through work design—it increases the number of tasks *and* gives workers the authority and control to make decisions about planning and executing their work. Job enrichment allows the employee to assume more responsibility. It has the same advantages as job enlargement. However, it also has the additional advantage of giving the employee autonomy and independence, and allowing for greater participation. The disadvantage with job enrichment is that the employee may see the autonomy as decisions that should be performed by someone at a higher level.

How does management enrich an employee's job? Figure 6.3 offers suggested guidelines based on the job characteristics model. **Combining tasks** puts fractionalized tasks back together to form a new and larger module of work. **Forming natural work units** makes an employee's tasks create an identifiable and meaningful whole. **Establishing client relationships** increases the direct relationships between workers and their clients. **Expanding jobs vertically** gives employees responsibilities and control formerly reserved for management. **Opening feedback channels** lets employees know how well they are doing and whether their performance is improving, deteriorating, or remaining constant.

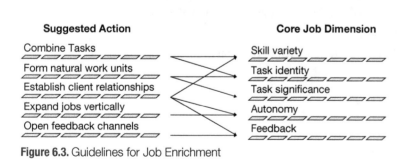

Figure 6.3. Guidelines for Job Enrichment

JOB SPECIALIZATION

The first widespread model of how individual work should be designed was **job specialization**. For example, a worker who applies safety decals to a piece of equipment as that equipment moves down an assembly line is performing a specialized job. On the surface, job specialization appears to be a rational and efficient way to structure jobs. The jobs in many factories, for instance, are highly specialized and are often designed to maximize productivity. In practice, however, performing those jobs can cause problems, foremost among them the extreme monotony of highly specialized tasks. Managers began to recognize that although job specialization might lead to efficiency, if carried too far, it could have a number of negative consequences.

Job specialization occurs when a job is composed of small, specific parts of a larger process or task. Specialized jobs are fast and easy to learn. Basic steps, low variety, and high repetition characterize specialized jobs. The primary advantage of specialized jobs is economic. Because a specialized job is fast and easy to learn, the organization can replace an employee with little down time or productivity loss. However, the primary disadvantage of specialized jobs is that they become boring just as fast. When employees become bored, job satisfaction declines. Commonly, declines in job satisfaction lead to high absenteeism and turnover and increases in workplace injury claims.

JOB MODIFICATION

Due to the efficiency of specialized jobs, organizations are generally slow in restructuring or eliminating them. Thus, job redesign efforts have generally focused on modifying jobs. The principle intent of modifying specialized jobs is to keep the benefits of specialized jobs while reducing the disadvantages. Organizations use job design to overcome the challenges associated with job specialization.

In the 1860s, the average workweek was 68 hours long. It wasn't until the 1930s that labor unions fought for legislation that created the 8-hour workday and the 40-hour workweek. Today, this arrangement no longer works for the majority of the American work force. The huge number of working women, including mothers of school-age children, the increase in two-career families, and the rise in single-parent families have forced companies to reconsider their work schedules.

Beyond the actual redesigning of jobs and the use of employee involvement, many organizations today are experimenting with a variety of **flexible work arrangements.** These arrangements are generally intended to enhance employee motivation and performance by giving workers more flexibility in how and when they work.

Among the more popular flexible work arrangements are flexible work schedules, job sharing, extended work schedules, variable work schedules, and telecommuting.

FLEXIBLE WORK SCHEDULING

Flexible work scheduling (flextime) has become extremely popular with both employees and their employers, with approximately 43% of the U.S. full-time workforce having flexible daily arrival and departure times. Employees must work a specific number of hours per week, but are free to vary their hours of work within certain limits. Figure 6.4 illustrates an example of a flextime schedule.

The benefits of flextime schedules are numerous, including reduced absenteeism, increased productivity, reduced overtime expenses, reduced hostility toward management, reduced traffic congestion around work sites, elimination of tardiness, and increased autonomy and responsibility for employees—many of which are known to increase employee job satisfaction. Two disadvantages to flexible work scheduling are **feelings of inequity**

Schedule One	
Percent Time:	100% = 40 hours per week
Core Hours:	9:00 am – 5:00 pm. Monday – Friday (1 hr. Lunch)
Work Start Time:	Between 8:00 am and 9:00 am
Work End Time:	Between 5:00 pm and 6:00 pm

Schedule Two	
Percent Time:	100% = 40 hours per week
Core Hours:	8:00 am – 6:30 pm. Monday – Thursday (1/2 hr. Lunch)
Work Start Time:	8:00 am
Work End Time:	6:30 pm

Schedule Three	
Percent Time:	90% = 36 hours per week
Core Hours:	8:30 am – 5:00 pm. Monday – Thursday (1/2 hr. Lunch) 8:00 am – Noon Friday (No Lunch)
Work Start Time:	8:30 am (Monday – Thursday) and 8:00 am (Friday)
Work End Time:	5:00 pm (Monday – Thursday); Noon (Friday)

Schedule Four	
Percent Time:	80% = 32 hours per week
Core Hours:	8:00 am – 6:00 pm. Monday – Wednesday (1/2 hr. Lunch) 8:00 am – 11:00 am. Thursday (No Lunch) Friday Off
Work Start Time:	Between 8:00 am and 9:00 am
Work End Time:	Between 5:00 pm and 6:00 pm

Figure 6.4. Example of Flextime Schedules

and **less teamwork**. Feelings of inequity can rise when an employer arbitrarily approves or disapproves flexible scheduling; this can create internal conflict among employees. If some employees find it unfair that co-workers are able to work flexible hours that they feel are more preferable, this can cause bitterness and lower morale among the ranks.

Employees that work with flextime cannot spend as much time in collaboration with co-workers as employees that work the same hours. Employees may only have a few hours a day for this collaboration. In some workplaces, work team communication takes place in an ongoing and spontaneous fashion that is hard to limit to just a few hours. Thus, flextime can actually slow down the pace of work team production because of this restricted collaboration.

JOB SHARING

Job sharing is a form of regular part-time work in which two people split a traditional 40-hour-a-week job. One might perform the job from 8:00 a.m. to noon and the other from 1:00 p.m. until 5:00 p.m., or the two could work full but alternate days. As described in the examples, these positions are regular part-time and as such must involve at least a 50% commitment. Therefore, the time commitment of each of the two individuals participating must be at least 20 hours per week.

Approximately 20% of large organizations now offer job sharing. Reasons it is not more widely adopted likely include the difficulty of finding a compatible partner to share a job and the historically negative perceptions of individuals not completely committed to their job and employer.

Job sharing can provide many benefits, including reduced absenteeism, improved recruitment and retention of valued staff who may not want full-time employment, improved scheduling and continuity, increased breadth of skills and experience, allowance for unusual schedule needs of staff, and experience in working as a successful team.

Job sharing does create some challenges, including the increased need for communication between the job share individuals, their colleagues, and their supervisor, so that division of responsibilities is clear, and the additional cost to the department to have two people on benefits for one position.

EXTENDED WORK SCHEDULES

Extended work scheduling refers to work schedules having longer than "normal" workdays. Although there is no clear consensus about the length of the extended workday, some sources consider it to be between 8 and 12 hours in length, while others insist that the term applies only when shifts are longer than 12 hours.

Usually, workers on extended workday schedules work fewer than five days a week. When the traditional 36-to-40-hour workweek is squeezed into three or four days, the number of days worked in a row is decreased and the number of consecutive days off is increased.

Many hospital, industrial, transportation, mining, and office organizations are adopting the extended workday, based on the assumption that it offers some advantages. However, the decision to set up longer work shifts (up to 12 hours or more) should not be made lightly. Studies on this subject cannot yet provide sufficient evidence to decide categorically in favor or against the use of extended work shifts.

Table 6.1 provides examples of the advantages and disadvantages of extended work scheduling.

Table 6.1. Advantages and Disadvantages of Extended Work Scheduling

Advantages	Disadvantages
More days off and more consecutive days off	More days off and more consecutive days off
More family and leisure time	Workers lose the touch with their operations
More rest days to recover from fatigue	Long traveling time or exhausting recreation may cause fatigue on return to work
Fewer consecutive workdays	Decline in safety and alertness
Improved morale	Slower pace of work
Increased job satisfaction	Workers need more breaks
Reduced absenteeism	
Reduced time of commuting	

VARIABLE WORK SCHEDULES

Do you know of a friend or colleague who is an early riser, who loves starting work early so they can leave work mid-afternoon? Or, perhaps your neighbor gets every other Friday off, having a three-day weekend to go skiing. Maybe you're the person who likes to sleep in late every morning because your work doesn't begin until 9am. All of these are examples of variable work scheduling; in other words, they are variation on the traditional 9-to-5, Monday-to-Friday workweek.

Variable work hour programs are becoming more and more popular with companies both large and small as employers realize they are good for employee morale and good for business. There are two popular variable work schedules: compressed workweek and staggered work hours.

Compressed workweek.   In a compressed workweek, employees complete their required number of work hours in fewer-than-normal days per week. This arrangement allows employees to have one or two days off each week or one day off every other week, depending upon which type of compressed workweek program you prefer. The three most popular compressed week schedules are the 4/40, where the employee works four 10-hour days each week with the fifth day off; the 9/80 programs, wherein the employee works 80 hours in nine days with the 10th day off; and the 3/12 programs, wherein the employee works three 12-hour days each week with two days off. Employees in this program often receive four additional hours to make a 40-hour week as credit for working longer days.

Staggered work hours.   This approach involves spreading out employee arrival and departure times by anywhere from 15 minutes to 2 hours. By staggering these shifts you can help reduce bottlenecks in employee parking lots, in streets at the entrance to your office, and even in elevators. Reducing congestion through staggered hours benefits air quality by reducing vehicle idling time in congested conditions or by allowing employees to avoid the peak travel period.

When implementing a staggered work hours program, you must determine whether participation will be voluntary or mandatory. In either case, it is wise to offer as many shift choices as possible so that employees can select a schedule that is convenient for them.

TELECOMMUTING

Telecommuting is as close as it gets to the ideal job for many people. Telecommuting provides the benefits of flexible hours, freedom to come and go as you please, few interruptions from co-workers, and no commuting.

As is apparent from our previous description, telecommuting is working from home for at least a portion of the workweek on a computer that is linked to the employer's office. In essence, you have a **virtual office** from home.

U.S. companies are increasingly turning to telecommuting to cut costs, allow their employees to balance work and life, and help the environment and, while only 2.9 million Americans consider the home to be their primary work location, the numbers are growing.

The Telework Research Network (TRN) reports that telecommuting job numbers increased by 61% between 2005 and 2009, with the average teleworker working from home 2.4 days a week.

The TRN also reports that over 70% of work-at-home employees hold sales, office, management, or professional positions. And while popular opinion claims that telecommuting is best suited to young, technologically savvy employees, the TRN discovered that older workers are more likely to hold telecommuting positions.

In addition to higher productivity, less turnover, improved morale, and the saving on real estate, office supplies, and utility costs, severe weather, traffic jams, and similar disruptions are less likely to interrupt a telecommuter's productivity. Such conditions can make it impossible for employees to reach the office, while telecommuters can continue to work without interruption.

What kinds of jobs are best suited for telecommuting? There are three categories: routine information-handling tasks, mobile activities, and professional and other knowledge-related tasks. Writers, attorneys, analysts, and employees who spend the majority of their time on computers or on the phone, such as telemarketers, customer service representatives, reservation agents, and product support specialists, are the best candidates.

While it's possible to work from home full time, most employees assign telecommuting duties on a part-time basis. Face-to-face communication remains important for weekly meetings, brainstorming sessions, and other team-related activity.

Coming into the office a few times a week prevents the telecommuting employee from feeling isolated, and helps maintain the sense of being part of a team.

EMPLOYEE INVOLVEMENT

Employee involvement is creating an environment in which people have an impact on the decisions and actions that affect their jobs. It is a participative process that uses employee inputs to increase their commitment to the organization's success. Employee involvement is not the goal nor is it a tool, as practiced in many organizations. Rather, it is a management and leadership philosophy about how people are most enabled to contribute to continuous improvement and the ongoing success of their work organization.

The logic behind employee involvement is quite simple. If we involve workers in decisions that affect them and increase their autonomy and control over their work lives, they will become more motivated, more committed to the organization, more productive, and more satisfied with their jobs.

Employee involvement takes on three major forms: **participative management**, **empowerment**, and **representative participation**. In most cases managers who use these techniques are attempting to enhance employee motivation. In a sense, all are extensions of job design because each fundamentally alters how employees in an organization perform their jobs. Participation occurs when employees have a joint voice and share a significant degree of decision-making power with their immediate supervisor.

Participative management has been promoted as a panacea for poor morale and low productivity. However, for it to work, trust and confidence must exist among all parties. The issues in which employees are engaged must also be relevant to their interests in order for them to be motivated. Finally, employees must have the competence and knowledge to make a useful contribution to the issues at hand.

Research on the effectiveness of participation-performance relationships indicate higher returns on stock, lower turnover rates, and marginally higher labor productivity.

Representative participation is the most widely legislated form of employee involvement around the world. Almost every country in Western Europe requires companies to practice representative participation.

The goal of representative participation is to redistribute power within an organization, putting labor on a more equal footing with management and stockholders by letting labor actually participate in the interests of the organization.

The two most common forms of representative participation are works councils and board representation.

A **works council** is a nominated or elected group of employees that represents a company's workers for the purpose of receiving information from and consulting with the company's management on decisions that affect employees. **Board representatives** are employees who sit on a company's board of directors and represent the interests of the firm's employees.

Although participation might increase the motivation and satisfaction of employee representatives, there is little evidence that this permeates to those employees they represent, as works councils are dominated by management and have little impact on employees or the organization. Hence, the greatest value of representative participation is symbolic and does little to change the attitudes of the employees or increase performance of the organization.

Empowerment is the process of enabling workers to set their own work goals, make decisions, and solve problems within their spheres of responsibility and authority. Thus, empowerment is a somewhat broader concept that promotes participation in a wide variety of areas, including, but not limited to, work itself, work context, and work environment.

ORGANIZATIONAL REWARD SYSTEMS

One of the primary purposes of performance management is to provide a basis for rewarding employees. We now turn our attention to rewards and their impact on employee motivation and performance.

The **reward system** consists of all organizational components, including people, processes, rules and procedures, and decision-making activities involved in allocating compensation and benefits to employees in exchange for their contributions to the organization.

Rewards constitute many of the inducements that organizations provide to employees as their part of the psychological contract. Rewards also satisfy some of the needs that employees attempt to meet through their choice of work-related behaviors. The purpose of the reward system in most organizations is to attract, retain, and motivate qualified employees.

The organization's compensation structure must be equitable and consistent to ensure equality of treatment and compliance with the law. Compensation should also be a fair reward for the individual's contributions to the organization, although in most cases these contributions are difficult, if not impossible, to measure objectively. Given this limitation, managers should be as fair and as equitable as possible.

Finally, the system must be competitive in the external labor market for the organization to attract and retain competent workers in appropriate fields. Beyond these broad considerations, an organization must develop its philosophy of compensation based on its own conditions and needs, and this philosophy must be defined and built into the actual reward system. The organization needs to decide what types of behaviors or performance it wants to encourage with a reward system, because what is rewarded tends to recur. Possible behaviors include performance, longevity, attendance, loyalty, contributions to the "bottom line," responsibility, and conformity. Performance measurement, as described earlier, assesses these behaviors, but the choice of which behaviors to reward is a function of the compensation system.

It is also important for the organization to recognize that organizational rewards have many meanings for employees. **Intrinsic** and **extrinsic rewards** carry both surface and symbolic value. The surface value of a reward to an employee is its objective meaning or worth. A salary increase of 5%, for example, means that an individual has 5% more spending power than before, whereas a promotion, on the surface, means new duties and responsibilities. However, managers must also recognize that rewards also carry symbolic value. If a person gets a 3% salary increase when everyone else gets 5%, one plausible meaning is that the organization values other employees more. But if the same person gets 3% and all others get only 1%, the meaning may be just the opposite; the individual is seen as the most valuable employee. Thus, rewards convey to people not only how much they are valued by the organization but also their importance relative to others. Managers need to tune in to the many meanings rewards can convey, not only to the surface messages but to the symbolic messages as well.

Most organizations use several different types of rewards. The most common are base pay, incentive systems, benefits, perquisites, and awards. These rewards are combined to create an individual's compensation package.

Base pay is, for most people, the most important reward—the pay they receive. Obviously, money is important because of the things it can buy, but it can also symbolize an employee's worth. An effectively planned and managed pay system can improve motivation and performance. Employee compensation is a major cost of doing business, as much as 50% to 60% in many organizations, so a poorly designed system can be an expensive proposition. Since pay is considered a major source of employee dissatisfaction, a poorly designed system can also result in problems in other areas, such as turnover and low morale.

Incentive systems are plans in which employees can earn additional compensation in return for certain types of performance. Examples of incentive programs include the following:

1. **Piecework** programs, which tie a worker's earnings to the number of units produced.
2. **Gain-sharing** programs, which grant additional earnings to employees or work groups for cost-reduction ideas.
3. **Bonus** systems, which provide managers with lump-sum payments from a special fund based on the financial performance of the organization or a unit.
4. **Long-term compensation**, which gives managers additional income based on stock price performance, earnings per share, or return on equity.
5. **Merit pay** plans, which base pay raises on the employee's performance.
6. **Profit-sharing** plans, which distribute a portion of the firm's profits to all employees at a predetermined rate.
7. **Employee stock option** plans, which set aside stock in the company for employees to purchase at a reduced rate.

Plans oriented mainly toward individual employees may cause increased competition for these rewards and some possibly disruptive behaviors, such as sabotaging a coworker's performance, sacrificing quality for quantity, or fighting over customers. A group incentive plan, on the other hand, requires that employees trust one another and work together. Of course, all incentive systems have advantages and disadvantages. Long-term compensation for executives is particularly controversial because of the large sums of money involved and the basis for the payments. Indeed, executive compensation is one of the more controversial subjects that U. S. businesses have had to face in recent years. When a firm is growing rapidly, and its profits are also growing rapidly, relatively few objections can be raised to paying the CEO well. However, objections arise when an organization is laying off workers because its financial performance is perhaps less than might be expected and the CEO is still earning a huge amount of money.

Another major component of the compensation package is **indirect compensation**, also commonly referred to as the employee benefits plan. Typical benefits provided by businesses include the following:

1. **Payment for time not worked** both on and off the job: On-the-job free time includes lunch, rest, coffee breaks, and wash-up or get-ready time. Off-the-job time not worked includes vacation, sick leave, holidays, and personal days.
2. **Social Security** contributions: The employer contributes half the money paid into the system established under the Federal Insurance Contributions Act (FICA). The employee pays the other half.
3. **Unemployment** compensation: People who have lost their jobs or are temporarily laid off get a percentage of their wages from an insurance-like program.
4. **Disability and workers' compensation** benefits: Employers contribute funds to help workers who cannot work due to occupational injury or ailment.
5. **Life and health insurance** programs: Most organizations offer insurance at a cost far below what individuals would pay to buy insurance on their own.
6. **Pension or retirement** plans: Most organizations offer plans to provide supplementary income to employees after they retire. A company's Social Security, unemployment, and workers' compensation contributions are set by law, but deciding how much to contribute for other kinds of benefits is up to each company. Some organizations contribute more to the cost of these benefits than others. Some companies pay the entire cost; others pay a percentage of the cost of certain benefits, such as health insurance, and bear the entire cost of other benefits. In many organizations today, benefits now account for 30% to 40% of the payroll.

Perquisites are special privileges awarded to selected members of an organization, usually top managers. For years, the top executives of many businesses were allowed privileges such as unlimited use of the company jet, motor home, vacation home, and executive dining room. In Japan, a popular perquisite is a paid membership in an exclusive golf club, while a common perquisite in England is first-class travel. More than anything else, though, perquisites seem to add to the status of their recipients and, thus, may increase job satisfaction and reduce turnover.

Award programs can be an effective means of motivation. At many companies, employees receive awards for everything from seniority to perfect attendance, from zero defects to cost reduction suggestions. Award programs can be costly in the time required to run them and in money if cash awards are given, but award systems can improve performance under the right conditions.

Managers can use a variety of methods to enhance performance in organizations (Table 6.2). The need- and process-based perspectives on motivation explain some of the factors involved in increasing the potential for motivated behavior directed at enhanced performance. Managers can then use such means as goal setting, job design, flexible work arrangements, performance management, rewards, and organizational behavior motivation to help translate this potential into actual enhanced performance.

Table 6.2. Enhancing Performance in Organizations

8 Ways Leaders Can Motivate Employees Beyond Money
Energize your team.
There's more to life than work.
Put your people first.
Act with integrity.
Be a great communicator.
Be a great listener.
Be a problem solver.
Lead through experience and competence, not through title or position.

Martin Zwilling, "8 Ways Leaders Can Motivate Employees Beyond Money," Forbes.com. Copyright © 2012 by Forbes.com, LLC.

VARIABLE PAY PROGRAMS

Companies often underestimate the importance of retaining top talent. Although pay is not the primary factor in motivating an employee, it is a major factor in keeping top performers. A 2006 study found that, while only 45% of employers thought pay was a key factor in losing top talent, 71% of top performers indicated it was a top reason.

Given the importance of pay, managers must make some strategic decisions. Should the organization lead, match, or follow the market in pay? In the following section we look at four areas for consideration: 1) how much should we pay employees, 2) how to pay employees (variable pay or skill-based pay), 3) what benefits and choices to offer employees (such as flexible pay), and 4) how to construct employee recognition programs.

The best pay system balances both internal and external equity. **Internal equity** is the worth of the job to the organization (usually established through a technical process called job evaluation) and **external equity** is the external competitiveness of an organization's pay relative to pay elsewhere in its industry (usually established through pay surveys). Hence, the best pay system pays what the job is worth (internal) while also paying competitively relative to the labor market.

Some organizations prefer to be the market pay leaders by paying above the market, and in doing so often get better qualified, more highly motivated employees who will stay with the organization longer. Others may lag behind the market because they can't afford to pay market rates, or they are willing to bear the costs of paying below market, with higher employee turnover and less motivated workers.

A study of 126 large organizations found that employees who believed they were receiving a competitive pay level had higher morale and were more productive, and customers were more satisfied as well.

Because pay is often the highest single operating cost for an organization, the decision to pay above or below market becomes a strategic decision with clearly defined trade-offs.

Variable pay programs base a portion of an employee's pay on some individual and/or organizational measure of performance. The employee's earning can therefore vary up or down. Examples of variable pay programs are piece-rate plans, merit-based pay, bonuses, skill-based pay, profit sharing, gainsharing, and employee stock ownership plans. The fluctuation in variable pay is what makes these programs attractive to management, as it turns the organization's fixed cost of labor into a variable cost, thus reducing expenses when performance declines. When pay is tied to performance, the employee's earnings also recognize contribution rather than being a form of entitlement. Overtime, low performers' pay stagnates, whereas high performers can enjoy increases in pay with their hard work. The following provides a closer look at each of the variable-pay programs.

Piece-rate plan.   This plan is a very common and very popular means of compensation for production workers. It pays workers a fixed sum for each unit of production completed. A pure piece-rate plan provides no base salary and pays the employee only for what they produce (or sell). For example, ballpark workers selling soda and peanuts are frequently paid on this plan. If they sell 100 bags of peanuts at $2 each, their take is $200. However, if they only sell 10 bags of peanuts their take is only $20. The harder they work, the more they earn. The drawback of this type of pay plan is that it does not work for many jobs. Kobe Bryant of the Los Angeles Lakers earns $23.5 million per year regardless of how many games he wins. Would it be better to pay him $500,000 for every game the team wins, thus in order to make his $23.5 million the team must win 47 games? It would seem very unlikely that any professional athlete would accept such a deal. Hence, although incentives are motivating and relevant for some jobs, it would be quite unrealistic to think they can work for all jobs.

Merit-based pay.   This plan pays for individual performance based on performance appraisal ratings. If designed correctly, merit-based pay plans help to provide individuals with a strong relationship between performance and the rewards they receive. Although this approach to pay seems appealing, there are several limitations to this plan. One is that they are typically based on an annual performance appraisal and, thus, are only as valid as the performance ratings. A second limitation is that the pay-raise pool fluctuates on economic or other conditions that have little to do with individual performance.

Bonuses.   A significant component to an employee's total compensation is an annual bonus. The incentive effects of performance bonuses should be higher than those of merit pay because rather than paying for performance over the years (merit based), bonuses reward recent performance. Moreover, when the firm has lean profit years they can cut bonuses to reduce compensation costs, which can be problematic if bonuses are a large percentage of the total pay package, or when employees come to take bonuses for granted.

Skill-based pay. Also known as **knowledge-based pay** or **competency-based pay**, this is an alternative to job-based pay that bases the employee pay levels on how many skills they have or how many jobs they can do. Employers find this pay approach attractive as it increases the flexibility of the workforce, making filling staffing needs an easier task when employees are interchangeable. An added benefit to this approach is the increased communication level between employees as a result of their cross training. The downside to this program is that employees can "top-out." That is, they learn all the skills the program calls for them to learn, which can frustrate employees after they have been challenged by an environment of learning, growth, and continual pay raises. One additional downside is that this approach only deals with whether an employee can perform the skill, not the level of the performance.

Profit-sharing plans. These are organization-wide programs that distribute compensation based on some established formula designed around the company's profitability. These profits may be distributed equally or based on seniority, performance, and so forth. Profit-sharing plans attempt to directly link employee pay with organizational economic health. These plans, at the organizational level, appear to have positive impact on the employee's attitudes, as they provide a greater feeling of psychological ownership. Compensation in this plan can be in the form of direct cash outlays or, particularly for top managers, come from stock options previously granted based on the company's profit performance.

Gainsharing. Gainsharing is a bonus incentive system designed to improve productivity through employee involvement, with the gains from "working smarter" shared between the employer and the employees according to a predetermined formula. Gainsharing is quite different from profit sharing in that it ties rewards to productivity gains rather than profits. Employees in a gainsharing plan can receive incentive awards even when the organization isn't profitable. Employers find this incentive program useful, as high-performing workers pressure weaker performers to work harder, improving performance for the group as a whole.

Employee stock ownership. An employee stock ownership plan (ESOP) is an employee benefit plan that provides a company's workers with an ownership interest in the company. The employer allocates a certain number of shares of the company to each eligible employee. Shares are allotted based on pay scale or some other similar form of distribution. Each employee's shares are held in the company's ESOP trust until he or she leaves or retires. Research has shown that ESOPs increase employee satisfaction, but their impact on job performance is less clear. ESOPs for top management can reduce unethical behavior. CEOs are more likely to manipulate firm earnings reports to make themselves look good in the short run when they don't have an ownership share, even though this manipulation will eventually lead to lower stock prices. However, when CEOs own a large value of stock, they report earnings accurately because they don't want the negative consequences of declining stock prices.

SUMMARY OF CHAPTER

1. Job design and employee involvement are the foundations of a motivating work setting.

2. The ways in which jobs are designed and the types of ways to involve employees have a tremendous effect on the performance and motivation of employees and the extent to which an organization is able to achieve its goals.

3. Job enlargement and job enrichment focus on the horizontal and vertical loading of jobs. Each approach attempts to raise intrinsic motivation.

4. The job characteristics model also focuses on intrinsic motivation. This model proposes five core dimensions (skill variety, task identity, task significance, autonomy, and feedback). These five dimensions lead to three critical psychological states (experienced meaningfulness of work, experienced responsibility for work outcomes, and knowledge of results) that in turn lead to several outcomes (intrinsic motivation, job performance, job satisfaction, and low absenteeism and turnover).

5. Individual differences (knowledge and skills, and satisfaction with the work context) affect the key relationships in the job characteristics model.

6. **Organizational reward systems** consists of all organizational components, including people, processes, rules and procedures, and decision-making activities involved in allocating compensation and benefits to employees in exchange for their contributions to the organization

7. **Variable pay programs** base a portion of an employee's pay on some individual and/or organizational measure of performance. The employee's earning can therefore vary up or down.

8. Employee involvement is creating an environment in which people have an impact on decisions and actions that affect their jobs.

9. There are three major forms of employee involvement: participative management, empowerment, and representative participation.

10. Empowerment is the process of enabling workers to set their own work goals, make decisions, and solve problems within their spheres of responsibility and authority.

DISCUSSION QUESTIONS

1. How might a manager redesign the job of a person who delivers newspapers to raise levels of the core job dimensions identified by the job characteristics model?

2. Do all employees want to be empowered and make the decisions that their bosses used to make? Why or why not?

3. Do all employees want their pay to be based on their performance? Why or why not?

4. Despite the positive effects of merit pay on motivation, when might an organization not want to use it?

AM I INTERNALLY MOTIVATED AT WORK?

INSTRUCTIONS

Indicate how often the following reasons for studying are true for you. Use the following scale:
1: Never | 2: Rarely | 3: Sometimes | 4: Often | 5: Always

1. I enjoy having a variety of tasks at work.
2. I am often bored at work.
3. I am aware of the significance of my job.
4. I am aware of the contribution my job makes to the company.
5. My bosses involve me in the decisions surrounding my job.
6. My job is highly structured.
7. I am given commands at work without the ability to offer suggestions.
8. I have autonomy in areas of my job.
9. My bosses provide routine feedback on my performance.
10. I only receive feedback when I do something wrong.

SCORING KEY:

To find your score, add up your points. Reverse score numbers 2, 6, 7, and 10 (1 = 5, 2 = 4, 3 = 3, 4 = 2, 5 = 1). The resulting number will be between 0 and 50.

ANALYSIS:

The importance of this assessment is to demonstrate that job characteristics affect your internal motivation at work. Variety, identity, significance, autonomy, and feedback all generate a higher and more satisfying job performance. Take a moment to think about your job. Consider your score and your degree of internal motivation at work.

A score of 40 to 50 reveals that you may be motivated at work and experience meaning at work, understand your contributions to the company, and feel responsible for certain outcomes at work. A score of 30 to 40 indicates that your job may be lacking the presence of key motivating job characteristics. A score of 0 to 30 indicates that you are likely not satisfied with your job and feel that you are not growing at work.

Adapted from: Hackman, J. R. and Oldman, G. R. (1976), "Motivation through the design of Work" T. Organizational Behavior and Human Performance Journal, August, p. 250-279.

CHAPTER 6 REFERENCES

Brown, D. (2002, November 18). Everybody loves flex. *Canadian HR Reporter*, p. 1.

Buchko, A. (1992). The effects of employee ownership on employee attitudes: A test of three theoretical perspectives. *Work and Occupations, 19*(1), 59–78.

Datta, K., Guthrie, J. P., & Wright, P. M. (2005). Human resource management and labor productivity: Does industry matter? *Academy of Management Journal, 48*(1), 135–145.

Doucouliagos, C. (1995). Worker participation and productivity in labor-managed and participatory capitalist firms: A meta-analysis. *Industrial and Labor Relations Review, 49*(1) 58–77.

Flextime gains in popularity in Germany. (2000, September). *Manpower Argus*, p. 4.

Grzywacz, J. G., Carlson, D. S., & Shulkin, S. (2008). Schedule flexibility and stress: Linking formal and flexible arrangements and perceived flexibility to employee health. *Community, Work, and Family, 11*(2), 199–214.

Hackman, J. R., & Oldman, G. R. (1976). Motivation through the design of work. *Organizational Behavior and Human Performance*, 16(2) 50–279.

Hackman, J. R., & Oldman, G. R. (1980). *Work redesign*. Reading, MA: Addison-Wesley.

Hanson, G., & Bell, W. D. (1987). *Profit sharing and profitability: How profit sharing promotes business success*. London: Kogan Page.

Humphrey, S. E., Nahrgang, J. D., & Morgeson, F. P. (2007). Integrating motivational, social, and contextual work design features: A meta-analytic summary and theoretical extension of the work design literature. *Journal of Applied Psychology, 92*(5), 1332–1356.

Huff, J. W., Wright, J. A., & Neuman, G. A. (1999). Flexible and compressed workweek schedules: A meta-analysis of their effects on work-related criteria. *Journal of Applied Psychology, 84*(4), 496–513.

Kossek, E., Lautsch, B. A., & Eaton, S. C. (2006). Telecommuting, control, and boundary management: Correlates of policy use and practice, job control, and work-family effectiveness. *Journal of Vocational Behavior, 68*(2), 347–367.

Morgeson, P., Johnson, M. D., Campion, M. A., Jedsker, G.J. & Mumford, T. V. (2006). Understanding reactions to job redesign: A quasi-experimental investigation of the moderating effects of organizational contact on perceptions of performance behavior. *Personal Psychology, 59(2),* 333–363.

Murray, B., & Gerhart, B. (1998). An empirical analysis of a skill-based pay program and plant performance. *Academy of Management Journal, 41(1),* 68–78.

Ortega, J. (2001). Job rotation as a learning mechanism. *Management Science*, 47(10), 1361–1370.

Ralston, D. A., & Flanagan, M. F. (1985). The effect of flextime on absenteeism and turnover for male and female employees. *Journal of Vocational Behavior*, 26(2), 206–217.

Riordan, C. M., Vandenberg, R. J., & Richardson, H. A. (2005). Employee involvement climate and organizational effectiveness. *Human Resource Management, 44*(4), 471–488.

Shaw, J. D., Gupta, N., Mitra, A., & Ledford Jr., G. E. (2005). Success and survival of skill-based pay plans. *Journal of Management, 31*(10), 1–22.

Takeuchi, R., Lepak, D. P., Wang, H., & Takeuchi, K. (2007). An empirical examination of the mechanisms mediating performance of Japanese organizations. *Journal of Applied Psychology, 92*(4), 1069–1083.

Welbourne, T. M., & Gomez-Mejia, L. R. (1995). Gainsharing: A critical review and a future research agenda. *Journal of Management, 21*(3), 559–609.

Zhang, X., Bartol, K. M., Smith, K. G., Pfarrer, M. D., & Khanin, D. M. (2008). CEOs on the edge: Earnings manipulation and stock-based incentive misalignment. *Academy of Management Journal, 51*(2), 241–258.

UNDERSTANDING AND MANAGING SOCIAL PROCESSES AND MAKING DECISIONS

3

COMMUNICATION IN ORGANIZATIONS

CHAPTER LEARNING OBJECTIVES

After reading this chapter, you should have a good understanding of

- the communication process and why effective communication is critical in the workplace;
- the difference between formal and informal communication channels;
- how perceptions interact with the communication process and the different methods of improving communication transmissions;
- how active and empathic listening can be utilized to improve reception;
- the importance of feedback and the steps involved in giving and receiving feedback effectively; and
- the four common types of group meetings and six important considerations for holding effective meetings.

"Today, communication itself is the problem. We have become the world's first overcommunicated society. Each year we send more and receive less."

- AL RIES

WHY IS COMMUNICATION IMPORTANT?

According to the National Association of Colleges and Employers (NACE), the most important proficiency a college graduate can possess is effective communication skills. Recently, NACE, a leading authority on the employment of college graduates, conducted a poll and found that 79% of those polled reported that most college students did not have effective communication skills (NACE, 2011a). Along with effective communication, NACE found that soft skills were important to adapt to different workplace environments. In a follow-up survey conducted in 2015, NACE reported that employers found new college graduates received low grades in two key areas—teamwork and communication. NACE reported, "Teamwork dropped from an A- among 2013–14 respondents to a B this year, making it the second lowest graded attribute. Written communication skills, the third key skill employers look for, received a B-, down from a B+ last year."

This research supports the thoughts and beliefs penned in 2004 by Henry Mintzberg in his book, *Managers Not MBAs: A Hard Look at the Soft Practice of*

Managing and Management Development. He offers a bold critique of how MBA programs have an overemphasized focus on science and analytics at the expense of critical management and leadership skills. Claiming that management has been misinterpreted as business education, Mintzberg believes the overemphasis of MBA analyses and techniques leave graduates with a distorted impression that management consists of applying formulas to situations. He suggests this practice has led to many of the corrupt, dehumanizing effects witnessed in businesses today.

Clearly, communication plays a pivotal role in the workplace. In order to succeed in business today, organizations are looking for individuals with sophisticated soft skills who can communicate with diverse employee groups in a variety of situations.

THE RISE OF MODERN COMMUNICATION

How to Win Friends and Influence People, written by Dale Carnegie and first published in 1936, was a small book dedicated to improving social skills. The book became immensely popular and launched Dale Carnegie into a successful career involving writing, speaking, and training. Before his death in 1955, Dale Carnegie had become the foremost expert on how to interact with people. Today, Dale Carnegie's book has become a landmark guide on how to communicate and interact with people, selling over 3 million copies.

During the 1900s, the nature of management was the focus of exploration and debate. Early discussions were centered on the hierarchy of positions, organizational structure, and division of work. As one of the first writers to link communication skills with managerial effectiveness, Carnegie suggested that employee commitment did not depend solely on economic factors, but was gained through interpersonal communication skills. Carnegie's notion that the interpersonal communication skills of a manager could influence employee commitment was a radical introduction to management conversations. Carnegie's beliefs paved the way for exploration and examination of the relationship between managers and employees.

During the 1950s, communication theories and conventions began to emerge. However, the nature of management communication remained largely intact until the era of empowerment. During the 1990s, the era of empowerment ushered in power sharing—the delegation of power and authority to employees. Debate and discussion focused on decentralization of power and information sharing. In 1989, *Fortune* reported that 74% of the CEOs surveyed declared they had become more participatory and less dictatorial, more consensus oriented than imperial, and now relied more on communication than command. Organizations and their leaders began to understand that giving up centralized power facilitated faster product development, increased organizational flexibility, and improved quality.

Recently, research conducted in 2013 to 2014 has identified effective communication as a leading indicator of financial performance, and proven that effective organizational communication can help a company significantly outperform their industry peers.

Unfortunately, effective communication is complicated in contemporary organizations. External environmental pressures, such as increased competition and regulatory constraints, and internal drivers, such as diverse work environments, are changing and increasing the complexity of workplace communication. Contemporary companies are adapting by employing a variety of information technologies and communication networks to ensure the rapid dissemination of information and facilitate decision making.

COMMUNICATION NETWORKS

A **communication network** is composed of a group of employees sharing regular lines of communication. **Centralized networks** exist when information is funneled through a limited number of employees within the organization. **Decentralized networks** exist when information is broadly shared among and flows through many individuals within the organization. Organizations managing turbulent and complex environments often find decentralized networks optimal because individuals can quickly communicate changes in the business environment. In a decentralized network, individuals can contribute ideas, share knowledge, and discuss solutions for managing these changes.

Global organizations have adopted a variety of communication network forms to help facilitate information acquisition, processing, and dissemination. Emphasizing the use of autonomous, self-managing teams, many of these networks employ flat hierarchies and use information technology to coordinate projects and employees located throughout different geographic locations.

Regardless of the type of communication network, employees working together need to communicate through formal and informal channels to share information and keep abreast of developments in the organization.

COMMUNICATION CHANNELS

The term **communication channel** is used to describe the means through which employees send and receive information. The communication of data from one individual to another requires some form of a pathway, known as a communication channel, which refers to the way information flows within the organization. There are two basic types of communication channels found in organizations: formal and informal.

FORMAL CHANNELS

Formal communication channels include the system of official organizational channels that carry approved information and messages. For example, the formal communication channel may carry organizational edicts, such as policies and procedures, and be transmitted via formal communication systems, such as company emails. Essentially, three formal communication channels exist: downward communication, upward communication, and horizontal communication.

Downward communication includes the communication that flows from upper to lower levels in an organization. Generally, downward communication contains the issuing of orders down the organizational hierarchy. Downward communication is utilized to give employees job-related information. Examples of downward communication include company newsletters and websites.

Upward communication includes the communication that flows from the lower levels to the upper levels in an organization. Generally, upward communication contains feedback about operations and situations. For example, upward communications help higher-level managers understand organizational performance problems and workplace situations. Common types of upward communication include progress reports.

Horizontal communication flows among employees at the same organizational level. For example, horizontal communication occurs when two supervisors coordinate the schedule of shared employees. Generally, horizontal communication facilitates coordination and cooperation between different personnel in the same company by allowing coworkers to share important information. Horizontal communication can also help coworkers discuss situations and resolve problems without involving upper levels of management. Examples of horizontal communication can include interdepartmental memos or requests for resources.

Breakdowns in a communication channel lead to an inefficient flow of information. For example, if information is incomplete and employees are unsure of what the company or their boss expects of them, it could cause employees to become suspicious of motives or to become less productive. When formal communication is incomplete or unclear, employees often seek information through informal communication channels.

Informal communication channels occur outside of the organization's established channels. Informal communication channels generally arise from a lack of information or truthfulness from the formal communication channel, as well as the increased ease of use, as informal channels are unregulated.

The **grapevine** is the most common informal communication channel. The grapevine is a network of employee-to-employee messages that occur outside of formal communication channels. Arising out of curiosity, the grapevine stems from the workers' need to know what is going on and how it might affect them or their coworkers. When formal communication channels do not supply sufficient or complete information, employees may create the information in order to fill gaps. An attempt by workers to understand a situation by creating a communication network designed to supply information about it, grapevine communication networks are about who knows whom in the organization. Organizations that have robust grapevines often develop formal communications that are encrypted in order to prevent the spread of misinformation. **Encryption** refers to the sending of messages that are not readily understood.

Interestingly, research has proven that grapevines contain highly accurate information. First, because grapevines help supply missing information that is not available through formal channels, information spreads rapidly. Second, because grapevine information is typically carried through face-to-face channels, senders can get feedback to make sure they understand the message, thus reducing misunderstandings. Third, because most of the information in an organization moves through the grapevine, workers usually verify the accuracy of information. This is accomplished by verifying the interpretation of the message with others.

All communication, both formal and informal, impacts the organization. When managers withhold information or send encrypted messages, it is generally a bad communication practice. The absence of information or the presence of encrypted information from upper-level management only fuels the grapevine. A better management strategy is to inform employees honestly and, when possible, completely.

THE COMMUNICATION PROCESS

Regardless of the way communication takes place within the organization, all communication proceeds through the basic communication process. The **communication process** is the exchange of information between two or more people.

The basic communication process is divided into three components once the sender develops an idea and composes a message. First, the sender transmits the message through a channel to the receiver. Then, the message is transmitted to the other party—the receiver. Lastly, the receiver interprets the message and receives meaning. The receiver may or may not provide feedback to the sender.

However, some workplace communication will proceed through a more advanced communication process. Expanding upon the basic communication progression, there are five components in the advanced communication process:

1. Sender (has the message to convey, transmits the message, encodes the message)
2. Message (the subject matter, opinion, fact, idea, information)
3. Communication channel (media through which message is delivered, links sender and receiver)
4. Receiver (receives messages, decodes message, interprets message, and may provide feedback)
5. Feedback (a signal from the receiver to the sender)

The **sender**, who begins the communication process, composes a message he or she wants to convey to another person. In essence, the message is what the sender wants someone else to know. The next step is encoding the message. **Encoding** means selecting a form for the message, such as written or verbal, that can be recognized and acknowledged by the receiver. The sender transmits the message using a communication channel. Selected by the sender, the communication channel includes the media through which the message is transmitted. The communication channel links the message from the sender to the receiver.

Once the message is received, the **receiver** decodes and interprets the message. **Decoding** is the process by which the receiver interprets the communication. The receiver will translate the message using their knowledge, background, and experience.

Feedback, a return message from the receiver to the sender, indicates the receiver's translation and understanding of the message. Some communication channels allow for immediate feedback. For example, using the phone or face-to-face conversation as the communication channel allows the sender to receive immediate feedback. Other communication channels do not allow the sender to receive immediate feedback. For example, using text or email as the communication channel does not allow the sender to receive immediate feedback, as they must wait for the receiver to respond. Feedback, the final link in the communication process chain, is extremely helpful as it makes senders aware of possible miscommunications.

At times, the message, as understood by the receiver, isn't the message the sender planned to send. Because of perceptual filters, receivers may translate a vastly different meaning to a message than that which the sender intended. Once the sender is aware of a miscommunication, he or she is able to offer continued communications, such as clarifications, until the receiver understands the message as intended. Feedback may take the form of a nonverbal, written, or oral response from the receiver to the sender. A **feedback signal** is the interpretation of the message by the receiver. Often, this signal is influenced by such factors as the receiver's experience, background, or emotional state.

HOW NOISE INTERFERES WITH THE COMMUNICATION PROCESS

Noise is the interference with the transmission of the intended message. It prevents the message from being interpreted by the receiver as intended by the sender. Noise causes an interruption in the flow of information (Figure 7.1).

Noise can be external or internal. **External noise** is related to the environment. Common examples of external noise are a noisy room or an interruption in technology. On the other hand, **internal noise** is generally semantic or psychological. Common examples of semantic noise include grammatical errors, acronyms, and technical language, while examples of psychological noise include preconceived notions we bring to conversations such as stereotypes, reputations, biases, and assumptions.

Both internal and external noise cause communication problems and prevent effective communication. Messages are transmitted with and against a backdrop of noise. In the communication process, noise may occur in any of the step in the communication process, for any of the following reasons:

1. Sender is not sure what message to communicate.
2. Message is not clearly encoded.
3. Wrong communication channel is chosen.
4. Message is not decoded or received properly.

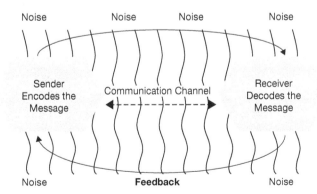

Figure 7.1. The Communication Process

Kipley, D., Jewe, R., & Helm-Stevens, R., A Foundation in the Principles of Management, pp. 258. Copyright © 2015 by Cognella, Inc. Reprinted with permission.

5.   The receiver doesn't have the knowledge, experience, or time to understand the message.

HOW PERCEPTION INFLUENCES THE COMMUNICATION PROCESS

As employees perform their work, they are exposed to a wide variety of stimuli, such as occurrences and communications, and arrange the information in a meaningful way. Employees experience stimuli through their perceptual filters, based on past experiences and exposures. Through the lens of perceptual filters, employees interpret and assign meaning to the stimuli. **Perception**, a subjective, active, and creative process, is defined as the process of experiencing the world around us. By creating awareness of objects and events in their world, individuals attend to, organize, interpret, and store information. The basic perception process occurs in four stages:

1.   Stimulation (an action on various nerve agents)
2.   Organization (arranging the information)
3.   Interpretation-evaluation (ability to reveal meanings and relationships in society)
4.   Storage-memory (ability to store and recall information)

Perception, a cognitive progression of interpretations, begins with how the receiver perceives the sender's communication and interprets what they sensed. Thus, different employees may end up with different interpretations and understandings of the same message.

Perception influences and often creates communication problems in the workplace. Frequently, employees exposed to the same organizational communication or information end up with dissimilar views, ideas, and understandings. Two of the most common perception problems are selective perception and closure.

Selective perception is defined as the tendency to notice and accept the stimuli that is consistent with our experiences, values, beliefs, and expectations, while discounting or ignoring stimuli that is inconsistent. On the other hand, **closure** is defined as the tendency to fill in the gaps when information is missing. Employees may make assumptions about missing information. Likely, the assumptions will be based on interpretations of past experiences and exposures.

A misalignment, or gap, in perception occurs when the intention and message set forth by the sender is misunderstood when received. When sending communications, clear and concise messages help minimize communication misunderstandings. It is critical to share information accurately and in the most complete manner appropriate. It is important for all levels of leaders in the organization to be transparent in order to reduce perception problems and build trust, resulting in improved employee morale. However, although a sender may make every effort to send a clear message, the receiver's ability to listen is just as essential to effective communication.

IMPROVING RECEPTION BY LISTENING

Many employees are proficient at hearing, but few are skilled at listening. Effective listening, a vital part of effective communication, is not just hearing. Although hearing and listening are used interchangeably, they mean two very different things. **Hearing**, involuntary and uncontrollable, involves receiving and perceiving sounds. On the other hand, **listening** requires attention, as it is a conscious effort to hear and understand. Typically, active and empathic listening are the two most important listening skills that managers must develop in order to possess competent listening skills.

Active listening is the process of participating in giving the speaker nonjudgmental feedback that demonstrates you accurately heard the sender's message. Active listening involves assuming half the responsibility for successful communication. Active listening involves seeking to understand (not just hear) the sender's message by verifying understanding prior to providing feedback. Individuals proficient at active listening put the speaker at ease by maintaining interest and eye contact. They show the sender that they are attentive by nodding and making short statements to gain more information or seek clarification. Three active listening tools are critical to understanding: clarifying, paraphrasing, and summarizing.

Clarifying, asking the sender to explain or provide more details, helps the receiver understand confusing or ambiguous statements. Similarly, **paraphrasing**, restating what was said to you in your own words, helps the receiver understand and provides the opportunity for the sender to further expand upon the message. **Summarizing** involves providing a review of the sender's main points or emotions. Since each of these key elements help the receiver understand and acknowledge the message, the receiver should refrain from interrupting. Instead, the receiver can use the natural breaks in the speaker's delivery as a time to clarify, paraphrase, or summarize.

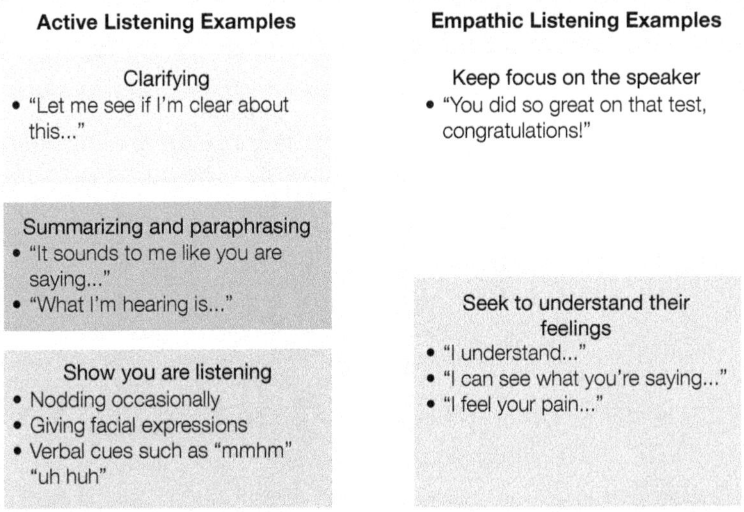

Active Listening Examples

Clarifying
- "Let me see if I'm clear about this..."

Summarizing and paraphrasing
- "It sounds to me like you are saying..."
- "What I'm hearing is..."

Show you are listening
- Nodding occasionally
- Giving facial expressions
- Verbal cues such as "mmhm" "uh huh"

Empathic Listening Examples

Keep focus on the speaker
- "You did so great on that test, congratulations!"

Seek to understand their feelings
- "I understand..."
- "I can see what you're saying..."
- "I feel your pain..."

Figure 7.2. Active and Empathic Listening Prompts

Active listeners make a conscious effort to hear the words, but, more importantly, they try to understand the complete message. Active listening is achieved by attentively listening without distraction and without forming counter arguments. It is important to withhold evaluation, counter arguments, or criticism until after the message is accurately and completely received. Until then, the receiver should respond with the intent to understand in order to receive the complete message accurately.

Empathic listening is defined as the ability to understand by paying attention to another person's feelings, concerns, or emotional state. This means understanding the sender's personal perspective–how they **feel**. Empathic listening is built upon active listening because, first, the sender must understand the message. However, more advanced than active listening, empathic listening requires the receiver to recognize and understand the feelings, perceptions, and motives of the sender. Simply, empathic listening is the receiver's ability and willingness to appreciate the situation without judgment. Unlike sympathy, listening empathically does not necessarily involve agreeing with the sender's perspective, or being affected by the sender's perceptions, but, instead, the ability to see the world through the other person's eyes. Two key elements can help employees become better empathic listeners: understanding feelings and reflecting feelings.

Effective empathic listeners depend on **understanding feelings**—the receiver's desire to understand and reflect the sender's feelings. It is critical to genuinely desire to understand the sender's perspectives and emotions. On the other hand, **reflecting feelings** involves indicating that you understand the sender's emotions. Unlike active listening, reflecting feelings is focused on the affective part of the message (Figure 7.2).

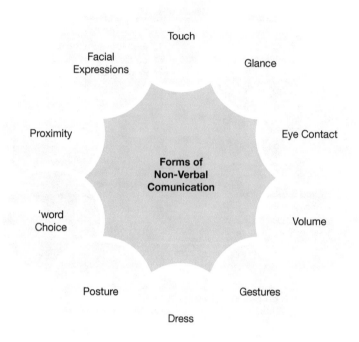

Figure 7.3. Forms of Nonverbal Communication

Kipley, D., Jewe, R., & Helm-Stevens, R., A Foundation in the Principles of Management, pp. 259. Copyright © 2015 by Cognella, Inc. Reprinted with permission.

NONVERBAL COMMUNICATION AS A SOURCE OF INFORMATION

Nonverbal communication provides richness and meaning to oral communication. **Nonverbal communication**, which includes gestures and facial expressions, is any communication that does not involve words (Figure 7.3). The transmission of messages by a medium other than writing or speech, nonverbal communication includes aspects of speech itself, such as accent, pitch, and tone. Certainly, the importance of nonverbal communication is well documented. Research suggests that 45% to 93% of oral communication is influenced by nonverbal feedback. Obviously, nonverbal feedback can demonstrate to the sender that the receiver accepts or discounts the message. Additionally, nonverbal communication can contradict the verbal communication message spoken by the sender. Two types of nonverbal communications are kinesics and paralanguage.

From the Greek word *kinesis*, meaning "movement," **kinesics** involves facial and body movements. These movements may include facial expressions, eye contact, and hand gestures, such as tapping fingers or jingling keys. Kinesics can be used to signal approval or disapproval of a message. For example, a smile or a nod can demonstrate the receiver's approval. Conversely, a finger to the lips may indicate that the receiver doesn't want to hear the message.

Paralanguage involves vocal characterizers and qualifiers. **Vocal characterizers** include laughing, yelling, and crying, while **vocal qualifiers** include volume, pitch, and tempo. Often, speaking patterns, such as silence, hesitation, or yelling, are utilized to send a signal. Pitch and tone can cause a sentence to become a command.

Nonverbal communication, a critical link in the feedback process of oral communication, has multiple functions. It can be used to repeat the message, augment, accent, or regulate the message. Regardless of the intended function, nonverbal communication is very helpful and informative. Although it is a complex source of information, nonverbal communication can complement, contradict, or be an adjunct to the spoken word. Nonverbal communication can convey emotions, such as happiness, satisfaction, anger, distrust, worry, or fear. It is communication without saying or writing anything.

USING FEEDBACK TO PROMOTE INDIVIDUAL AND ORGANIZATIONAL GROWTH

In the communication process, **feedback** is the response of a receiver or an audience to a message. Due to the usefulness of feedback in bringing clarity to communication and aiding in understanding, the term feedback is also used to describe responses or return of information about a workplace activity. **Performance feedback** is defined as a return of information about a workplace activity, process, or result. Although there are several types of performance feedback in the workplace, effective feedback is descriptive, not judgmental. It is focused on workplace behavior, not personal behaviors or characteristics. Effective feedback is designed to be a collaborative effort and intended to help the individual.

Critical to workplace success, effective feedback conveys important information to help promote individual and organizational growth. Feedback is important because it gauges understanding. For example, it can help determine whether the instructions provided were understood. Feedback also promotes productivity and quality. For example, it can help explain whether or not the standard of work was acceptable. Effective feedback is also a sign of healthy communication in the workplace, as it creates trust and facilitates open relationships between individuals.

A significant study by Bandura and Cervone in 1983 showed the importance of feedback on performance. Their research and published trials resulted from studying the effects of feedback on a group of cyclists. Bandura and Cervone split a group of 80 cyclists equally into four smaller training groups. The performance improvement of the four cycling groups was closely monitored. Group One received clear performance goals. Group Two did not receive goals, but did receive regular performance feedback. Group Three received goals in the beginning and feedback throughout the trial. Group Four, the control group, did not receive goals or performance feedback. As expected, Group Four showed the least performance improvement. The study found Group Three, which received goals and benefitted from feedback, improved almost three times more than Group Four. The Bandura and Cervone study illustrates how important giving helpful feedback is to the development of individuals and their team.

GIVING FEEDBACK

Team leaders, supervisors, and managers use feedback to help employees focus on important issues. In the workplace, feedback should be delivered to help workers do the right things, do things the right way, and perform at higher levels. Indeed, many productive employees are likely to be motivated by well-delivered feedback.

Although performance appraisals are scheduled on a regular basis in most organizations, feedback does not need to be limited to a scheduled date and time; it can occur when most appropriate. Formal feedback, such as a performance appraisal, is generally scheduled. Conversely, informal feedback generally occurs throughout the workday. Regardless of the time or formality, feedback must be effective in order to improve job performance, reduce confusion regarding expectations and current performance, promote professional and personal growth in employees, and maintain or improve workplace morale.

Basic Rules for Delivering Positive Feedback

1. Describe the positive behavior. Be specific in providing details.
2. Explain why the behavior was positive. It is helpful to describe how the positive behavior impacted the organization, department or customer.
3. Thank the employee. Acknowledge the employee's contribution with a verbal 'thank you.' If necessary, help the employee accept credit.

Figure 7.4. Basic Rules for Delivering Positive Feedback

In order for feedback to be effective, it should be balanced. There should be a mix of positive and constructive feedback. Giving feedback is not always easy, but there are five basic principals essential to delivering effective feedback.

1. Feedback should be delivered in the right setting. As a rule, it is acceptable to deliver positive feedback in public. However, this rule is general and can be tricky. It is best to consider the employee's personality and preference. On the other hand, constructive feedback should be delivered privately.

2. Feedback should be specific. Specific feedback focuses on incidents that are within the worker's control. It is important for the manager to supply specific information, such as when and where it happened and what the results were. For example, if a manager witnesses an employee arriving late to work, it is not helpful to tell the employee, "You are always late." It would be better to say, "In the last two weeks, you have been more than 15 minutes late four times." Remember to focus on observations and facts rather than inferences.

3. Feedback should be timely. As a rule, feedback should occur promptly following the observation or incident. Feedback is more effective when both the manager and the employee can recall the incident. When the feedback occurs closely following the observation, the incident is vivid and can be discussed in detail. Delayed feedback, for example attempting to discuss an incident that happened three months ago, is often problematic due to lack of recall and memory. Additionally, performance deficiencies should be addressed at the earliest possible opportunity. This will prevent the employee from forming poor habits.

4. Feedback should be task oriented as opposed to employee oriented. Task-oriented feedback focuses on the problem or the deficient performance rather that the personality of the employee. Feedback should be based on what an employee does or did, rather than personality traits or generalizations. In order to be effective, it is important for managers to be nonjudgmental while providing feedback. For example, it is not helpful for a manager to say, "You always talk too much." It is better to say, "I noticed that you talked during much of the department meeting. This prevented me from covering the agenda."

5. Feedback should be balanced. There are two important focuses when balancing feedback. First, employees should be provided with a balance of praise and criticism. Second, employees should be provided with frequent feedback, but not overloaded with it. If an employee is overloaded with feedback, he or she can be confused about what needs to be improved.

In addition to understanding the basic skills needed to deliver feedback, it is important to recognize that feedback can be positive, constructive, or destructive. Positive feedback (acknowledging good performance), and constructive feedback (addressing areas in need of improvement), should occur in the workplace. Conversely, every effort should be made to avoid delivering destructive feedback.

Positive feedback is used to reinforce desired behavior. Positive feedback includes information or input to a staff member about a job well done. Perhaps, the news could stem from a customer comment or, perhaps, the manager may observe a staff member providing great customer service. Research suggests that positive feedback should outnumber constructive feedback. Consider the following steps when giving positive feedback, as well as reinforcing great performance:

Table 7.1. Steps to provide positive feedback and reinforce great performance

1. Describe the positive behavior
   Be specific, have details

2. Explain why the behavior was positive
   Describe how the behavior impacts the organization, customer, or department in a positive way

3. Thank the employee
   Give a verbal 'thank you' and the appropriate credit

Constructive feedback addresses areas of improvement, with the intention to be helpful or corrective. Generally, based on observation, constructive feedback is information specific or issue focused, and aimed at correcting performance deficiencies, providing additional information or resources to correct the deficiency, and motivating employees. With all these situations, giving feedback is the only way to make certain the behavior is likely to change.

Consider the following steps when giving constructive feedback.

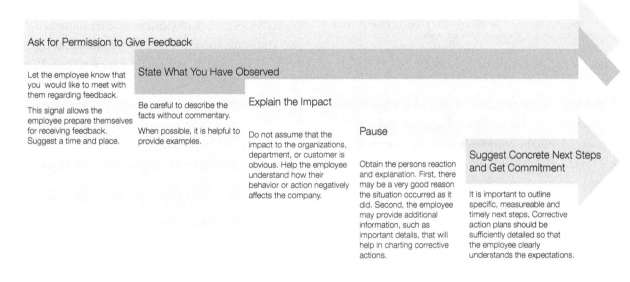

Figure 7.5. Giving Constructive Feedback

Kipley, D., Jewe, R., & Helm-Stevens, R., A Foundation in the Principles of Management, pp. 265. Copyright © 2015 by Cognella, Inc. Reprinted with permission.

1. Ask for permission to give feedback. Let the employee know that you would like to meet with them regarding feedback. This signal allows the employee to prepare himself or herself for receiving feedback. Suggest a time and place.

2. State what you have observed. Be careful to describe the facts without commentary. When possible, it is helpful to provide examples.

3. Explain the impact. Do not assume the impact to the department or customer is obvious. Help explain how the behavior or action negatively affects the company.

4. Pause. Obtain the person's reaction and explanation. First, there may be a very good reason the situation occurred as it did. Second, the employee may provide additional information, such as important details, that will help in charting corrective actions.

5. Suggest concrete next steps. It is important to outline specific, measurable, and timely next steps. Corrective action plans should be sufficiently detailed so that the expectations are clearly understood.

6. Get commitment. It is important to have commitment to the corrective action plan.

Not being kind
• Be careful not to refrain from making personal or generalized comments. It is important to be professional and focus on the issues and not the employee.

Being too kind
• Be careful not to get caught up in being tactful or sugarcoating the issues. It is important to address the issue in clear and specific terms.

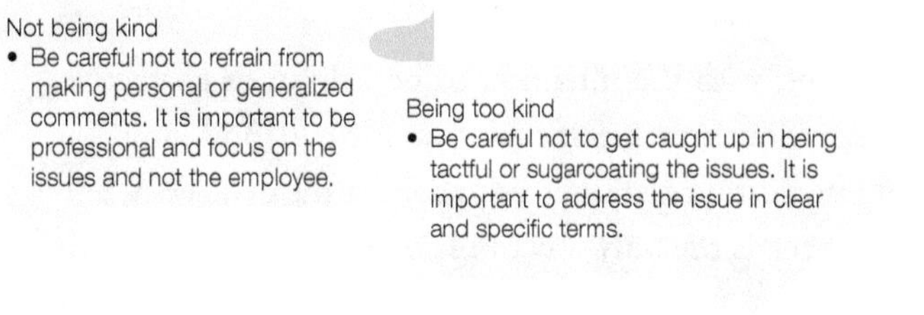

Figure 7.6. Common Mistakes in Delivering Feedback

Kipley, D., Jewe, R., & Helm-Stevens, R., A Foundation in the Principles of Management, pp. 266. Copyright © 2015 by Cognella, Inc. Reprinted with permission.

In order for feedback to be constructive instead of destructive, it should be focused on specific behaviors and be problem/solution oriented. **Destructive feedback**, which tends to occur in the form of generalized or subjective comments, is critical and disapproving without any intention of being helpful. Although destructive feedback often occurs when poor performance is witnessed or when there is a lack of agreed-upon performance standards, it is delivered in a way that negatively impacts the employee. In the worst of scenarios, destructive feedback is a personal criticism that does not improve performance. Often, destructive feedback produces a negative or defensive reaction from the recipient. At times, employees respond to destructive feedback with verbal or physical aggression. In order to reduce the chances of delivering destructive feedback, managers should be cautious in entering conversations with subordinates when frustrated.

Providing one-on-one feedback is one of the most powerful tools available to develop employees and, since giving regular and frequent feedback is part of supervising and managing, it is important to be aware of the most common mistakes new managers make when learning to give feedback. Many new managers and supervisors make one of the two most common mistakes when delivering feedback. (See also Figure 7.6.)

1. Being too harsh. Refrain from making personal or generalized comments, as they impede reception. It is important to be professional. Focus on the issue and not the individual.

2. Being too kind. Don't get caught up in being tactful or sugarcoating the issue to the extent of the message being obscured. It is important to address issues clearly and succinctly.

RECEIVING FEEDBACK

Receiving feedback is critical to effective workplace performance, as it provides an opportunity to change and modify behaviors. However, receiving feedback requires skill, especially when the feedback is focused on a sensitive area or if the sender isn't skilled at delivering feedback. In order to accept and understand feedback, you need to listen first.

Don't think about a response or justification. Just listen to the entire message with the goal of fully understanding the feedback. Use different types of active listening questions to clarify the situation, and reflect back your understanding. Ask clarifying questions to seek more information and ensure that you have fully understood the entire meaning or situation. Use paraphrasing to reflect back your understanding and summarizing to check for understanding. Be aware of your emotions. In order to receive feedback, you must be able to exercise self-control.

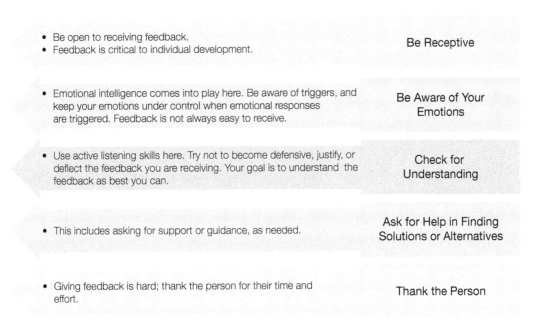

- Be open to receiving feedback.
- Feedback is critical to individual development.

Be Receptive

- Emotional intelligence comes into play here. Be aware of triggers, and keep your emotions under control when emotional responses are triggered. Feedback is not always easy to receive.

Be Aware of Your Emotions

- Use active listening skills here. Try not to become defensive, justify, or deflect the feedback you are receiving. Your goal is to understand the feedback as best you can.

Check for Understanding

- This includes asking for support or guidance, as needed.

Ask for Help in Finding Solutions or Alternatives

- Giving feedback is hard; thank the person for their time and effort.

Thank the Person

Figure 7.7. Receiving Feedback

Consider the following steps when receiving feedback.

1. Be receptive. Be open to receiving feedback.
2. Be aware of your emotions. Manage your emotions by keeping them under control. Remind yourself that feedback is not always easy to receive.
3. Check for understanding. Utilize active listening to ensure understanding.
4. Ask for help in finding solutions or alternatives. If appropriate, ask for support, guidance, or training.
5. Thank the person. Remind yourself that it is not always easy to give feedback. If appropriate, apologize (Figure 7.7).

When receiving constructive feedback, the emotional intelligence components of self-awareness and self-control are essential. It is necessary to be aware of your emotions and be able to keep them under control when a trigger causes an emotional response. Try not to become defensive or take it personally. Allow the person to finish their feedback. Do not interrupt. Do not attempt to justify, deflect, or minimize the feedback. Keep the discussion focused on observable facts. If the feedback involves a person or group, do not attempt to track the feedback by seeking out contributing parties. Be honest with yourself and do not discount or doubt the validity of the data you are receiving. Remember that positive and negative feedback are critical to individual growth. Well-delivered feedback helps us learn and grow. Negative feedback alerts us to areas of weakness, while positive feedback helps us understand our strengths.

When receiving positive feedback, a common response is one of embarrassment, such as minimizing or downplaying the accomplishment. At times, individuals find it difficult to answer in a confident or assertive manner without sounding conceited. When positive feedback is given, listen to it. Positive feedback is essential for personal and professional development. If we do not understand what we are doing well and why, it can be difficult to build on our strengths. When offered a compliment or praise, say "thank you" and consider responding with a phrase similar to those listed below:

- I'm glad to hear that.
- Thank you, I worked hard on that.
- I am pleased that it worked out.
- Thank you, I thought that worked well.

WORKPLACE MEETINGS

Increasingly, contemporary organizations utilize a variety of different types of meetings to rapidly share and disseminate information. An important part of workplace communication, meetings continue to be useful to coordinate work functions, gain broader perspectives, find facts, and solve complex problems. Additionally, because many organizations are utilizing team-based work environments as a key personnel configuration, the need for building working relationships and maximizing team effectiveness has become essential. There are four common categories of workplace meetings:

1. **Informational**: Explain the importance of new decisions or company activities.
2. **Fact-finding**: Tap into the expertise of several employees from different levels or functional areas to obtain facts for decision making or planning.
3. **Problem-solving**: Sometimes referred to as decision-making meetings, members are invited to pool their expertise with the goal of finding a solution.
4. **Coordination**: Generally used for project management with the goal of keeping everyone informed and up to date on progress, and assigning tasks and responsibilities.

SUMMARY OF CHAPTER

1. This chapter focused on outlining the basic components of the communication process and the importance of effective communication.
2. We learned about the differences between formal and informal communication channels.
3. We explored how active and empathic listening strategies can be utilized to improve reception.
4. We examined how perceptions interact with the communication process and the different methods of improving communication transmissions.
5. This chapter discussed the importance of nonverbal communication and the effect of nonverbal communication on perception.
6. We learned about the basic types of feedback and the steps needed to effectively give and receive feedback to employees.
7. We explored the importance of feedback to improving individual and organizational performance.
8. We discussed the common mistakes new managers make when giving feedback.

DISCUSSION QUESTIONS

1. Explain how perceptions interact with the communication process and the different methods of improving communication transmissions.
2. What strategies can supervisors utilize to improve communication transmissions?
3. Identify the techniques needed to deliver effective positive and constructive feedback.
4. Why is feedback necessary for individual and organizational performance improvement?

AM I AN EFFECTIVE LISTENER?

INSTRUCTIONS

Use the scale below to answer the following statements.
1: Strongly disagree | 2: Disagree | 3: Neutral | 4: Agree | 5: Strongly agree

1. I take time to think about my responses when someone has finished talking.
2. I want to hear the whole story/big picture, not just the facts, when deciding my opinion on something.
3. I think about and evaluate what is being said to me while it is being said.
4. I ask for clarification when things are unclear to me.
5. I focus on listening only to the conversation I am a part of.
6. I focus more on what is actually being said than what I am wanting to hear.
7. At times, I only pretend to be paying attention.
8. I purposely use nonverbal cues to let someone know I am listening to them.
9. I try to understand what is being said through the other person's point of view.
10. I believe that I pick up nonverbal communications well.
11. I wait until the speaker has finished to create a response.
12. Even if we disagree, people would say I understand the point they are making.
13. When I am bored of a conversation, I end it by removing attention from the speaker.
14. I can listen attentively despite the speaker's way of delivering the information.
15. Most of the time I know what is going to be said.

SCORING KEY:

Add up your total for all 15 statements. Reverse score items 3, 7, 13, and 15 (5 = 1, 4 = 2, 3 = 3, 2 = 4, 1 = 5).

ANALYSIS:

Listening skills are important for effective communication. An effective listener takes the time to understand the message being spoken, and show that they are listening. They utilize aspects of active listening throughout the conversation.

Your score will be between 15 and 75; the higher the score, the better the listening skills. If you score 40 and below, you may want to consider improving your listening skills. Scores 60 and above, though you could still improve upon them, indicate well-tuned listening skills.

Adapted from: Robbins, S. P. (2009). II.A.2: How good are my listening skills?, Self-assessment library (52-53). Upper Saddle River, NJ: Pearson Education Inc.
Original Source: Glenn, E. C., & Pood, E. A. (1989). Listening self-inventory. Supervisory Management. p. 12-15.

CHAPTER 7 REFERENCES

Angell, P. (2004). Business communication design. Boston, MA: McGraw Hill Irwin.

Argenti, P. (2007). Corporate communication. New York, NY: McGraw-Hill/Irwin.

Austen, J. L. (1962). *How to do things with words.* Oxford: Oxford University Press.

Axley, S. (1984). Managerial and organizational communication in terms of the conduit metaphor. *Academy of Management Review, 9*(3), 428–437.

Barge, J. K. (2004). Reflexivity and managerial practice. *Communication Monographs, 71*(1), 70–96.

Barge, J. K., & Little, M. (2002). Dialogical wisdom, communicative practice, and organizational life. *Communication Theory, 12*(4), 375–397.

Berlo, D. K. (1960). *The process of communication: An introduction to theory and practice.* New York: Holt, Rinehart & Winston.

Berlo, D. K. (1971). Human communication: The basic proposition. In *Essay on Communication.* East Lansing, MI: Department of Communication.

Bryant, J., Miron, D. (2004) Theory and Research in Mass Communication, Journal of Communication, 54(4), 662–704.

Bryne, J. A. (2005, November 28). The man who invented management: Why Peter Drucker's ideas still matter. *BusinessWeek,* 97–106.

Carnegie, D. (1936). *How to win friends and influence people.* New York: Simon & Schuster.

Colvin, J. (2009, April 5). You've got voice mail, but do you care? *Houston Chronicle,* p. G6.

Conger, J. A. (1989). *The charismatic leader.* San Francisco: Jossey-Bass.

Conrad, D., Newberry, R. (2011). 24 Business Communication Skills: Attitudes of Human Resource Managers versus Business Educators, American Communication Journal, 13(1), 4–23.

Conrad, C., & Poole, M. S. (2005). *Strategic organizational communication in a global economy* (6th ed.). Belmont, CA: Wadsworth.

Daft, R. L., Lengel, R. H., & Trevino L. K. (1987). Message equivocality, media selection, and manager performance: Implications for information systems. *MIS Quarterly, 11*(2), 355–366.

Daft, R. L., & Weick, K. E. (1984). Toward a model of organizations as interpretation systems. *Academy of Management Review, 9*(2), 284–295.

Dilenschneider, R. L. (1992). A briefing for leaders: Communication as the ultimate exercise of power. New York, NY: HarperCollins.

Du-Babcock, B. (2006). Teaching business communication: Past, present, and future.
Journal of Business Communication, 43(3), 253–264.

Duiek, R. E., & Fielden, J. S. (1990). *Principles of business communication.* New York: Macmillan.

Eisenberg, E. M., Goodall, H. L., & Trethewey, A. (2007). *Organizational communication: Balancing creativity and constraint* (5th ed.). Boston: Bedford/St. Martin's.

Fairhurst, G. (2001). Dualisms in leadership research. In F. M. Jablin & L. L. Putnam (Eds.), *The new handbook of organizational communication* (p. 379–439). Newbury Park, CA: Sage.

Fairhurst, G. (2007). *Discursive leadership.* Thousand Oaks, CA: Sage.

Feldman, M. S., & March J. G. (1981). Information in organizations as signal and symbol. *Administrative Science Quarterly, 26*(1), 171–186.

Gottschalk, Jr., E. C. (1983). Firms are cool to meetings by television. *The Wall Street Journal*, p. 1.

Hanna, M. & Wilson, G. (1998). Communicating in business and professional settings. New York, NY: The McGraw-Hill Companies.

Hargie, O. (2002). Communication audits and the effects of increased information: A follow-up study, The Journal of Business Communication 39, 414

Hollander, E. P., & Offerman, L. R. (1990). Power and leadership in organization. *American Psychologist, 45*(2), 179–189.

Hynes, G. (2005). Managerial communications: Strategies and Applications. New York, NY: McGraw-Hill/Irwin.

Jablin, F. M., & Putnam, L. L. (Eds.). (2001). *The new handbook of organizational communication.* Newbury Park, CA: Sage.

Jones, E, Watson, B., Gardner, J., Gallois, C. (2006). Organizational Communication: Challenges for the New Century, Journal of Communication, 54(4), 722–750.

Katzenbach, J. R., & Smith, D. K. (2003). *The wisdom of teams: Creating the high-performance organization.* New York: Collins Business Essentials.

Kouzes, J. M., & Posner, B. Z. (2007). *The leadership challenge.* San Francisco: Jossey-Bass.

LaFasto, M. J. F., & Larson, C. (2001). *When teams work best: 6,000 team members and leaders tell what it takes to succeed.* Thousand Oaks, CA: Sage.

Maes, J. D., Weldy, T. G., & Icenogle, M. L. (1997). A managerial perspective: Oral communication competency is most important for business students in the workplace. The Journal of Business Communication, 34(1), 67–80.

Miller, K. (2005). *Organizational communication: Approaches and processes* (4th ed.). Belmont, CA: Wadsworth.

Mintzberg, H. (2004). Managers not MBAs: A hard look at the soft practice of managing and management development. San Francisco, CA: Berrett-Koehler Publishers.

Monge, P., & Fulk, J. (1999). Communication technologies for global network organizations. In G. DeSanctis & J. Fulk (Eds.), *Communication technologies and organizational forms* (pp. 71–100). Thousand Oaks, CA: Sage.

Murranka, P. A. & Lynch, D. (1999). Developing a competency-based fundamentals of management communication course, Business Communication Quarterly, 62(3), 9–23.

National Association of Colleges and Employers (NACE). (2011a). Job outlook: College hiring to increase 9.6 percent. Retrieved from http://www.naceweb.org/s04152015/job-outlook-spring-update-hiring-plans.aspx?mainindex-recslide1-spot-jospr-04242015

National Association of Colleges and Employers (NACE). (2011b). NACE poll: College students' communication skills. Retrieved November 28, 2011, from http://www.naceweb.org

National Association of Colleges and Employers (NACE). (2015). Job Outlook 2015 Report. Retrieved December 10, 2015, from http://www.naceweb.org/s01212015/job-outlook-majors-in-demand.aspx

Rice, R. E. (1984). Evaluating new media systems. In J. Johnson (Ed.), *Evaluating the new information technologies: New directions for Program Evaluation* (pp. 53–71). San Francisco: Jossey-Bass.

Rusk, T. (1993). The Power of Ethical Persuasion. New York, NY: Penguin Books.

Sapp, D., Zhang, Q. (2009). Trends in industry supervisors' feedback on business communication internships. Business Communication Quarterly, 72(3), 274-288.

Roethlisberger, F. L., & Dickson, W. (1939). *Management and the workers.* New York: Wiley & Sons.

Smeltzer, L. R., & Thomas, G. F. (1994). Managers as writers: Research in context. *Journal of Business and Technical Communications, 8*(2), 186.

Smith R. C., & Turner, P. K. (1995). A social constructionist reconfiguration of metaphor analysis. *Communication Monographs, 62*(2), 152–180.

Stewart, T. A. (1989, November 6). New ways to exercise power. *Fortune*, pp. 52–64.

Towers Watson Inc. (2013-2014). Change and communication ROI: The 10th anniversary report. Retrieved from www.towerswatson.com

Ulinski, M., O'Callaghan, S. (2002). A comparison of MBA students' and employers' perceptions of the value of oral communication skills for employment, Journal of Educaiton for Business, 7794), 193–197.

Weick, K. (1979). *The social psychology of organizing* (2nd Ed.). Reading, MA: Addison-Wesley.

Waner, K.(1995).Business communication competencies needed by employees as perceived by business faculty and business professionals, Business Communication Quarterly, 58(4), 51–56.

Wise, K. (2005). The importance of writing skills, Public Relations Quarterly,50(3), 37–38.

Young, M. & Murphy, W. (2003). Integrating communications skills into the marketing curriculum: A case study, Journal of Marketing Education, 25(1), 57–70.

DECISION MAKING

CHAPTER LEARNING OBJECTIVES

After reading this chapter, you should have a good understanding of

- the difference between non-programmed and programmed decisions and why non-programmed decision making is a complex, uncertain process;
- the differences between the main models of decision making and the main sources of error in decision making;
- the advantages and disadvantages of group decision making;
- the importance of ethical decision making in the practice of management;
- how to identify different ethical perspectives and ethical decision-making models;
- the importance of understanding the four different styles of decision making;
- the advantages and disadvantages of different decision-making methods; and
- the four categories of consideration for evaluating alternatives.

"High office teaches decision-making, not substance. It consumes intellectual capital; it does not create it. Most high officials leave office with the perceptions and insights with which they entered; they learn how to make decisions but not what decisions to make."

- HENRY A. KISSINGER

DECISION MAKING

Effective decision making is an important skill for all employees, and is particularly important for supervisors, managers, and leaders. **Decision making** is defined as the process of choosing a solution from available alternatives. Simply put, it is the thought process of selecting a choice from several alternative options.

The first part of this chapter will examine the importance of decisions and the various approaches to decision making. It is important to understand the various decision-making styles so that you will be able to recognize your own style and utilize different approaches. Through an understanding of the advantages and disadvantages of the different styles, you will be able to utilize different styles according to the situation. Additionally, throughout your career, you will work with people with different decision-making styles. You will also learn about programmed and non-programmed decisions and the different non-programmed decision-making methods.

The second part of this chapter will examine ethical decision making and introduce the basic models for ethical decision making. Successful decision making requires the consideration and evaluation of alternatives. You will learn the four key considerations when evaluating alternatives. At best, missing a consideration could result in a less-than-optimal decision. At worst, missing a consideration could result in serious implications and harm the organization.

Lastly, this chapter will introduce the importance of utilizing ethics training to prepare employees for facing ethical dilemmas. Ethics training provides employees with a framework for decision making and an understanding of the company's expectations from them.

TYPES OF DECISIONS

All organizations face decisions daily. In the workplace, you will be faced with two types of decisions—programmed and non-programmed. **Programmed decisions** are routine, almost automatic. Programmed decisions generally involve situations that have occurred before, so policies and processes already exist for how to handle them. Responding is simply a matter of following the guidelines on how to handle the situation. On the other hand, **non-programmed decisions** occur in unusual situations that have not been addressed often. Policies or guidelines do not exist yet and so these types of decisions are made on a managers' intuition or best judgment.

NON-PROGRAMMED DECISIONS

When members of an organization must choose how to respond to a new or novel opportunity or problem they engage in non-programmed decisions. Hence, non-programmed decisions are unique decisions that require a custom-made solution, such as when a manager is confronted with an ill-structured or novel problem and there is no cut and dry solution.

For example, the creation of a marketing strategy for the new Apple watch represents a non-programmed decision. Non-programmed decisions involve searching for the extra information needed to make the right choice. Because the problem or opportunity has not been experienced before, members of the organization are uncertain about how they should respond, and thus they search for any information they can find to help them make their decision.

PROGRAMMED DECISIONS

Members of an organization make non-programmed decisions to respond to new opportunities or problems, and they also need to engage in programmed decisions to respond to issues or problems that are routine or recurring. Hence, programmed decisions are made in routine, repetitive, well-structured situations with predetermined decision rules. These may be based on habit or established policies, rules, and procedures, and stem from prior experience or technical knowledge about what works or does not work in a given situation.

For example, organizations often have standardized routines for handling customer complaints or employee discipline. Decisions are programmed to the extent that they are repetitive and routine, and that a definite approach has been worked out for handling them. Because the problem is well defined or recurring, the manager does not have to go to the trouble and expense of working through an involved decision-making process.

To make a programmed decision, organizational members use a **decision rule**, a standard sequence or automated responses that they follow routinely whenever they encounter a specific type of problem or opportunity. For

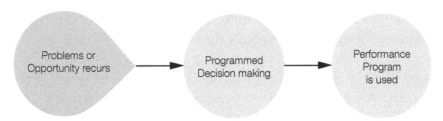

Figure 8.1. Programmed Decision Making

example, Nordstrom's developed a decision rule that specifies how salespeople should respond to customers who return items that have been worn or that are simply defective. Best Buy has developed a decision rule that indicates how sales clerks should respond when a sale item is out of stock.

Organizations develop decision rules or decision guidelines whenever the identical or similar kinds of opportunities or problems keep occurring. Once a decision rule is developed, members of the organization utilize the program almost automatically when the specific problem is encountered. They do not have to search for information or think about what they should do in response. Decision rules often evolve from non-programmed decisions over time (Figure 8.1). When a novel problem or opportunity starts to recur over time, it becomes something that requires a programmed decision and the organization comes up with a standard response or rule.

DECISION-MAKING STYLES

Individuals differ along two dimensions in the way they approach decision making. The first is based on an individual's way of thinking. Some individuals tend to be rational and orderly in how they process information. These individuals tend to be linear, while other individuals tend to be holistic, viewing decisions from an aerial perspective. These individuals are often intuitive and may not process information in a linear order.

The second dimension is based on an individual's tolerance for ambiguity. Some individuals tend to have a low tolerance for ambiguity. These individuals crave consistency and order. Consequently, they prefer to structure information to eliminate or minimize ambiguity. Other individuals are able to tolerate high levels of ambiguity. Consequently, they often have the ability to process several thoughts at the same time. These two dimensions are the basis of the four decision-making styles: directive, analytic, conceptual, and behavioral.

Directive.   Individuals with a directive style are efficient, rational, and logical. They tend to have a low tolerance for ambiguity. They often view issues and decisions in the short term and make quick decisions. The disadvantage of the directive style can be decisions made with minimal information and minimal consideration of available alternatives.

Analytic.   The opposite of the directive style, individuals with an analytical style of decision making have a high tolerance for ambiguity. Careful decision makers, individuals with the analytic decision-making style prefer to be well informed, as they want to carefully evaluate options. They tend to easily adapt to new situations and cope well with unique challenges.

Conceptual.   Individuals with a conceptual style of decision making are usually broad in their approach and prefer to consider all options and alternatives. They tend to think long term and be goal oriented. Quite often, they are able to understand how different parts and structures work together. They tend to be able to visualize long-term consequences and formulate innovative solutions.

Behavioral.   Individuals with a behavioral decision-making style work well with others and tend to be more open to ideas and suggestions. These individuals are generally concerned about the recognition of team members along with the achievements of their team, and generally try to avoid conflict. Because these individuals tend to place a high importance on their acceptance by others and being in the in-group, the disadvantage of this style can be a less-than-optimal decision due to political or social concerns.

RATIONAL DECISION MAKING

Rational decision making is a systematic process in which managers define problems, evaluate alternatives, and choose the optimal solution that provides the maximum benefits to their organization. In addition, your solution has to be optimal because your company will be investing a tremendous amount of time, money, and resources to support your decision.

The six steps for the rational decision-making process are as follows.

1. Define the problem.   It is impossible to make a rational decision unless you can clearly define the problem or context in which the decision needs to be made. A **problem** exists when there is a gap between a desired state (what is wanted) and an existing state (the situation you currently face). Why does a decision need to be made? What will be the outcome if no decision is made? What outcome is desired? What is preventing that outcome from being realized?

2. Identify decision criteria.   This step is critical because this is the process of selecting what needs to be done. Once a decision maker has defined the problem, he or she needs to identify the decision criteria that will be important in solving the problem. Typically, the more criteria a potential solution meets, the better that solution will be. In this step, the decision maker determines what is relevant in making the decision. This step adds the decision maker's interests, values, and similar personal preferences into the process. Identifying the criteria that are important is critical because what one person thinks is relevant another person may not. Also, keep in mind that any factors not identified in this step are considered irrelevant to the decision maker.

3. Weigh the criteria. The third step requires the decision maker to weigh the previously identified criteria in order to give them their correct priority in the decision. Although there are numerous mathematical models for weighing decision criteria, all require the decision maker to provide an initial ranking of the criteria.

One method used to weigh the criteria is called **absolute comparisons**, in which each criterion is compared with a standard or ranked on its own merits. Decision makers will rank these criteria differently depending on what they value or require from each alternative. An example of absolute comparison is illustrated in Figure 8.2.

Another method used by decision makers is **relative comparisons**, in which each of the listed criteria is compared directly with every other criterion. Figure 8.3 shows

Absolute Weighting of Decision Criteria for a Car Purchase

Circled numbers indicate how important the particular criterion is to a car buyer. Your ranking may be different.

	CU	NVI	SI	I	CI
1. Owner Satisfaction	1	2	3	4	(5)
2. Reliability	1	2	3	(4)	5
3. Depreciation	1	2	(3)	4	5
4. Avoiding Accidents	1	2	(3)	4	5
5. Fuel Economy	1	(2)	3	4	5
6. Crash Protection	1	2	3	(4)	5
7. Acceleration	1	2	3	4	(5)
8. Ride	1	(2)	3	4	5
9. Entertainment	1	2	3	4	(5)

CU – completely unimportant, NVI – not very important,
SI – somewhat important, I – important, CI – critically important

Figure 8.2. Absolute Comparison of Decision Criteria

Kipley, D., Jewe, R., & Helm-Stevens, R., A Foundation in the Principles of Management, pp. 77. Copyright © 2015 by Cognella, Inc. Reprinted with permission.

five criteria that someone might use when buying a house. In the first column, we see that the time of the daily commute has been rated less important (-1) than the school system quality; more important (+1) than having a pool or a quiet street; and just as important as the house being brand new (0). Total weight is determined by summing the scores in each of the columns. Now we can see that the daily commute and school system quality are the most important factors to this home buyer, while a pool and a quiet street are the least important.

Relative Comparison of Home Characteristics

Home Characteristics	DC	SSQ	P	QS	NBH
Daily Commute (DC)		+1	−1	−1	0
School System Quality (SSQ)	−1		−1	−1	−1
Pool (P)	+1	+1		0	+1
Quiet Street (QS)	+1	+1	0		0
Newly Built House (NBH)	0	+1	−1	0	
Total Weight	+1	+4	−3	−2	0

Figure 8.3. Relative Comparison of Decision Criteria

Kipley, D., Jewe, R., & Helm-Stevens, R., A Foundation in the Principles of Management, pp. 78. Copyright © 2015 by Cognella, Inc. Reprinted with permission.

4. Generate alternative courses of action.   The key to this step is to not focus on the obvious alternatives or do what has worked in the past. High-quality decisions come from being open to multiple alternatives. It is often helpful to involve consultants or experts in the area in which the decision needs to be made. Once the alternatives have been generated, the decision maker must critically analyze and evaluate each one.

5. Evaluate each alternative.   As you evaluate each alternative, you should be looking at the likely positive and negative consequences associated with each. It is unusual to find one alternative that would completely resolve the problem and is without a doubt better than all others. As you consider positive and negative consequences, you must be careful to differentiate between what you know for a fact and what you believe might be the case. The decision maker needs to determine not just what results each alternative could yield, but how probable it is that those results will be realized. The more fact-based the evaluation, the more confident the decision maker can be that the expected outcome will occur.

6. Compute the optimal decision.   The final step in this model requires computing the optimal decision. Evaluating each alternative using the weighted criteria and selecting the alternative with the total higher score determines the optimal decision.

ASSUMPTIONS OF THE MODEL.
The success of the rational decision-making process just described contains a number of assumptions:

- **Problem clarity**: The problem is clear and unambiguous. The decision maker is assumed to have complete information regarding the decision situation.
- **Known options**: It is assumed the decision maker can identify all the relevant criteria and can list all the viable alternatives. Furthermore, the decision maker is aware of all the possible consequences of each alternative.
- **Clear preference**: Rationality assumes that the criteria and alternatives can be raked and weighted to reflect their importance.
- **Constant preferences**: It's assumed that the specific decision criteria are constant and that the weights assigned to them are stable over time.

- **No time or cost constraints:** The rational decision maker can obtain full information about criteria and alternatives because it's assumed that there are no time or cost constraints.
- **Maximum payoff:** The rational decision maker will choose the alternative that yields the highest perceived value.

Testing the model.   Every decision is intended to fix a problem. The final test of any decision is whether or not the problem was fixed. Did it go away? Did it change noticeably? Is it better now, or worse, or the same? What new problems did the solution create? If the problem remains or has worsened, the steps of the decision-making process need to be repeated until an acceptable resolution has been found.

LIMITS TO RATIONAL DECISION MAKING

In general, following the six steps in the rational decision-making model will generate better decisions that when not using the model. It is advised that, whenever possible, managers should follow the steps, especially for important decisions with long-range consequences.

However, given the fact that businesses and managers do not exist in a perfect world with no real-world constraints, it is highly doubtful that the rational decision-making method can always generate the optimal solution to provide maximum benefits to their organizations, for the following six reasons:

1. Decision makers do not have complete knowledge of all the facts surrounding the problem and cannot foresee future events with complete accuracy. Therefore, it is not always possible to choose the optimum solution.
2. The search for a decision is often stopped as soon as the minimum acceptable level of rationality is reached. Most decisions involve too many complex variables, all of which cannot be examined fully by a decision maker.
3. A decision-making situation may involve multiple goals, all of which cannot be maximized simultaneously.
4. The environment of decision making is often uncertain. The making and implementation of decisions are influenced by several uncontrollable factors and the consequences of various alternatives cannot be anticipated accurately.
5. A decision in one area may have an adverse effect on another area of operations. For example, a decision to produce high-quality goods may result in an increased production costs and it may not be possible to sell the product with a sufficient profit margin.
6. Human factors are the main limits on rational decision making. Personal value systems, perceptions, and economic and social factors are the main human limits on rationality.

The rational decision-making method model describes the way decisions *should* be made. In other words, decision makers wanting to make optimal decisions should *not* have to face time and cost constraints. Certainly, very few managers actually make rational decisions the way they should. The way that managers actually make decisions is more accurately described as bounded (or limited) rationality. **Bounded rationality** states that the rationality of individuals is limited by the information they have, the cognitive limitations of their minds, and the finite amount of time they have to make decisions. In theory, fully rational decision makers maximize decisions by choosing the optimal solutions. However, as pointed out previously, because of limited resources, including attention, memory, and expertise, managers don't maximize—they **satisfice**, choosing the alternative that is simply "good enough."

It is often argued that the primary job of management is making sound decisions. Yet, several authors claim that over half of the decisions made in the workplace fail. Thus, over the years, several frameworks have been developed to help managers and employees when faced with non-programmed decisions or decisions that are partially non-programmed. These frameworks are all designed for quick resolution of problems in the workplace. Many of these frameworks are simple to use and easy to remember—a key component in quick, successful decision making (Table 8.1).

Table 8.1. Individual Decision-Making Frameworks

Model	Description
Blanchard and Peale Model	This model presents three questions that managers should ponder when resolving ethical dilemmas: 1) Is it legal? 2) Is it balanced? and 3) How does it make me feel? If the answer to the first question, "Is it legal?" is no, you should stop there and refrain from illegal action. "Is it balanced?" requires a manager to step back and view a problem from another perspective, such as those of other parties involved. "How does it make me feel?" asks a manager to conduct a self-evaluation of his or her comfort level with a decision. Even though they may be legal and may appear balanced, some decisions can make a manager uncomfortable, sending a cautionary signal.
Wall Street Journal Model	The *Wall Street Journal* model consists of three components: 1) Am I in compliance with the law? 2) What contribution does this choice of action make to the company, the shareholders, the community, and others? and 3) What are the short- and long-term consequences of this decision? Any proposed conduct must first be in compliance with the law. The next step requires an evaluation of a decision's contributions to the shareholders and stakeholders. Lastly, managers are asked to envision the consequences of a decision. A decision that seems costly in the short term may actually provide a long-term benefit for the company.
Warren Buffett Front-Page-of-the-Newspaper Test	This simple ethical test requires that a decision maker envision how a reporter would describe a decision or action on the front page of newspaper. During the aftermath of the bond market scandal at Salomon Brothers, the interim chairman, Warren Buffett, told employees, "Contemplating any business act, an employee should ask himself whether he would be willing to see it immediately described by an informed and critical reporter on the front page of his local paper, there to be read by his spouse, children, and friends. At Salomon we simply want no part of any activities that pass legal tests but that we, as citizens, would find offensive."
Jennings National Enquirer Test	The purpose of this test is to have you step back from the business setting in which decisions are made and view the issue and choices from the perspective of an objective outsider. Named for its author, the test asks the individual to "make up the worst possible headline you can think of and then re-evaluate your decision." The aim of this model is to help managers envision how their actions and decisions look to the outside world.
Peter Drucker Model	*Primum non nocere* is Latin for "Above all, do no harm." Dr. Peter Drucker adapted this concept from the motto of the medical profession. This simple ethical test encourages us to make decisions that do not harm others. For example, this idea would keep us from producing a product that could cause injury or would compel us be deficient in the working conditions we provide for workers in other countries.

ETHICAL DECISION MAKING

Is everything that is legal, ethical? It would be tempting to think so. However, if we consider some of the laws of the past, we can easily see that they were not ethical. Consider the Virginia Slave Codes of 1705 that permitted slavery, laws of the past that prohibited women from voting, and laws allowing child labor, for example. Thus, defining what is ethical does not necessarily depend on its legal position.

Ethics is defined as the code of moral principles that sets standards of good or bad, right or wrong, in our conduct. **Personal ethics** are guides for our behavior, helping us make moral choices among alternative courses of action. **Ethical behavior** is the term often used to describe what we accept as right or wrong, or good or bad.

Business ethics is a form of applied ethics or professional ethics that examines ethical principles and moral or ethical problems that arise in a business environment. It applies to all aspects of business conduct and is relevant to the conduct of individuals and entire organizations. Business ethics is often guided by law, while other types of ethical frameworks provide a basic framework that businesses may choose to follow in order to gain public acceptance.

Ethical decision making is making a decision that is both legally and morally acceptable to the larger community, utilizing all ethical perspectives and models to inform and influence the decision, to produce the best possible outcomes for all stakeholders.

ETHICAL BEHAVIOR AND VALUES

Not everything that is legal is ethical, and many ethical problems arise at work when people are asked to do something that violates their personal beliefs, even though the act is legal. So how do we go about making the decision when it extends beyond legality and moves into your individual beliefs and judgments of what is right and wrong, your personal **values**?

Values are the underlying beliefs and judgments regarding what is right or desirable and that influence individual attitudes and behaviors. Psychologist Milton Rokeach delineates two types of values: terminal and instrumental.

Terminal values are the goals that we work towards and view as most desirable. These values are desirable states of existence and are the goals that we would like to achieve during our lifetime, such as family, security, true friendship, a comfortable life, self-respect, a sense of accomplishment, and happiness, to name a few.

Instrumental values concern the means for accomplishing these ends. Instrumental values are core values and as such are permanent in nature, comprising personal characteristics and character traits. Instrumental values refer to preferable modes of behavior and include values like honesty, sincerity, ambition, independence, obedience, imaginativeness, courageousness, competitiveness, and also some negative traits, too. Organizations also have instrumental values (which can be ascertained from the organizational culture); these are permanent in nature and difficult to change.

Southwest Airlines is one example of an organization with clearly defined instrumental values that significantly contribute to its overwhelming success. Some of Southwest's instrumental values are low cost, hard work, family, fun, individuality, ownership, and profitability. The low-cost concept enables people who generally cannot afford an airline flight the opportunity to fly short flights in a short amount of time. Southwest employees do a great job servicing their customers by working very hard. The employees understand the importance of working hard and fast to ensure every flight meets their scheduled flight time. They are not just working hard to meet the mission; they work hard because they are part owners of the company.

ETHICAL PERSPECTIVES

Ethical perspectives provide a philosophical basis for evaluating behavior and decision making. A variety of influences inform our decision making, many of which are rooted in classical thought concerning morality and what constitutes right and good in a world of competing interests. The following section examines four of the major ethical philosophical views: utilitarian, individualism, justice, and moral rights. See Figure 8.4.

Nineteenth-century philosopher John Stuart Mill argued that the resolution of ethical dilemmas requires a balancing effort in which we minimize the harms that result from a decision, while maximizing the benefits. Accordingly, the **utilitarian view** considers that ethical decisions should be resolved by delivering the greatest good to the greatest number of people, as long as the majority of those involved are helped and a minimum number are harmed. For example, a manager decides to cut the workforce by 30% in order to keep the company profitable and save the remaining jobs, rather than lose them all to a business failure. Utilitarianism challenges us to look at the impact of proposed solutions to ethical dilemmas from the viewpoint of all stakeholders and attempt to provide the greatest amount of good for the greatest number of people.

The **individualism view** of ethical behavior would focus on the long-term advancement of self-interests. The cornerstone of this view is that people become self-regulating over time as they strive for individual advantage; ethics are maintained in the process. For example, suppose that you might think about cheating on your next exam. However, you realize that this short-term gain might lead to a long-term loss if you get caught and fail the course. For this reasoning, you reject the idea.

The **justice view** of moral reasoning considers the behavior ethical when people are treated impartially and fairly according to legal rules and standards. This view judges the ethical aspects of any decision on the basis of how equitable it is for everyone affected, arguing that we should always choose the fairest and most just or equitable resolution of any ethical dilemma. Recently, researchers have identified three aspects of justice in the workplace: procedural justice, distributive justice, and interactional justice.

Procedural justice refers to the idea of fairness and transparency in the processes that resolve disputes and allocate resources. It reflects the extent to which an individual perceives that outcome decisions have been fairly made. The use of fair procedures helps to communicate to the employees that they are valued members of the organization. Procedural justice focuses on the formal procedures used to make decisions and then communicating to the employees that the process involves fair procedures.

Distributive justice involves the perceived fairness of the allocation of outcome without respect to individual characteristics, such as ethnicity, race, age, or gender. For example, when workers of the same job are paid different salaries, group members may feel that distributive justice has not occurred. To determine whether distributive justice has occurred, individuals often seek the distributive norm of their group. A **distributive norm** is the standard of behavior that is required, desired, or designated as normal within a particular group (length of employment with the company). If rewards and costs are allocated according to the designated distributive norms of the group, distributive justice has occurred.

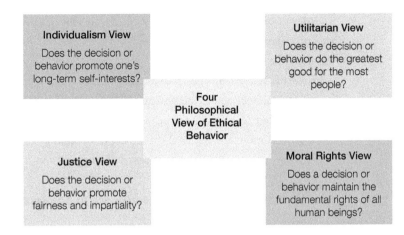

Figure 8.4. The Four Views of Ethical Behavior

Interactional justice focuses on the treatment of others with dignity and respect received when procedures are implemented. For example, does a bank loan officer take the time to fully explain to an applicant why he or she was denied a loan?

The **moral rights view**, based on the teachings of John Locke and Thomas Jefferson, considers the rights of people to life, liberty, and fair treatment. The moral rights approach asserts that human beings have fundamental rights and liberties that cannot be taken away by an individual's decision. Thus, an ethically direct decision is one that best maintains the rights of those people affected by it.

Six moral rights should be considered during decision making:

1. *The right of free consent*: Individuals are to be treated only as they knowingly and freely consent to be treated.
2. *The right to privacy*: Individuals can choose to do as they please away from work and have control of information about their private life.
3. *The right of freedom of conscience*: Individuals may refrain from carrying out any order that violates their moral and religious norms.
4. *The right of free speech*: Individuals may criticize the truthful ethics or legality of the actions of others.
5. *The right to due process*: Individuals have a right to an impartial hearing and fair treatment.
6. *The right to life and safety*: Individuals have a right to live without endangerment or violation of their health and safety

To make ethical decisions, managers need to avoid interfering with the fundamental rights of others. For example, a decision to eavesdrop on employees violates the right to privacy. Sexual harassment is also unethical because it violates the right to freedom of consent. The right of free speech would support whistle-blowers who call attention to illegal or inappropriate actions within a company.

ETHICAL INTENSITY OF A DECISION

Managers don't treat all ethical decisions the same. A manager whose decision is to lay off 10 employees is going to treat that decision differently than if an employee was caught taking paper home for personal use. **Ethical intensity** is the degree of moral importance given to an issue. It is influenced by six factors:

1. The first factor is **magnitude of consequences**—the harm or benefits accruing to individuals affected by a decision or behavior. An action that causes 1,000 people to suffer a particular injury has greater consequences than an action that causes 20 people to suffer the same injury.
2. The second factor is **probability of effect**—the likelihood that if a decision is implemented it will lead to the harm or benefit predicted. The production of an automobile that would be dangerous to occupants during normal driving has greater probability of harm than the production of a NASCAR racecar that endangers the driver when curves are taken at high speed.
3. The third factor, **social consensus**, is the amount of public agreement that a proposed decision is bad or good. For example, actively discriminating against minority job candidates is worse than not actively seeking out minority job candidates.
4. The fourth factor is **temporal immediacy**—the length of time that elapses between making a decision and when the consequences of that decision are known. A shorter length of time implies greater immediacy. An example of this is if Pfizer releases a drug that causes 1% of the people who take it to have acute nervous

reactions within one week. This has greater temporal immediacy than releasing a drug that will cause 1% of those who take it to develop nervous disorders after 25 years of use.

5. The fifth factor, **proximity of effect**, is the sense of closeness (social, cultural, psychological, or physical) that the decision maker has for victims or beneficiaries of the decision. For example, recently, Citigroup cut approximately 53,000 jobs. This reduced its labor force to 300,000 employees, with even more layoffs anticipated. This action had a greater impact on the remaining employees than the personal impact the news reporters feel when announcing this layoff.

6. The sixth factor is **concentration of effect**—the inverse function of the number of people affected by a decision. A change in an insurance policy denying coverage to 40 people with claims of $50,000 each has a more concentrated effect than a change denying coverage to 4,000 people with claims of $500 each.

ETHICAL DECISION-MAKING MODELS

Ethical decision-making models combine both ethical perspectives and ethical models to provide a systematic process to produce ethical decisions. Ethical decision-making models provide managers and employees with a method to evaluate situations through ethical reflection or clarifying questions, in order to identify the issues and the potential outcomes of an action or behavior (Box 8.1). In addition to understanding the framework for basic models of ethical decision making, two particular approaches are noteworthy.

BOX 8.1: A BASIC MODEL OF ETHICAL DECISION MAKING[1]

7. **Identify the problem** – What makes an ethical problem? Think in terms of rights, obligations, fairness, relationships. and integrity. How would you define the problem if you stood on other side of the fence?

8. **Identify the constituents** – Who has been hurt? Who could be hurt? Who could be helped? Are they willing players, or are they victims? Can you negotiate with them?

9. **Diagnose the situation** – How did it happen in the first place? What could have prevented it? Is it going to get worse or better? Can the damage now be undone?

10. **Analyze your options** – Imagine the range of possibilities. Limit yourself to the two or three most manageable. What are the likely outcomes of each? What are the likely costs? Look to the company mission statement or code of ethics for guidance.

11. **Make your choice** – What is your intention in making this decision? How does it compare with the probable results? Can you discuss the problem with the affected parties before you act? Could you disclose without qualm your decision to your boss, the CEO, the board of directors, your family, or society as it whole?

12. **Act** – Do what you have to do. Don't be afraid to admit errors. Be as bold in confronting a problem as you were in causing it.

---

1   Kipley, D., Jewe, R., & Helm-Stevens, R., A Foundation in the Principles of Management, pp. 52. Copyright © 2015 by Cognella, Inc. Reprinted with permission.

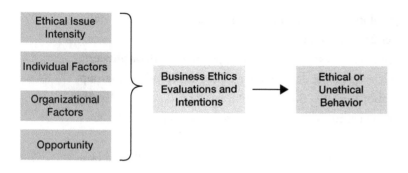

Figure 8.5. Ferrell Ethical Decision-Making Framework

The Ferrell ethical decision making framework considers four factors when evaluating ethical dilemmas: ethical issue intensity, individual factors, organizational factors, and opportunity (Figure 8.5).

Ethical issue intensity is the perceived relevance or importance of an ethical issue to the individual, work group, or organization. This reflects the ethical sensitivity of the individual or work group and triggers the ethical decision-making process. Individuals can be subject to six spheres of influence: 1) the workplace, 2) the legal system, 3) family, 4) community, 5) religion, and 6) profession. Outcomes will be affected by the degree of **moral intensity** involved, which is the person's perception of social pressure and the harm his or her decision will inflict on others.

Individual factors refers to the notion that people base their ethical decisions on their own values and principles of right or wrong. Values are learned through socialization. Good personal values decrease unethical behavior and increase positive work behavior, but values are subjective and may vary across cultures. While an organization may intend to do right, organizational or social forces can alter this intent. Gender, education, work experience, nationality, and age can affect ethical decision making.

Organizational factors refers to the consideration that organizational culture can have a stronger influence on employees than an individual's values. A corporate culture is a set of values, norms, and artifacts that the members of an organization share, while an ethical culture reflects whether the firm has an ethical conscience, and is a function of many factors. Significant others within the organization are those who have influence in a work group. An organizational culture where obedience to authority is valued can explain why many employees unquestioningly follow superior's orders.

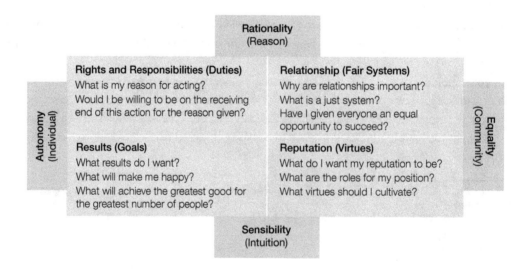

Figure 8.6. The Baird Decision-Making Framework

Opportunity is defined as the conditions within an organization that limit or permit ethical or unethical behavior. Opportunities for misconduct can be reduced by establishing formal codes, policies, and rules. However, aggressive enforcement is often required to limit opportunities for unethical behavior. Also, knowledge can sometimes lead to unethical behavior. A person who has an information base, expertise, or information about competition has an opportunity to exploit knowledge.

THE BAIRD DECISION-MAKING FRAMEWORK

The Baird decision-making framework examines ethical situations through four lenses: the rights lens, the relationship lens, the results lens, and the reputation lens. This framework assumes that leaders are predisposed to a particular lens or set of lenses, and will seek to evaluate ethical dilemmas from the values represented by each lens (Figure 8.6).

Rights lens: An action is ethical if I fulfill my duties and do the right thing as I claim my individual rights. Values that take priority in this lens are life/safety, truthfulness, privacy, freedom of conscience, free speech, financial transparency, and the right to contract.

Relationship lens: An action is ethical if it supports a framework for continuous systemic ethical improvement for both the organization and the institutions supporting it. Values that take priority in this lens are fair treatment, fair administration of rules, fair compensation, fair blame, and due process.

Results lens: An action is ethical if good ends and good results come from the action. Values that take priority in this lens are maximizing satisfaction, efficiency, loyalty, and avoidance of conflicts of interest.

Reputation lens: An action is ethical if it is consistent with the habitual development of sound character traits, including thoughtful reflection, good intentions, and noble human virtues. Values that take priority in this lens are integrity, justice, courage, and civility.

EVALUATING ALTERNATIVES

Four key considerations must be taken into account when evaluating alternatives: legality, ethicality, feasibility, and practicality. At best, missing a consideration could result in a less-than-optimal decision. At worst, missing a consideration could result in serious implications and harm to the organization.

- Legal: Managers must be sure that all alternatives are legal.
- Ethical: Managers must be sure that all alternatives are ethical and will not cause harm to employees, stakeholders, or shareholders.
- Feasible: Managers must be sure that all alternatives are sustainable.
- Practical: Managers must be sure that the organization has the capabilities and resources to carry the decision through.

TRAINING FOR ETHICAL DECISION MAKING

Preparing employees for facing ethical dilemmas is one of the main benefits of work **ethics training**. It provides employees with a framework for decision making and an understanding of the company's expectations of them.

The first objective in ethics training is guiding employees into making more ethical decisions. Even when not faced with a large ethical dilemma, employees make decisions requiring a solid foundation in ethics on a daily basis. For instance, the employee may regularly take home some office supplies without thinking of how it is costing the company. If an employee witnesses someone going against the company's ethical guidelines, he or she will know what to do and how to report the incident.

The second objective for ethics training is to achieve credibility with employees. Employees often complain that outside instructors and consultants are teaching theory that has nothing to do with their jobs and the practical dilemmas they are facing. Training reinforces and becomes more credible when top management teach the initial classes to their subordinates, who then in turn teach the classes to their subordinates.

The final objective of ethics training is to teach employees a practical model of ethical decision making. Providing employees with a basic model should help them think through how to make the different choices.

SUMMARY OF CHAPTER

1. We learned the difference between programmed and non-programmed decisions.
2. This chapter revealed that there are six steps in the rational decision-making process, in which managers define problems, evaluate alternatives, and compute optimal solutions.
3. We examined the Baird Decision Making Framework and the four lenses – rights and responsibilities, relationships, results, and reputation.
4. We explored the Ferrell Ethical Decision-Making Framework including ethical issue intensity, individual factors, organizational factors, and opportunity.
5. The rational decision-making process describes how decisions should be made in an ideal world, without limits. However, bounded rationality recognizes that, in the real world, managers' limited resources, incomplete and imperfect information, and limited decision-making capabilities restrict their decision-making process.
6. Making a decision that satisfies the necessary criteria is not always the decision that will be the most ethical, and decision makers should always take ethics into account when making decisions.
7. We learned about the important considerations in evaluating alternatives.
8. We explored how companies prepare employees for facing ethical dilemmas.

DISCUSSION QUESTIONS

1. What is the difference between non-programmed and programmed decisions?
2. What are the four different styles of decision making? What are the differences between them?
3. What are the advantages and disadvantages of group decision making?
4. Why is ethical decision making important in management? Identify the different ethical perspectives and ethical decision-making models.

HOW DELIBERATE AM I WHEN MAKING DECISIONS?

INSTRUCTIONS

Read the following statements and indicate which you use when making decisions, using the following scale:
1: Rarely | 2: Not Often | 3: Sometimes | 4: Often | 5: Almost Always

1. I act without thinking.
2. I often question why I do things.
3. I think through all my options before deciding.
4. I am careful with my words.
5. I go with my gut when making decisions.
6. I am quick to make a decision.
7. I identify the best course of action among several alternative possibilities.

SCORING KEY:

To score, add responses for questions 3, 4, and 7. Then reverse score questions 1, 2, 5, and 6 so that 1 = 5, 2 = 4, 3 = 3, 4 = 2, and 5 = 1. Finally, add up your total for all six items. Scores will be between 7 and 35.

ANALYSIS:

This scale assesses how deliberate you are when making decisions. If you scored at or above 28, you tend to be quite deliberate. If you scored at or below 14, you tend to be rash. Scores between 14 and 27 reveal a more blended style of decision-making.

Decision making is the process of choosing between two or more courses of action. When decision making occurs during the course of problem solving, it generally involves choosing between different possible alternatives. Decisions can be made through either an intuitive or reasoned process, or a combination of the two.

There are times when an intuitive decision will suffice, while at other times a more deliberate process may be needed. Individuals differ in how they make decisions. Some people prefer to collect information, carefully weigh alternatives, and then select the best option, while others prefer to make a choice as quickly as possible.

Adapted from: L.R Goldburg, J.A. Johnson, H.W. Eber, R. Hogan, M.C. Ashton, C.R. Cloninger, and H.G. Gough, "The International Personality Item Pool and the Future of Public-Domain Personality Measures," Journal of Research in Personality, 2006, 40, 84-96.

CHAPTER 8 REFERENCES

Baird, C. A. (2012). *Everyday ethics: Making wise choices in a complex world* (2nd ed.). Denver, CO: Ethics Game Press.

Barry, Vincent, *Moral Issues in Business* (Belmont, Calif.: Wadsworth, 1979).

Beauchamp, Tom and Norman Bowie, *Ethical Theory and Business* (Englewood Cliffs, NJ: Prentice-Hall, 1979; 6th ed, 2001)

Baumhart, Raymond, "How Ethics Are Businessmen?," *Harvard Business Review*, 39 (4) (1961)).

Bowie, Norman E., "Business Ethics," in *New Directions in Ethics*, ed. Joseph P. DeMarco and Richard M. Fox, New York: Routledge & Kegan Paul, 1986.)

Cooper, R. K., and Sawaf, A. Executive EQ: Emotional Intelligence in Leader-ship and Organizations. N.Y.: Grosset/ Putnam, 1996.

De George, Richard Business Ethics (N.Y.: Macmillan, 1982; 5th ed., Prentice-Hall, 1999).

De George, Richard T., "The Status of Business Ethics: Past and Future," *Journal of Business Ethics*,6 (1987), pp. 201–211.

De George, Richard, *Competing with Integrity in Internal Business* (New York: Oxford University Press, 1993)

Donaldson, Thomas and Patricia Werhane, *Ethical Issues in Business: A Philosophical Approach* (Englewood Cliffs, NJ: Prentice-Hall, 1979; 7th ed., 2002)

Donaldson, Thomas, *The Ethics of Business Ethics* (New York: Oxford University Press, 1989).

Ferrell, O. C., Fraedrich, J., & Ferrell, L. (2013). *Business ethics: Ethical decision making and cases* (9th ed.). Mason, OH: South Western Cengage Learning.

Ireland, R. D., & Miller, C. C. (2004). Decision making and firm success. *Academy of Management Executive*, *18*(4), 8–12.

Jennings, M. M. (2012). Business ethics (7th ed.). Mason, OH: South Western Cengage Learning.

Moberg, D. (1999). When Good People Do Bad Things at Work, Ethics, 10(2), 19–29.

Nash, L. (1993). *Good intentions aside: A manager's guide to resolving ethical problems*. Boston: Harvard Business School Press.

Nutt, P. C. (1999). Surprising but true: Half the decisions in organizations fail. *Academy of Management Executive*, *13*(4), 75–90.

Nutt, P. C. (2002). *Why decisions fail*. San Francisco: Berrett-Koehler.

Opotow, S. "Moral Exclusion and Injustice: An Introduction." Journal of Social Issues 46 (1990): 120.

Rawls, John, *A Theory of Justice* (Cambridge, Mass., Belknap Press of Harvard University Press, 1971).

Smith, Adam, *An Inquiry into the Nature and Causes of the Wealth of Nations; The Theory of Moral Sentiments*.

Stackhouse, Max L., Dennis P. McCann and Shirley J. Roels, with Preston N. Williams, eds, *On Moral Business: Classical and Contemporary Resources for Ethics in Economic Life* (Grand Rapids, Mich.: William B. Eerdmans Publichsing Company, 1995).

Solomon, R. (1999). *A better way to think about business.* New York: Oxford University Press.

Tawney, R. H. *Religion and the Rise of Capitalism* (New York: Harcourt, Brace and Co., 1926).

Velasquez, Manuel G, *Business Ethics: Concepts and Cases* (Englewood Cliffs, NJ: Prentice-Hall, 1982; 5th ed., 2002)

Walton, Clarence, *Corporate Social Responsibilities* (Belmont, Calif., Wadsworth Pub. Co.,1967).

WORKING IN TEAMS

CHAPTER LEARNING OBJECTIVES

After reading this chapter, you should have a good understanding of

- the difference between groups and teams;
- the importance of managing workplace teams and enhancing their effectiveness;
- the advantages and disadvantages of using teams;
- the different types of workplace teams;
- the stages of team development and effective leadership behaviors in each stage;
- the five components of designing successful teams; and
- the two kinds of conflict and their definitions.

"Unity is strength. When there is teamwork and collaboration, wonderful things can be achieved."

- MATTIE STEPANEK

MANAGING TEAMS

In response to complex environments, organizations have begun to utilize team-based work environments to compete. Recognizing that the success of any business requires individuals to work together to achieve organizational goals and objectives, companies are beginning to utilize and leverage the benefits of teamwork. Today, a growing number of organizations are significantly improving their effectiveness and efficiency by adopting team-based environments, but not all workplace groups become effective work teams. So what makes some teams effective and others not?

The first half of this chapter will present research from an area originating in the fields of psychology and the social sciences, called group dynamics. The study of how individuals work in small groups, group dynamics research has been gathering over the decades. Because organizations have rapidly expanded the use of team-based work environments, management researchers have concentrated on understanding

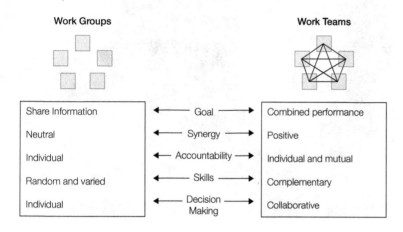

Figure 9.1. Comparing Work Groups and Work Teams

Kipley, D., Jewe, R., & Helm-Stevens, R., A Foundation in the Principles of Management, pp. 177. Copyright © 2015 by Cognella, Inc. Reprinted with permission.

group dynamics in the workplace with the goal of helping businesses increase the effectiveness of their teams.

The second half of this chapter will examine conflict and present strategies designed to minimize group conflict. Information will be presented on how to conduct different types of brainstorming sessions to encourage participation and creative thinking. Additionally, this chapter will explore multiple techniques for group decision making, designed to ensure a participatory process in which multiple individuals act collectively to analyze problems or situations, consider and evaluate alternative courses of action, and select from among the alternatives a solution or solutions.

WORK GROUP VERSUS WORK TEAM

A **work group** is a collection of individuals operating towards a business goal, with little or no collaboration between the members of the group. For example, the work group may be responsible for work on separate parts of project or for assisting different customers. A **work team** is a collaborative group of individuals with complementary talents and skills joined together to accomplish a common organizational objective or goal. Work teams are not the solution for every situation or organization. Yet, when organizations create high-functioning teams and the teams are utilized properly and in the right settings, work teams can dramatically improve effectiveness, efficiency, and overall company performance. When composed and managed properly, work teams can achieve higher productivity and better results than other traditional management approaches.

Similar to work teams, a **high-functioning team** is generally regarded as a tight-knit team, aligned with and committed to a common goal, capable of achieving a high level of collaboration and innovation. In high-functioning teams, the output of the team generally exceeds the sum of the output of individual members (Figure 9.1).

TYPES OF WORK TEAMS

In today's workplace, team-based environments are growing in popularity. Different teams are utilized by organizations to help the business respond to both specific and complex problems and challenges. Generally, the type of team an organization utilizes varies from business to business and depends upon the need and purpose or goal.

Prior to creating a team, managers need to think through the purpose, scope, design, and level of autonomy of the team. **Autonomy** is the degree to which workers have the independence and authority to utilize resources, access information, and decide how and when to accomplish their tasks. There are four types of workplace teams commonly found in organizations:

- problem-solving teams;
- self-managed teams;

- cross-functional teams; and
- virtual teams.

Problem-solving teams, designed for specific issues, help to solve organizational problems by offering suggestions and advice to management. They share ideas and offer suggestions on how processes and methods can be improved in areas such as manufacturing safety, product quality, and customer satisfaction. Typically, although problem-solving teams look at improving quality, effectiveness, and efficiency, they are rarely given the authority to implement their ideas or suggestions.

Self-managed teams have the greatest degree of autonomy, as they generally take on supervisory responsibilities. Self-managed teams are generally granted responsibility over their schedules, meeting times, task assignments, and processes. Typical responsibilities include managing and controlling resources and having oversight over projects and tasks. At times, a self-managed team may select their own members and evaluate and provide feedback on each other's performance.

Cross-functional teams are intentionally composed of employees at about the same hierarchical level but from different functional areas of the organization. Typically, cross-functional teams coordinate complex projects or attempt to accomplish a specific task that requires one or more areas of expertise. Because members have different functional backgrounds and specialties, cross-functional teams are effective at exchanging information and perspectives. Communication and coordination between different functional areas of expertise helps organizations build better designs and improve quality.

Virtual teams are composed of geographically or organizationally dispersed employees who use technology to meet and accomplish assigned tasks. Technology allows virtual team members to collaborate online and eliminates the need meet face to face. Because the team members don't meet in person, the ability to overcome time and space constraints is an advantage. Virtual teams allow team members greater flexibility, demand less of a time commitment, and are less costly for organizations to support.

ADVANTAGES OF TEAMS

Organizations are finding that working in teams creates advantages for the organization and also benefits the employee. The three primary reasons organizations adopt team-based environments are to increase in efficiency, share ideas to foster collaboration and innovation, and promote better decision making. Increased efficiency, a key advantage of teamwork, results when team members work together to accomplish tasks. A team can work more quickly and with greater efficiency than an individual. Shared ideas, another key advantage of teamwork, results when team members contribute different perspectives and approaches. The ability to share and bounce ideas among team members produces innovation and collaboration. Decision making in teams improves due to the sharing of ideas, perspectives, and approaches. Because members possess different experiences, knowledge, skills, and abilities, the team is able to gather multiple perspectives. This generally leads teams to make better decisions.

Diverse viewpoints help the team to generate multiple approaches to problems and brainstorm alternative solutions. The increased knowledge generated from multiple perspectives provides the team with a bed of information from which to generate more alternative solutions. Diverse viewpoints also assist the team in identifying and solving the fundamental causes of the problem, rather than simply dealing with the symptoms. Additionally, team members are more committed to the solution when they are involved in the decision-making process. Many organizations are finding the major advantages of teamwork lead to additional benefits, such as increased speed and efficiency in product development; increased customer satisfaction, product, and service quality; improved organizational communication; and employee job satisfaction.

In addition, the advantages of teamwork are more than just organizational; generally, there are personal benefits for the employee as well. Several advantages work teams offer the team member include improved office relationships, development of ability or expansion of knowledge through the sharing of work, a feeling of connectedness, and job satisfaction.

DISADVANTAGES OF TEAMS

Although work teams can produce significant benefits for the organization and the employee, there can also be disadvantages. Simply creating and using workplace teams does not guarantee the organization or the employee positive outcomes, as there are several inherent problems in work teams. The two most crucial disadvantages of teamwork are social loafing and the problems associated with groupthink. Closely connected to unequal participation, social loafing is a key disadvantage of work teams.

First documented by 19th-century German scientist Max Ringelmann (1913), **social loafing** occurs when team members do not participate, or participate minimally, and instead deliberately exert less or entirely withhold their efforts. In other words, they do not perform their share of the work.

While working on rope pulling exertion, Ringelmann found that the larger the team, the less the individual effort. Social loafing is more likely to occur in larger groups because it can be difficult to categorize the efforts and the individual team members. Social loafers are less likely to assume responsibility for a task; they count on blending into the background, where their lack of efforts isn't easily spotted. In some cases, social loafers are armed with a variety of excuses and delay tactics. In some instances this can lead to conflict, resentment, and low workplace morale. In teamwork, there can be a tendency for unequal participation as some members to contribute less and others contribute more. Unlike unequal participation, social loafing is a conscious and intentional action. Due to the importance of team-based class projects, most students already know about social loafers or "slackers."

REDUCING SOCIAL LOAFING

Dan Rothwell (1999) claims utilizing the three Cs of motivation can reduce social loafing: collaboration, content, and choice.

- **Collaboration**, a way to involve team members, is achieved by assigning special and meaningful tasks to all members of the team.
- **Content**, giving meaning to involvement, is achieved by assigning worthy and meaningful tasks to team members.
- **Choice**, the opportunity to have input into involvement, is achieved by providing members the opportunity to choose their tasks.

In addition to the three motivational considerations presented above, there are three additional practical tools to help reduce social loafing:

1. Assign due dates and **milestones** for checking in to ensure that group members are progressing on their assigned tasks.
2. As group members to provide **feedback** on task progress during group meetings. Involve the group in helping those group members in need.
3. Create a system of **accountability** and ownership (Figure 9.2).

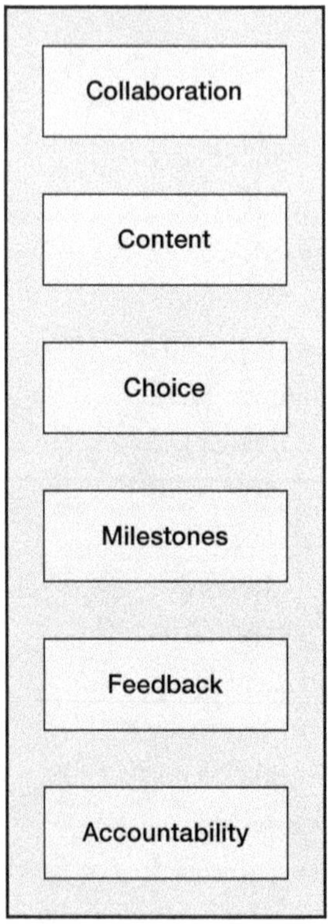

Involvement, responsibility, and motivation are deterrents to social loafing. For example, assigning group roles and tasks can cause lack of motivation, disagreements, and frustration. Conversely, involving group members in the planning and discussion of assignments and the

Figure 9.2. The Six Keys to Reducing Social Loafing

Collaboration

Content

Choice

Milestones

Feedback

Accountability

freedom to choose tasks encourages collaboration and responsibility while reducing social loafing (Figure 9.2). In addition to allowing group members to volunteer for tasks and projects, when possible, align group member strengths to tasks and projects. It is also important to clearly communicate expectations, including due dates and milestones, to team members. Prior to due dates, allow time in group meetings for individuals to share their progress and update the team on any challenges they encountered. This will help create a sense of ownership and accountability.

Groupthink, the second key disadvantage of teamwork, can have disastrous affects. Pioneered and documented by Irving Janis (1971), groupthink is a psychological phenomenon. **Groupthink** occurs when the desire for harmony or conformity among group members results in illogical, irrational, or unscientific decision making. In highly cohesive groups or groups constructed with unequal power distributions, group members feel tremendous pressure to agree with each other so the group can continue a particular course of action. Generally evidenced by an inadequate number of alternative solutions, a hallmark of groupthink is the lack of independent critical thinking. Additional characteristics of groupthink include restricted discussion, elimination of diverse perspectives, and poor decision making. Janis noted three antecedent conditions to groupthink: high group cohesiveness, structural faults, and situational context.

- **High group cohesiveness** leads to lack of individuality. The group becomes more important than the individual or their opinions and ideas.
- **Structural faults** include insulation of the group, lack of rules or norms for decision making, lack of impartial leadership, and lack of diverse experience, background, and knowledge among group members.
- **Situational context** includes recent group failures, moral dilemmas, overwhelming difficulties in decision making, and disproportionate or overpowering external threats.

These conditions underpin groupthink. However, it is not necessary for each of the three to be present in order for groupthink to occur. In order to help individuals identify the possible occurrence of groupthink, Irving Janis documented eight symptoms. The eight symptoms indicative of groupthink can help managers, leaders, and groups recognize the signs of groupthink (Figure 9.3).

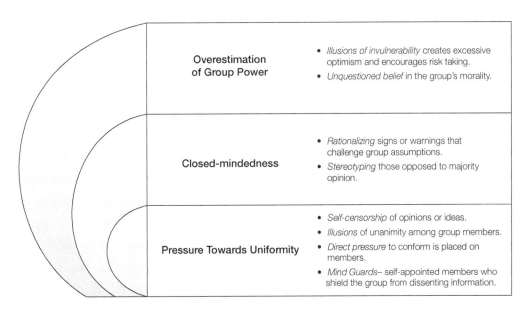

Figure 9.3. The Signs of Groupthink

Type I: Overestimations of the group—its power and morality

1. **Illusions of invulnerability** include creating excessive optimism and encouraging risk taking.
2. **Unquestioned belief** in the group's morality. Members believe in the rightness of the cause and, therefore, ignore the consequences of their actions.

Type II: Closed-mindedness

3. **Rationalizing** signs or warnings that might challenge the assumptions of the group.
4. **Stereotyping** those who are opposed to the majority opinion of the group as, for example, stupid or biased.

Type III: Pressure towards uniformity

5. **Self-censorship**—opinions or ideas that deviate from the seeming group consensus are not expressed.
6. **Illusions of unanimity** among group members. Silence is viewed as agreement and majority views and judgments are assumed to be unanimous.
7. **Direct pressure** to conform is placed on members who question the group. Members are under pressure not to express dissenting arguments.
8. **Mind guards**—self-appointed members who shield the group from dissenting information. Members who shield the group leader and members from information that is problematic or contradictory to existing information.

Not surprisingly, Janis also devoted a considerable amount of time to investigating and documenting strategies designed to prevent groupthink. Although not every decision-making group is destined to groupthink, Janis devised eight tactics to aid in preventing it:

1. Leaders should assign each member the role of "critical evaluator." This allows each member to freely air objections and doubts.
2. Leaders should not express an opinion, preference, or expectation when assigning tasks to the group.
3. Leaders should remove themselves from most group meetings. This will help leaders avoid excessively influencing the outcome.
4. The organization should set up several independent groups. These independent groups should be assigned to work on the same assignment or task.
5. Each effective alternative should be examined.
6. Each member should discuss the group's ideas with trusted people outside of the group.
7. The group should invite one or more outside experts into meetings. Group members should be allowed to discuss with and question the outside experts, while the outside experts should challenge the members' views.
8. At least one group member should be assigned the role of devil's advocate. This role should question assumptions and plans. This role should also be rotated.

ADVANTAGES AND DISADVANTAGES OF TEAMS

Managers and leaders must consider the advantages and disadvantages of teams before deciding to transition individual projects to team-based projects and assigning tasks to teams (Table 9.1).

Table 9.1. Team Advantages and Disadvantages

G.J. Medsker, and M.A. Campion, Adapted from Table 14.1, "Job and Team Design," Handbook of Human Factors and Ergonomics, ed. Gavriel Salvendy, pp. 465. Copyright © 1997 by John Wiley & Sons, Inc.

Team Advantages	Team Disadvantages
• Team members have the opportunity to learn from each other.	• Some individuals are not compatible with teamwork.
• Potential exists for greater work force flexibility with cross-training.	• Workers must be selected to fit the team as well as the requisite job skills.
• Opportunity provided for synergistic combinations of ideas and abilities.	• Some members may experience less motivating jobs as part of a team.
• New approaches to tasks may be discovered.	• Organization may resist change.
• Team-membership can provide social facilitation and support for difficult tasks and situations.	• Conflict may develop between team members or other teams.
• Communication and information exchange may be facilitated and increased.	• Teams may be time consuming due to need for coordination and consensus.
• Teams can foster greater cooperation among team members.	• Teams can stymie creativity and inhibit good decision-making if "group think" becomes prevalent.
• Interdependent work flow can be enhanced.	• Evaluation and rewards may be perceived as less powerful.
• Potential exists for greater acceptance and understanding of team-made decisions.	• "Free-riding" within the team may occur.
• Greater autonomy, variety, identity, significance, and feedback for workers can occur.	• Less flexibility may be experienced in personnel replacement or transfer.
• Team commitment may stimulate performance and attendance.	

Source: Adapted from Medsker and Campion (1997).

DESIGNING WORK TEAMS

As more organizations adopt team-based environments and utilize different types of teams, it is imperative for managers to understand how to effectively construct and lead work teams. Part of this success hinges on understanding the characteristics, features, or attributes that create the setting for high-functioning teams. Team member composition, selecting the right people for the team, is an essential foundational factor for creating well-functioning and high-performing teams. Although, there is ongoing discussion regarding effective team member composition, a common set of components is recognized as essential in designing effective work teams (Figure 9.4):

1. Team norms
2. Team cohesiveness
3. Team roles
4. Team size
5. Group diversity

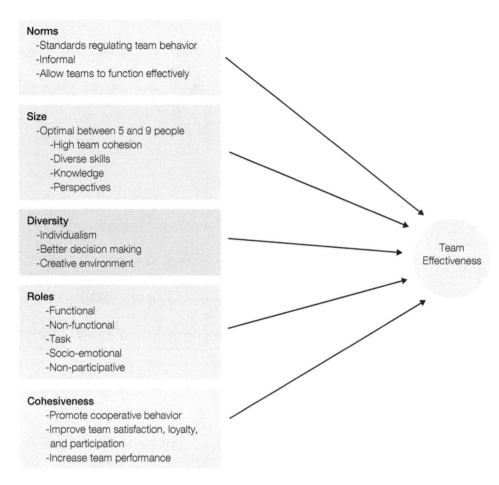

Figure 9.4. The Five Components of Team Effectiveness

Kipley, D., Jewe, R., & Helm-Stevens, R., A Foundation in the Principles of Management, pp. 186. Copyright © 2015 by Cognella, Inc. Reprinted with permission.

TEAM NORMS

Team norms are implicit agreed-on standards that regulate team behavior. Although team norms are informal and develop over time, they are understood codes that govern the behaviors of team members. Valuable because they let team members know what is expected of them, norms regulate team behavior and allow teams to function effectively. Often linked to positive organizational outcomes, team norms can influence stronger organizational commitment, improved job and organizational satisfaction, and a deeper trust in management. For example, effective work teams develop positive and constructive norms about individual behavior, such as timeliness, accountability, quality, job performance, absenteeism, safety, professionalism, and transparency. Research has proven that norms are one of the most powerful influences on an individual's work behavior.

Similar to positive team norms, destructive or negative team norms are informal and develop over time. Destructive team norms can harm the organization, other employees, and team members. For example, deliberately bending or breaking the rules, developing passive-aggressive behaviors, or intentionally ignoring the chain of command are all negative team norms that can harm the organization and it's employees. Although research demonstrates that team norms develop in the early stages of group development, they can also develop over time.

Because destructive team norms can negatively influence a teams' behavior, it is critical that teams establish positive norms as early as possible.

TEAM COHESIVENESS

Cohesiveness, a critical characteristic of successful work teams, is the extent to which team members are attracted to a team and motivated to stay as a part of the team. Important for many reasons, team cohesiveness promotes cooperative behavior. Primarily, research has proven that high cohesiveness increases team member satisfaction, loyalty, and participation, which leads to improved team performance. Typically, morale is higher due to better communication among the group, because members share a feeling of being in on things. Additionally, highly cohesive teams are committed to team decisions and therefore experience a higher shared accountability. Because cohesive groups are able to retain their members, they experience lower turnover.

Research has established that cohesive teams are able to attain high levels of performance quickly as compared to teams with low cohesiveness. Conversely, teams low in cohesion may experience disagreements, conflicts, lack of participation, and poor communication. Typically, teams with low cohesion are often lacking in organization, coordination, and commitment to the team. Teams with low cohesiveness may have members not fully committed to team decisions, strategies, schedules, or goals. As a result, teams low in cohesion take much longer to reach the same levels of performance.

TEAM ROLES

Team roles are broadly categorized as functional or non-functional. **Functional roles** assist the team to successfully and productively attain their goal. **Non-functional roles** detract from the team and hinder performance. Differentiation of functional roles within a team leads to better team cohesiveness and productivity and helps minimize group conflict. Although there are many different kinds and levels of contributions by individuals in a team, there are five key roles—three functional and two non-functional.

FUNCTIONAL TEAM ROLES.

Functional roles include task, socio-emotional, and dual roles. **Task roles** include individual actions that help the project stay on task and move forward. Individuals who fulfill task roles think about what it takes to do the job. They are generally organized and proficient at sequencing. Task roles directly contribute to the productivity of the team.

Socio-emotional roles include individual actions that help communication and participation, and preserve team relationships. Individuals who fulfill socio-emotional roles work at strengthening and maintaining relationships. They are generally inclusive and encouraging. Socio-emotional roles directly contribute to the cohesiveness of the team. Although many individuals will have a dominant strength in their functional role, other individuals may operate as more of a dual role.

Dual roles include individuals equally comfortable contributing in either the task or the socio-emotional role. If a group is to become a high-functioning team, then the task and the socio-emotional roles must both be present, as either role may be required by the team at any given time. When necessary, a team composed of dual role individuals can help balance the lack of either a task or socio-emotional role team member. If a team lacks balance, then it will have difficulty attaining its goal in an effective and efficient manner. A lack of socio-emotional role contributions is likely to cause quarrels and disagreements to fester and become destructive conflict. On the other hand, a lack of task role contributions is likely to cause a lack of focus and productivity.

The two common non-functional roles include the non-participative and hindering roles. **Non-participative roles** refer to the actions of individuals that are absent either physically or mentally. Individuals who are non-participative are generally absent, inattentive, or unengaged. Typically, they are not engaged, lack participation, and often miss deadlines. **Hindering roles** include individual actions that impede the team's progress. Individuals who fulfill hindering roles often delay or obstruct the team's progress. Hindering actions may include such behaviors as being uncooperative and withholding information or resources. At times, those in hindering roles engage in unethical behavior such as degrading or gossiping about others, or employing manipulative or passive-aggressive behaviors.

As team size increases, the need to differentiate between the roles of individuals increases. With time, the roles that team members occupy may change or evolve. Regardless of the level and type of contribution, team members should always behave in a way that furthers the objectives of the team and advances the organization.

TEAM SIZE

Research has established a preliminary link between team size and team performance. The size of the team has a significant effect on performance. In smaller groups, members have a tendency to participate, while in larger groups members are more likely to appear busy.

For most traditional types of work teams, the optimal number of team members is between five and nine. As it is easy for members to contribute in positive ways and get to know other team members, people can participate without getting lost in a large team. It is easier to instill a sense of responsibility and accountability in the team, while also having enough members to enable the team to take advantage of the diversity in team members' experience, skills, and knowledge.

Obviously, very small teams or very large teams come with significant concerns. Generally, a very large or very small team will not perform as well as moderately sized teams. If a team is too small (three or fewer members) there may be a lack of differences in ability, experience, skills, and knowledge. Lack of diversity may impact the team in the areas of generating alternatives, decision making, and innovation. On the other hand, if a team is too large (10 or more members) then the team is not likely to be cohesive. When teams become too large, it is difficult for members to get know each other. Often, this leads large teams to fragment into smaller sub-groups. The creation of sub-groups may create minority domination, where a few of the team members control and dominate.

TEAM MEMBER DIVERSITY

Although the need for team diversity has already been discussed, it is important to note that diversity in teamwork is not limited to racial or ethnic diversity. **Team member diversity** refers to individualism, such as variances in ability, experience, personality, education, and background. Simply put, team member diversity is the significant uniqueness of the personalities on the team. By definition, diverse representation from the team members provides an increased likelihood that a broad range of views and perspectives will be presented. This existence and presentation of diverse views is essential for effective decision making. From fully understanding the problem to identifying a greater number of alternative solutions, diversity fosters a creative environment and allows for exploration of a task, assignment, or problem from various angles. Research has proven the role of diverse contributions in improving and increasing team performance.

While constructing diverse teams, organizations must make sure that the individuals selected are focused on teamwork (individualism-collectivism). Hofstede's cultural dimensions theory defines **individualism-collectivism** as "the degree to which individuals are integrated into groups"—the degree to which loyalty to oneself is more important than loyalty to one's team or company. **Individualists**, who put their welfare and interest and those of their immediate family first, generally prefer independent tasks. They may prefer to work alone. In contrast, **collectivists**, who put group, team, or company interests ahead of self-interest, generally prefer interdependent tasks. They prefer to work with others. Still, the degree of individualism-collectivism should not preempt the need for team member diversity, as individualists may be appropriate when garnering wide variances within a team.

STAGES OF TEAM DEVELOPMENT

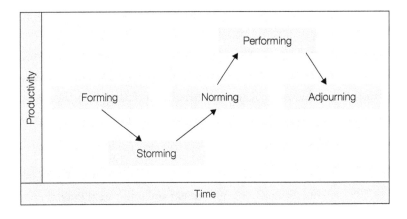

Figure 9.5. Tuckman's Stages of Team Development

Bruce Tuckman (1965), a prominent scholar in group dynamics theory and research, published his model of group development. Initially, Tuckman's stages of team development offered four stages—forming, storming, norming, and performing (Figure 9.5). In 1977, Tuckman and colleague Mary Jensen added a fifth stage—adjourning. Understanding that teams mature experientially and in stages, Tuckman explained that teams must traverse these phases in order to mature into well-functioning and high-performing teams. Tuckman's team development model suggests that, as teams mature, they pass through five separate and distinct stages of development. These stages are necessary for the growth of teams as they learn to overcome obstacles, develop solutions, and deliver results. Moreover, individual relationships and leadership styles change throughout the different phases—from the formation (forming) through the dissolution (adjourning)— of the team. Tuckman's model of group development has become the foundation for later models.

The initial stage of team development, **forming** is characterized as the "meet and greet" stage. When team members first meet each other, they are polite and try to avoid controversy and conflict. They do, however, form initial impressions, gather information, and try to assess how they fit into the group. A few of the first team norms will be established during this stage, as team members begin discussing expectations and discovering acceptable behaviors. During the forming stage, team leaders should facilitate the meet and greet, ensuring that all group members get to know each other and participate in conversations regarding preliminary roles, rules, and structure. During this stage, leaders should allow time for team members to get to know each other. If possible, team leaders should help the team set early ground rules and begin preliminary discussions on the methods of selecting and deciding upon team structure.

The second stage of team development, **storming**, is often distinguished by disagreements and conflicts. As team members become acquainted with each other, the level of comfort in expression increases. Generally, team members become more assertive at this stage and are more willing to state their opinions. Often, as team members begin voicing opinions, disagreements and arguments erupt. During this stage, team members also announce their intentions and politic for positions. Different personalities, agendas, and work styles clash and cause conflict. In addition to attempting to establish favorable roles for themselves, team members are likely to have disagreements about goals, objectives, and processes. During the disagreements and conflicts of the storming stage, it is important for the leaders to ensure that differences are channeled in a productive manner. It is also critical that team leaders do not attempt to squash or bury the difference, but instead foster an environment of respecting different opinions and remaining professional in conversations and actions. Additionally, leaders must keep driving the focus towards team goals and team performance. If a team remains in the storming stage or continues to the next stage without resolving the issues present, then the team is likely to be ineffective.

The establishment and acceptance of team roles and structure characterize **norming**, the third stage of team development. Having resolved differences, team members can begin the process of learning to work together productively. Team members begin settling into their roles and the group makes big decisions about goals and objectives. At this stage, the team should be working together to develop agreements and expectations about processes, methods, and working styles in preparation for the work that needs to be done. Leaders should ensure that participation and engagement among team members is high and that team norms are positive and performance oriented. While monitoring for groupthink, team leaders should ensure that members are beginning to operate as a cohesive unit. If commitment and unity are strong, then team members may participate in social activities. If so, leaders should help the group avoid cliques or factions.

In the fourth stage of team development, **performing**, is distinguished by performance. The team has become a well-oiled machine—an effective, efficient, fully functioning team. Because team roles and structure were settled in the previous stage, brainstorming and ideas are now debated instead of personal agendas. The team improves because it can now focus on creative and innovative problem solving. During this stage, it is common for cohesiveness to be high, as team members are committed to the team and feel responsible to other group members and accountable for the success or failure of the team. Leaders should ensure that productivity remains high by making certain the team has access to all required resources, such as information and materials.

Adjourning, which occurs after the completion of the project or task, involves closing the project and reviewing successes and failures. During this stage, leaders should conduct any outstanding evaluations, help the team celebrate successes, identify strengths to retain, and explore possible improvements for future team projects. Leaders should also recognize the personal involvement and investment of members and help the team transition from thinking of themselves as members of the team to preparing for the next project or returning to their previous assignment. The last stage of team development, adjourning, does not necessarily contribute to the main task of managing a team. However, it is important and relevant to individual development and critical for team development and organizational improvement.

Arguably, not all teams pass through each of these stages. However, teams that do progress through each stage tend to be better-performing teams. Conversely, ineffective teams may begin a process of decline and pass through the stages of de-norming, de-storming, and de-forming. If team cohesiveness destructs, teams may become complacent. If ineffective leadership transpires, then the team is likely to become ineffective and inefficient.

A reversal of the norming stage, **de-norming** is characterized by the deterioration of team performance. A natural erosion of group guidelines and norms may occur as the interests and expectations change and group members go in different directions. De-norming can also be caused by significant shifts to the team, such as changes to the size, scope, or goals of the team. When new members are introduced, they may question, challenge, or reject group norms or previously established roles, structures, methods, or work styles.

A reversal of the storming phase, **de-storming**, is distinguished by a decrease in group cohesiveness. Instead of the rapid and openness of disagreements found in the storming phase, a slow undercurrent of discontent resides among group members. The team's comfort level is disturbed as team unity weakens and group members increasingly resist conforming to team norms.

A reversal of the forming stage, **de-forming** is characterized by team member isolation. As the team begins to fall apart, members battle to gain control of pieces of the project or team. As team members struggle to position themselves, they begin to avoid other members and isolate themselves from the leaders. Team performance declines and those tasks or pieces of the project that are unclaimed go abandoned as the team quits caring.

Even if teams are proactively managed, decline is not inescapable. Leaders must not become complacent with a high-performing team. Additionally, in order to recognize the destruction of the deconstructive stages managers must be aware and informed of current team performance and group dynamics. When necessary, the leader or the manager should take the necessary steps to reinforce group norms, bolster cohesiveness, reiterate team and organizational goals, and negotiate disruptive conflict.

GROUP DECISION MAKING

Studies have shown that groups consistently outperform individuals in making decisions. **Group decision making** is a type of participatory process in which multiple individuals acting collectively analyze problems or situations, consider and evaluate alternative courses of action, and select from among the alternatives a solution or solutions. The number of people involved in group decision making varies greatly, but often ranges from two to seven. The individuals in a group may be demographically similar or quite diverse. Decision-making groups may be relatively informal in nature, or formally designated and charged with a specific goal. The process used to arrive at decisions may be unstructured or structured. The nature and composition of groups, their size, demographic makeup, structure, and purpose all affect their functioning to some degree.

ADVANTAGES

Group decision making has some advantages over individual decision making, as it takes advantage of the diverse strengths and expertise of its members. By tapping the unique qualities of group members, it is possible that the group can generate a greater number of alternatives that are of higher quality than can the individual. If a greater number of higher-quality alternatives are generated, then it is likely that the group will eventually reach a superior solution.

Group decision making may also lead to a greater collective understanding of the eventual course of action chosen, since it is possible that many affected by the decision implementation actually had input into the decision. This may promote a sense of ownership of the decision, which is likely to contribute to a greater acceptance of the course of action selected and greater commitment on the part of the affected individuals to make the course of action successful.

DISADVANTAGES

There are many potential disadvantages to group decision making. Groups are generally slower to arrive at decisions than individuals, so sometimes it is difficult to utilize them in situations where decisions must be made very quickly. One of the most often cited problems is groupthink. Although we examined groupthink earlier in the chapter, it is important to remember that groupthink occurs when individuals in a group feel pressure to conform to what seems to be the dominant view in the group. Opposing views of the majority opinion are suppressed and alternative courses of action are not fully explored.

Research suggests that certain characteristics of groups contribute to groupthink. First, if the group does not have an agreed-upon process for developing and evaluating alternatives, it is possible that an incomplete set of alternatives will be considered and that different courses of action will not be fully explored. Many of the formal decision-making processes (e.g., nominal group technique and brain storming) are designed, in part, to reduce the potential for groupthink by ensuring that group members offer and consider a large number of decision alternatives. Second, if a powerful leader dominates the group, other group members may quickly conform to the dominant view. Additionally, if the group is under stress and/or time pressure, groupthink may occur. Finally,

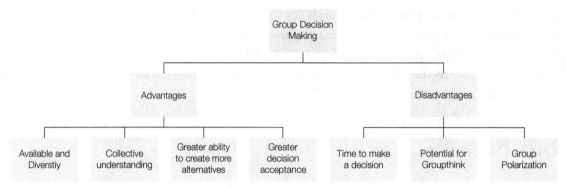

Figure 9.6. Group Decision Making Advantages and Disadvantages

studies suggest that highly cohesive groups are more susceptible to groupthink. Utilizing group decision-making techniques helps minimize the possibility of groupthink.

Group polarization is another potential disadvantage of group decision making. This is the tendency of the group to converge on more extreme solutions to a problem. The "risky shift" phenomenon is an example of polarization that occurs when the group decision is a riskier one than any of the group members would have made individually. This may result because individuals in a group sometimes do not feel as much responsibility and accountability for the actions of the group as they would if they were making the decision alone (Figure 9.6).

DELPHI TECHNIQUE

In the **Delphi technique**, a series of questionnaires, surveys, and so on are sent to a selected panel of experts (the Delphi group) through a facilitator, who oversees their responses. The group does not have to meet face to face, affording the panel the flexibility of working from their office, thus providing efficient use of the expert's time. All communication is normally in writing (letters or email). Members of the groups are selected because they are experts or they have relevant information.

The responses are collected, analyzed, and summarized to determine conflicting viewpoints on each point and then fed back to the group. The process continues in order to work towards synthesis and building consensus. The Delphi technique works as follows:

1. Members are selected for the Delphi panel due to their expertise.
2. They are kept separated and answer through open-ended questionnaires, surveys, and so on, in order to solicit specific information about a subject or content area. Keeping them separated avoids the negative effects of face-to-face discussions and avoids problems associated with group dynamics.
3. Members are asked to share their assessment and explanation of a problem or predict a future state of affairs.
4. The facilitator controls the interactions among the participants by processing the information and filtering out irrelevant content.
5. Replies are gathered, summarized, and then fed back to all the group members.
6. Members then make another decision based upon the new information.
7. The process is repeated until the responses converge satisfactorily, that is, it yields consensus.

Managers should not use the Delphi technique for common decisions because it is a time-consuming, labor-intensive, and expensive process. The Delphi technique is most appropriate for important long-term issues and problems.

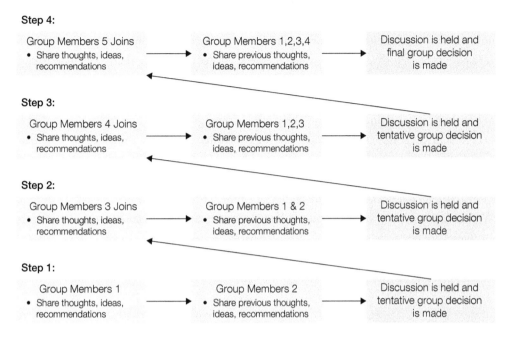

Figure 9.7. Stepladder Technique for Group Decision Making

STEPLADDER TECHNIQUE

The **stepladder technique** is a simple and effective tool to improve group decision making by determining how and when people enter the decision-making process. The stepladder theory assumes that members contribute to the group on an individual level before being influenced by anyone else, thus ensuring that each member's contributions are independent and are considered and discussed by the group. Such an approach brings a wider variety of new ideas, flexible thinking, and creative points of view (Figure 9.7).

Before a group is formed, you should present the task list or the problem list to all participants. Give everyone enough time to think over and carefully investigate what needs to be done. Each member will generate their own opinion on how to accomplish the tasks or solve the problems.

The following four basic steps illuminate how to implement the stepladder technique:

1. Form a core group of two members. They will dispute and find a solution.
2. Add a third member to the core group. This member will bring new ideas before hearing the first two members' conclusions and solutions. After new ideas are discussed and solutions are presented, the three members start discussing new options together.
3. Run this process repeatedly. A fourth member, a fifth member, and so on will be added to the core group.
4. Generate the final decision only after all members have been added to the group and they've presented their new ideas.

RINGI TECHNIQUE

Developed in Japan, the Ringi decision-making technique is generally used with controversial issues or situations. Allowing for conflict without face-to-face confrontation, the Ringi technique begins with the creation of a document that outlines and presents the issue or situation. The document is then circulated to group members anonymously. The group members contribute to the document by editing and adding comments individually. Once a group member has completed their contributions, the document continues to circulate anonymously. However, after a complete cycle through the group members, the document is revised to include all comments and suggestions. The process continues until group members stop editing and making suggestions.

In the Ringi approach, the final document that presents the issue and the resolution is a group effort and has been developed and refined anonymously. The major advantage of the Ringi technique is that it allows for group members to state their true beliefs while avoiding confrontation with another group member. The major disadvantage of the Ringi technique is the time consumed by the process. Additionally, there is no guarantee that the group members will produce an optimal decision.

Team decision making takes a considerable amount of time. Often, team meetings can be unproductive and inefficient. At times, a minority of group members dominate team discussions and restrict critical debates. When this occurs, problems are not fully defined and few alternative solutions are generated. These types of situations can cause team members to not feel accountable for team decisions. However, in order for teams to make better decisions, time and careful consideration of the topics at hand are required.

SUMMARY OF CHAPTER

1. We examined the advantages and disadvantages of teams.
2. We explored strategies to minimize the disadvantages of workplace teams. We learned how the three Cs can reduce social loafing and the eight preventative measures to employ in order to minimize the threat of groupthink.
3. We examined the four common types of workplace teams and the typical characteristics of each were discussed.
4. We explored the five core components of designing effective workplace teams.
5. Norms are implicit agreed-upon standards that regulate team behavior.
6. Cohesiveness is the extent to which team members are attracted to a team and motivated to stay part of the team.
7. We learned why differentiation of roles within a team leads to better team cohesiveness and productivity.
8. We learned the importance of team size and team member diversity are essential components for designing high-quality teams.
9. We explored Tuckman's stages of team development.

DISCUSSION QUESTIONS

1. What are the differences between work groups and work teams? What are the advantages and disadvantages of using teams?
2. Identify the eight preventive measures used to minimize the threat of groupthink.
3. Describe the five core components of designing effective workplace teams.
4. How do norms and cohesiveness contribute to developing high-quality teams? How does team size and member diversity help produce a high-functioning team?

WHAT DO I THINK ABOUT WORKING IN GROUPS?

INSTRUCTIONS

Indicate how much you agree with each statement using the following scale:
1: Strongly disagree | 2: Disagree | 3: Neutral | 4: Agree | 5: Strongly agree

1. I tend to keep to myself.
2. I prefer to work on my own.
3. I try to give other team members support when they need it.
4. I never miss meetings for groups I am in.
5. I work best in a group setting.
6. I respect the decisions the team or group makes.
7. I like being in a group or team.
8. I find it important to socialize with others.
9. I work best when I work on my own.

SCORING KEY:

To find your score, add up your total. First, reverse score items 1, 2, and 9, so 1 = 5, 2 = 4, 3 = 3, 4 = 2, and 5 = 1.

ANALYSIS:

Not everyone enjoys group work. Some people would prefer to work alone on projects and tasks. Those who scored 18 or below would be these kinds of people. If you scored 36 or above, you generally enjoy group work.

The workplace environment is increasing its use of team and group work. Those who prefer individual work will have to find ways to balance their preference with the reality of group work. Fortunately, your attitudes on group work can change. The key is to find a way to enjoy each group to which you are assigned.

Adapted from: Robbins, S. P. (2009). IV.E.1: What's My Attitude Toward Working I Groups?, Self-assessment library (116-117). Upper Saddle River, NJ: Pearson Education Inc.

Original Source: Goldberg, L.R., Johnson, J. A., Eber, H. W., Ashton, M. C., Cloninger, C. R., & Gough, H. G. (2006). The international personality item pool and the future of public-domain personality measures. Journal pf research in Personality, *40*(1), p. 84-96.

CHAPTER 9 REFERENCES

Alessandra, T., & Hunsaker, P. (1993). *Communicating at work.* New York: Fireside Publishers. (See especially p. 92.)

Amason, A. C., & Sapienza, H. J. (1997). The effects of top management, team size, and interaction norms on cognitive and affective conflict. *Journal of Management, 23*(4), 495–516.

Blanchard, K., & Parisi-Carew, E. (2009). *The one minute manager builds high performing teams.* New York: William Morrow.

Cappozzoli, T. K. (1995). Resolving conflict within teams. *Journal for Quality and Participation, 18*(7), 28–30.

Chidambaram, L., & Tung, L. L. (2005). Is out of sight, out of mind? An empirical study of social loafing in technology-supported groups. *Information Systems Research, 16*(2), 149–168.

Chung, J. E., Park, N., Wang, H., Fulk, J., & McLaughlin, M. (2010). Age differences in perceptions of online community participation among non-users: An extension of the Technology Acceptance Model. *Computers in Human Behavior, 26*(6), 1674–1684.

Earley, P. C. (1989). Social loafing and collectivism: A comparison of the United States and the People's Republic of China. *Administrative Science Quarterly, 34*(4), 565–581.

Edwards, G.C., Wattenberg, M. P., & Lineberry, R. L. (2005). *Government in America: People, politics, and policy* (12th ed.). New York: Pearson Longman.

Eidelson, R. J., & Eidelson, J. I. (2003). Dangerous ideas: Five beliefs that propel groups toward conflict. *American Psychologist, 58*(3), 182–192.

Fischer, M. D. (2012). Organizational turbulence, trouble and trauma: Theorizing the collapse of a mental health setting. *Organization Studies, 33*(9), 1153–1173.

Fischer, M. D., & Ferlie, E. (2013). Resisting hybridisation between modes of clinical risk management: Contradiction, contest, and the production of intractable conflict. *Accounting, Organizations and Society, 38*(1), 30–49.

Forsyth, D. R. (2009). *Group dynamics.* New York: Wadsworth.

Gilovich, T., Keltner, D., & Nisbett, R. E. (2006). *Social psychology.* New York: W.W. Norton. (See especially p. 60.)

Guffey, M. E., Rhodes, K., & Rogin, P. (2010). *Business communication: Process and product.* Toronto: Thomson South-Western.

Hofstede, G. (1984). *Culture's consequences: International differences in work-related values* (2nd ed.). Beverly Hills, CA: SAGE Publications.

Hofstede, G. (2010, September). *Whatsonmymind.*

Hofstede, G., Hofstede, J. G., & Minkov, M. (2010). *Cultures and organizations: software of the mind* (3rd ed.). New York: McGraw-Hill.

Hoon, H., & Tan, M. L. (2008). Organizational citizenship behavior and social loafing: The role of personality, motives, and contextual factors. *The Journal of Psychology, 142*(1), 89–108.

Ingham, A. G., Levinger, G., Graves, J., & Peckham, V. (1974). The Ringelmann effect: Studies of group size and group performance. *Journal of Experimental Social Psychology, 10*(4), 371–384.

Jackson, J. M., & Harkins, S. G. (1985). Equity in effort: An explanation of the social loafing effect. *Journal of Personality and Social Psychology, 49,* 1199–1206.

Janis, I. L. (1971). Groupthink. *Psychology Today, 5*(6), 43–46, 74–76.

Jehn, K. A., & Mannix, E. A. (2001). The dynamic nature of conflict: A longitudinal study. *Academy of Management Journal, 44*(2), 238–251.

Jowett, S., & Lavallee, D. (2007). Social psychology in sport. *Human Kinetics. 10,* 34.

Karau, S. J., & Williams, K. D. (1993). Social loafing: A meta-analytic review and theoretical integration. *Journal of Personality and Social Psychology, 65*(4), 681–706.

Kassin, S., Fein, S., & Markus, H. R. (n.d.). *Social psychology* (8th ed.). Belmont, CA: Cengage Wadsworth. (See especially p. 312).

Kraut, R. E., & Resnick, P. (n.d.). *Encouraging online contributions. The science of social design: Mining the social sciences to build successful online communities.* Cambridge, MA: MIT Press. (See especially p. 39.)

Kravitz, D. A., & Martin, B. (1986). Ringelmann rediscovered: The original article. *Journal of Personality and Social Psychology, 50*(5), 936–941.

Krumm, D. J. (2000). *Psychology at work: An introduction to industrial/organizational psychology.* New York: Worth Publishers. (See especially p. 178.)

Latané, B., Williams, K., & Harkins, S. (1979). Many hands make light the work: The causes and consequences of social loafing. *Journal of Personality and Social Psychology, 37*(6), 822–832.

Latham, G., & Baldes, P. (1975). James, J. *Journal of Applied Psychology, 60*(1).

Medsker, G. J., Campion, M. A. (1997). Job and team design. In G. Salvendy (Ed.), *Handbook of Human Factors and Ergonomics* (pp. 450–489). *Interscience,* 18 Apr 1997.

Nicholson, M. (1992). *Rationality and the analysis of international conflict.* Cambridge: Cambridge University Press. (See especially p. 13.)

Pattern: Collaboration in small groups. CSCW, The Computing Company, October 31, 2005.

Piezon, S. L., & Donaldson, R. L. (2005). Online groups and social loafing: Understanding student-group interactions. *Online Journal of Distance Learning Administration, 8*(4).

Piezon, S. L., & Ferree, W. D. (2008). Perceptions of social loafing in online Learning Groups: A study of Public University and U.S. Naval War College students. *The International Review of Research in Open and Distance Learning, 9*(2).

Resolve Hot Topics with Cooler Heads. (2007, May). Negotiation: 12-12.

Ringelmann, M. (1913). Recherches sur les moteurs animés: Travail de l'homme [Research on animate sources of power: The work of man]. *Annales de l'Institut National Agronomique,* 2nd series, *12,* 1–40.

Rothwell, J. D. (1999). *In the company of others: An introduction to communication.* New York: McGraw-Hill.

Shiue, Y., Chiu, C., & Chang, C. (2010). Exploring and mitigating social loafing in online communities. *Computers and Human Behavior, 26*(4), 768–777.

Snook, S. A. (2000). *Friendly fire: The accidental shootdown of U.S. Black Hawks over Northern Iraq.* Princeton, NJ: Princeton University Press. (See especially p. 135.)

Social Loafing: when groups are bad for productivity. PsyBlog. 29 May 2009 (citing, inter alia, Latane).

Sue, D. W., Bingham, R. P., Porché-Burke, L., & Vasquez, M. (1999). The diversification of psychology: A multicultural revolution. *American Psychologist, 54*(12), 1061–1069.

Thompson, L. L. (2003). *Making the team: A guide for managers.* Upper Saddle River, NJ: Pearson/Prentice Hall. (See especially pp. 31–32.)

Tuckman, B. (1965). Developmental sequence in small groups. *Psychological Bulletin* 63(6), 384–399.

Weldon, E., & Jehn. (1991). K. *Journal of Personality and Social Psychology, 61*(4).

White, A. K. (2009). *From comfort zone to performance management.* White & MacLean Publishing.

MANAGING AND LEADING ORGANIZATIONAL PROCESSES

4

CHAPTER LEARNING OBJECTIVES

After reading this chapter, you should be able to

- define what leadership is, when leaders are effective and ineffective, and the difference between formal and informal leaders;
- define leadership and contrast leadership with management;
- explain the contingency theory of leadership and differentiate between four different contingency approaches;
- address challenges to the effectiveness of leadership; and
- explain the strengths and limitations of each leadership theory and approach.

"Leaders become great, not because of their power, but because of their ability to empower others."

- JOHN MAXWELL

LEADERSHIP

What is the difference between management and leadership? John Kotter of the Harvard Business School writes that management is about coping with complexity and that good management brings about order and consistency by drawing up formal plans, designing rigid organizational structures, and monitoring results against the plans. Leadership is about coping with change. Hence, **leadership** is defined as the ability to influence a group toward the achievement of a vision or a set of goals. The source of this influence may be formal, such as that provided by managerial rank in an organization. Leaders establish direction by developing a vision of the future and then aligning people by communicating this vision and inspiring them to overcome hurdles. But, all leaders are not managers, nor, for that matter, are all managers leaders.

The focus of leadership research can include group processes, a personality perspective, an act or behavior, the power relationship between leaders and followers, and an instrument of goal achievement. Leadership involves influence and goal attainment, and occurs within a group context.

Management Produces Order & Consistency	Leadership Produces Change & Movement

• **Planning and Budgeting**
  – Establish agendas
  – Set timelines
  – Allocate resources
• **Organizing and Staffing**
  – Provide structure
  – Job placements
  – Establish rules and procedures
• **Control, Problem Solving**
  – Develop incentives
  – Generate solutions
  – Take corrective action
	• **Establish Direction**
	  – Create a vision
	  – Clarify the big picture
	  – Develop strategies
	• **Aligning People**
	  – Communicate goals
	  – Seek commitment
	  – Build teams and coalitions
	• **Motivate and Inspire**
	  – Inspire and energize
	  – Empower subordinates
	  – Satisfy unmet needs

Figure 10.1. Management Versus Leadership

All leaders exert influence over members of a group or organization. Some leaders, however, are given the formal or legal authority to do so. **Formal leaders** are those managers who are given legal authority to influence other members in the organization to achieve its goals. This legal authority gives them the power to control and make the best use of an organization's resources, including its money and capital and the abilities and skills of its employees. **Informal leaders** have no legal authority to influence other employees, but their personal skills and qualities give them the ability to exert influence in an organization, sometimes as much influence as its formal leaders. The ability of informal leaders to influence other people often stems from special skills or talents they possess, skills an organization's members realize will help achieve its goals.

Leaders influence and control the actions and beliefs of employees who directly report to them, those who work in the specific groups or teams they directly control, and even those who work across an entire organization. The various approaches to leadership that we describe in this chapter seek to explain why some people become leaders and others do not, and why some leaders are more effective than others in their attempts to influence people and groups.

LEADERSHIP AND MANAGEMENT

Although there are similarities, leadership is different from management (Figure 10.1). Leadership is largely motivational in nature, whereas management focuses on maintaining performance. Kotter notes that managers produce order and consistency while leaders produce change and movement.

However, while the activities of management and leadership may be played out differently, both are essential for an organization to prosper, as can be seen in Figure 10.2.

LEADERSHIP THEORIES AND APPROACHES

THE LEADER TRAIT APPROACH

This approach focuses exclusively on leaders and the traits that leaders exhibit. Organizations can use personality assessments to find the "right" people, on the assumption that certain leadership traits will increase organizational effectiveness. Position descriptions specify certain characteristics or traits for specific positions and personality assessment measures, such as the Leadership Trait Questionnaire and the Myers–Briggs Personality Inventory, are used to establish the right fit.

The strength of such an approach is that it is intuitively appealing given the perception that leaders are different in that they possess special traits. People want to view their leaders as being gifted or possessing special characteristics. This approach also has a degree of credibility due to a century of research support, and it highlights the leadership component in the leadership process. It provides a deeper level understanding of how personality is related to the leadership process, as well as providing benchmarks for what to look for in a leader.

How Leadership Complements Management

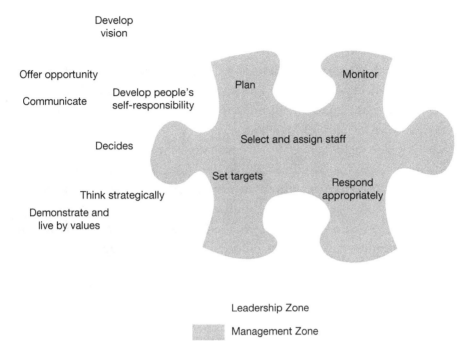

Figure 10.2. How Leadership Complements Management

The limitation of such an approach is that it fails to establish a definitive list of leadership traits and, thus, endless lists have emerged. It also doesn't take into account situational effects; leaders in one situation may not be leaders in another situation. The list of the most important leadership traits is highly subjective, as is the experience and observations that serve as the basis for the identified leadership traits. Also, because it is assumed that effective leadership traits are inherent to an individual, as opposed to something that is acquired, it is not useful for training and development.

The following traits seem to have the strongest relationship to effective management:

- **Intelligence**: Helps leaders solve complex problems.
- **Task-relevant knowledge**: Ensures that a leader knows what has to be done, how it should be done, and what resources are required for a group and organization to achieve its goals.
- **Dominance**: Helps a leader channel followers' efforts and abilities towards achieving group and organizational goals.
- **Self-confidence**: Helps a leader influence followers and motivate followers to persevere in the face of obstacles or difficulties.
- **High energy/activity levels**: Helps a leader deal with the many demands or activities encountered day to day.
- **Tolerance for stress**: Promotes a leader's ability to deal with the uncertainty or ambiguity inherent in any complex decision-making situation.
- **Integrity and honesty**: Indicates that a leader will behave ethically at all times and is worthy of followers' trust and confidence.

- **Emotional maturity:** Shows that a leader is not overly self-centered and can control his or her feelings as well as accept constructive criticism.

THE LEADER BEHAVIOR APPROACH

Rather than just looking at the personal traits of leaders, a group of researchers, including Carroll Shartle, John Hemphill, and Ralph Stogdill, began to focus on what leaders actually do. That is, they focused on the **specific behaviors** performed by effective leaders. Rather than focusing on the styles or traits of successful leaders, they studied leader behaviors when interacting with followers.

These researchers at The Ohio State University pioneered the leader behavior approach, arguing that one of the main ways in which leaders influence followers is through their personal, day-to-day decisions and behaviors. The behavior approach seeks to identify which leader behaviors help employees, groups, and organizations achieve their goals. Of all the studies, the Leader Behavior Approach is the most comprehensive and replicated behavioral theories which resulted from the Ohio State studies in the late 1940s. Seeking to identify independent dimensions of leader behavior, their research began with more than 1,000 dimensions. Throughout their research, the studies narrowed the list to two that substantially accounted for most of the leadership behavior described by employees. Researchers called these initiating structure and consideration.

Initiating structure is the extent to which a leader is likely to define and structure his or her role and those of his or her employees in the search for goal attainment. It includes behavior that attempts to organize work, work relationships, and goals. A leader who is high in initiating structure is someone who assigns group members to particular tasks, expects workers to maintain definite standards of performance, and emphasizes the meeting of deadlines.

Consideration is the extent to which a person's job relationships are characterized by mutual trust, respect for employees' ideas, and regard for their feelings. A leader high in consideration helps employees with personal problems, is friendly and approachable, treats all employees as equals, and expresses appreciation and support.

Note that consideration and initiating structure are complementary, though independent, leader behaviors. They are complementary because leaders can engage in both types of behaviors. They are independent because knowing the extent to which a leader engages in consideration says nothing about the extent to which they engage in initiating structure, and vice versa.

Leadership studies at the University of Michigan's Survey Research Center had similar objectives: to locate the behavioral characteristics of leaders that appeared related to performance effectiveness. Led by Rensis Likert, the Michigan research group also came up with two behavioral dimensions. The **employee-oriented leader** emphasized interpersonal relationships by taking a personal interest in the needs of employees and accepting individual differences among them. **Production-oriented leaders** emphasized the technical or task aspects of the job, focusing concerns on the accomplishment of the group's tasks. These dimensions are closely related to the Ohio State dimensions. Employee-oriented leadership is similar to consideration, and production-oriented leadership is similar to initiating structure.

Leaders who have certain traits and who display consideration and structuring behaviors do appear to be more effective. However, as important as traits and behaviors are in identifying effective or ineffective leaders, they do not guarantee success. The context matters as well.

THE SKILLS APPROACH

The focus of the skills approach is primarily descriptive in that it describes leadership from a skills perspective and provides a structure for understanding the nature of effective leadership. Developed by Katz, the Leadership

Skills Approach suggests that the importance of particular leadership skills varies depending on where leaders reside in the management hierarchy. Katz proposed that the three different abilities a manager should posses are technical ability, human relational skills, and conceptual skills. Human skill was defined as the ability to work with different people. Conceptual skill was defined as the ability to with ideas and concepts. Moreover, the level of importance of each skill varies in direct correlation to the persons' responsibility.

In 2000, Mumford and his colleagues developed a capability Skills Approach Model, figure 10.3. Examining the relationships

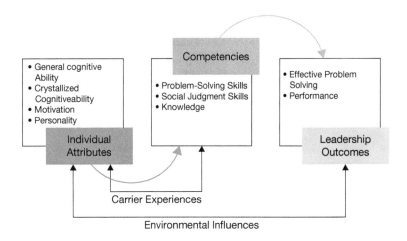

Figure 10.3. Mumford's Skills Approach Model

between a leader's knowledge, skill, and performance, the model proposes that skill make effective leadership possible. Mumford et al. suggest that leadership outcomes are a direct result of a leader's skilled competency in problem solving, social judgment, and knowledge. The Capability Model has five components: individual attributes, competencies, leadership outcomes, career experience, and environmental influences.

One of the strengths of this approach is that it is the first approach to conceptualize and create a structure of the process of leadership around skills and, by doing so, makes leadership available to everyone. It also provides an expansive view of leadership that incorporates a wide variety of components (e.g., problem-solving skills and social judgment skills) and provides a structure consistent with leadership education programs (Figure 10.3).

However, one shortcoming of this approach is that the breadth of the skills approach appears to extend beyond the boundaries of leadership, making it more general, less precise. It is also weak in predictive value in that it does not explain how skills lead to effective leadership performance.

FIEDLER'S CONTINGENCY THEORY

Similar to the trait approach, **Fiedler's theory** acknowledges that personal characteristics influence the effectiveness of leaders, and he was particularly interested in styles of leadership, or how a person approaches the task of leadership. Fiedler identified two distinct leadership styles: **relationship-oriented** and **task-oriented** styles, and proposed that one style or the other may characterize leaders.

Fiedler believes a key factor in leadership success is the individual's basic leadership style. He created the **least preferred co-worker (LPC) questionnaire** to identify that style by measuring whether a person is task or relationship oriented. The LPC questionnaire asks respondents to think of all the co-workers they have ever had and describe the one person they least enjoyed working with by rating that person on a scale of 1 to 8 for each of 16 sets of contrasting adjectives (such as pleasant/unpleasant, efficient/inefficient, open/guarded, supportive/hostile). If you describe the person you are least able to work with in favorable terms (a high LPC score), Fiedler would label you *relationship oriented*. In contrast, if you see your least preferred co-worker in relatively unfavorable terms (a low LPC score), you are primarily interested in productivity and are *task oriented*.

Fiedler assumes an individual's leadership style is fixed. This means that if a situation requires a task-oriented leader and the person in the leadership position is relationship oriented, either the situation has to be modified or the leader has to be replaced to achieve optimal effectiveness.

ASSESSING THE SITUATION

After assessing an individual's basic leadership style through the LPC questionnaire, we match the leader with the situation. Fiedler has identified three contingency or situational dimensions:

1. **Leader–member relations:** When the relationship between the leader and his or her followers is good, followers appreciate, trust, and feel a certain degree of loyalty toward their leader, and the situation is favorable for leading. When this relationship is poor, followers dislike or distrust their leader and the situation is unfavorable for leading.
2. **Task structure:** This is the degree to which the job assignments are clearly defined and understood. When a group has specific goals that need to be accomplished and every group member knows how to go about achieving these goals, task structure is high. When group goals are vague or uncertain and members are unsure about how to perform the tasks need to achieve these goals, task structure is low—the higher the task structure, the more favorable the leadership position.
3. **Position power:** Position power is the degree of influence a leader has over power variables such as hiring, firing, discipline, promotions, and salary increases. If a leader has the power to reward and punish subordinates by granting them pay raises and bonuses or docking their pay, the position power is high. If a leader can do little to reward or punish subordinates, then the position power is low. A situation is more favorable for leading when position power is high.

The next step is to evaluate the situation in terms of these three variables. Fiedler states that the better the leader–member relations, the more highly structured the job, and the stronger the position power, the more control the leader has.

MATCHING THE LEADER TO THE SITUATION

Combining the three contingency dimensions yields eight possible situations in which leaders can find themselves. The Fiedler model proposes matching an individual's LPC score and these eight situations to achieve maximum

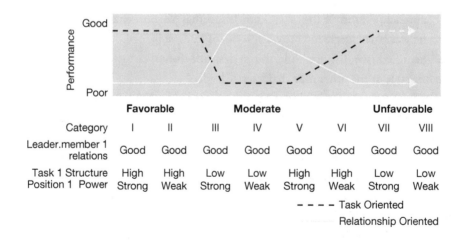

Figure 10.4. Favorable Situations for Leading

leadership effectiveness. Fiedler concluded that task-oriented leaders perform better in situations very favorable to them or very unfavorable. So, when faced with a category I, II, III, VII, or VIII situation, task-oriented leaders perform better. Relationship-oriented leaders perform better in moderately favorable situations, such as categories IV, V, and VI (see Figure 10.4).

Fiedler has since simplified these eight situations down to three. He now says task-oriented leaders perform best in situations of **high** and **low control**, while relationship-oriented leaders perform best in **moderate control** situations.

APPLYING FIEDLER'S FINDINGS

Using Fiedler's approach, you would match leaders in terms of their LPC scores with the type of situation, based on leader–member relationships, task structure, and position power, for which they are best suited.

However, remember that Fiedler views an individual's leadership style as fixed; hence, there are only two ways to improve leader effectiveness:

1. *Change the leader to fit the situation:* If a group situation rates highly unfavorable but is currently led by a relationship-oriented manager, the group's performance could be improved under a manager who is task oriented.
2. *Change the situation to fit the leader:* Restructure tasks or increase or decrease the leader's power to control factors such as salary increases, promotions, and disciplinary actions.

THE PATH-GOAL THEORY

Robert House, a respected researcher on leadership, realized that much of what leaders try to do in organizations involves motivating their followers. House's **path-goal theory** describes how leaders can motivate their followers to achieve group and organizational goals, and the kinds of behaviors they can engage in to accomplish that.

The path-goal theory maintains that it is the leader's job to help subordinates reach their goals by directing, guiding, and coaching them along the way. Leaders must evaluate task and subordinate characteristics and adapt their leadership style to fit those characteristics. The theory suggests which style is most appropriate for specific characteristics, and leaders should choose a leadership style that best fits the needs of subordinates and their work. Path-goal theory provides a set of assumptions about how different leadership styles will interact with subordinate characteristics and the work situation to affect employee motivation. Path-goal theory is complex, but also pragmatic in its approach.

One of the strengths of this theory is that it is a useful theoretical framework for understanding how various leadership behaviors affect the satisfaction of subordinates and their work performance. It also attempts to integrate the motivation principles of expectancy theory into a theory of leadership. Path-goal theory provides a practical model that underscores and highlights the important ways in which leaders help subordinates.

Path-goal theory suggests that effective leaders follow three guidelines to motivate their followers. The guidelines are based on the expectancy theory of motivation. Effective leaders who follow these guidelines have highly motivated subordinates who are likely to meet their work goals and perform at high levels:

1. *Determine what outcomes subordinates are trying to obtain in the workplace*: Identify what needs they are trying to satisfy, or what goals they are trying to meet. After gaining this information, the leader must have control over those outcomes or over the ability to give or withhold the outcomes from the subordinate.

2. *Reward subordinates for performing at high levels or achieving their work goals by giving them desired outcomes*: When subordinates meet these goals they will be performing at a high level—make certain that the desired outcomes are such that motivate goal attainment.

3. *Make sure the subordinates believe they can obtain their work goals and perform at high levels*: Leaders can do this by showing subordinates the paths to goal attainment (hence, path-goal), by removing any obstacles that might come up along the way, and by expressing confidence in their subordinates' capabilities.

House identified four types of behaviors that leaders can engage in to motivate subordinates:

1. **Directive behavior**: Similar to initiating structure, it lets subordinates know what tasks need to be performed and how they should be performed.

2. **Supportive behavior**: Similar to consideration, it lets subordinates know their leader cares about their well-being and is looking out for them.

3. **Participative behavior**: Enables subordinates to be involved in making decisions that affect them.

4. **Achievement-oriented behavior**: Pushes subordinates to do their best. Such behavior includes setting difficult goals for followers, expecting high performance, and expressing confidence in their capabilities.

The path-goal theory enhances our understanding of effective leadership in organizations by specifying how leaders should motivate their followers. Motivation is one of the key determinants of performance in an organization, and the ability to motivate followers is a crucial aspect of a leader's effectiveness.

THE LMX THEORY

The **Leader–Member Exchange (LMX) theory** works in two ways: it describes leadership and it prescribes leadership. The central concept is the dyadic relationship between leaders and their subordinates. It suggests that it is important to recognize the existence of ingroups and outgroups within an organization. There are significant differences in how goals are accomplished using ingroups versus outgroups, and relevant differences in ingroup versus outgroup behaviors.

The theory is best understood within the Leadership Making Model. In this model, leaders should form special relationships with all subordinates, offer each subordinate an opportunity for new roles and responsibilities, and

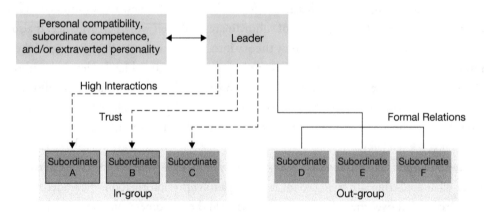

Figure 10.5. LMX Leadership Model

nurture high-quality exchanges with all subordinates. Rather than concentrating on differences, leaders focus on ways to build trust and respect with all subordinates, resulting in the entire work group becoming an ingroup (Figure 10.5).

The strength of LMX theory is that it validates our experience of how people within organizations relate to each other and to their leader. It also is the only leadership approach that makes the dyadic relationship the centerpiece of the leadership process. LMX theory directs our attention to the importance of communication in leadership and has a solid research foundation on how the practice of LMX theory is related to positive organizational outcomes.

However, critics of this approach argue that it inadvertently supports the development of privileged groups in the workplace and appears unfair and discriminatory. Also, the basic theoretical ideas of LMX are not fully developed and not enough is known about creating high-quality leader–member exchanges, nor the means to achieve building trust, respect, and obligation. Also, because of various scales and levels of analysis, the precise measurement of leader–member exchanges is questionable.

THE STYLE APPROACH

Developed by Blake and Mouton, the Managerial Grid is a popular framework for classifying a leaders' take versus person focus. The focus of the style approach is to provide a framework for assessing leadership in a broad way, as behavior with a task and relationship dimension. It offers a means of assessing in a general way the behaviors of leaders. The style approach marked a major shift in leadership research from being exclusively trait focused to including the behaviors and actions of leaders. At the conceptual level, a leader's style is composed of two major types of behaviors: task and relationship.

One of the strengths of this approach is the broad range of studies on leadership style that validates and gives credibility to the basic tenets of the approach. Also, the style approach is heuristic and leaders can learn a lot about themselves and how they come across to others by trying to see their behaviors in light of the task and relationship dimensions.

The model is built upon two behavioral dimensions – concern for people and concern for tasks. Concern for people is the degree to which a manager is person-centered. How much he or she considers the needs of their employees. Concern for tasks, also known as concern for results, is the degree to which a manager is task-centered. How much he or she emphasizes productivity.

The Impoverished manager does emphasize results or accomplishing tasks. Additionally, the Impoverished manager does not take the time to create a team atmosphere to a work environment that is motivating. Results can include disorganization and disharmony.

The Country Club manager is overly concerned with the feelings and emotions of employees but neglects production matters. The workplace is fun and relaxed but there is a lack of direction and control.

The Authority-Compliance manager believes that employees' needs are secondary to production. Generally autocratic, these managers have strict rules and regulations. They rely on layers of processes and procedures and often view punishment and an effective way to motivate their team.

The Middle-of-the-Road manager is able to create a balance between the concern for production and people. This may appear to be an ideal compromise; however, it is common that these leaders settle for average production and average performance.

The Team manger has a high concern for people and a high concern for production. According to Blake and Mouton, this is the effective managerial / leadership style (Figure 10.6)

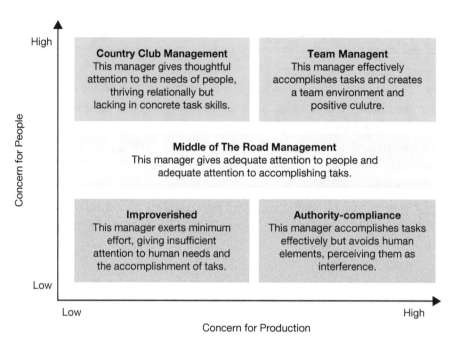

Figure 10.6. Blake and Moutons' Managerial Grid

Robert R. Blake and Anne A. McCanse, Leadership Dilemmas-Grid Solutions, pp. 29. Copyright © 1991 by Taylor & Francis Group (UK).

The Managerial Grid was later republished, by Blake and Adams, as the Leadership Grid. However, research has not adequately demonstrated how leaders' styles are associated with performance outcomes. Also, there is no universal style of leadership that could be effective in every situation. It also implies that the most effective leadership style is a high task and a high relationship combination, but research to support this finding is limited.

THE SITUATIONAL LEADERSHIP APPROACH

Developed by Hersey and Blanchard, the focus of this approach is centered on the idea that subordinates vacillate along the developmental continuum of competence and commitment, and therefore leader effectiveness depends upon assessing subordinates' developmental position and adapting leadership style to match the subordinate developmental level. The situational leadership approach, figure 10.7, requires leaders to demonstrate a strong degree of flexibility.

One of the strengths of this approach is that it is perceived as providing a credible model for training employees to become effective leaders. It is a straightforward approach that is easily understood and applied in a variety of settings. It also clearly outlines what you should and should not do in various settings. Situational leadership stresses that effective leaders are those who can change their style based on task requirements and subordinate needs and the premise that leaders need to treat each subordinate according to his/her unique needs.

The foundational premise of the Hersey and Blanchard theory is that there is no 'best' style of leadership. The leaders' style is dictated by the individual or groups' maturity. Built with four quadrants, the S1 Telling style is characterized by one-way communication from the leader. In the Telling style, the leader provides information on who, how, why and when. In the S2 Selling style, the leader still provides direction. However, there is two-way

Directive Behavior			
DIRECTING	COACHING	SUPPORTING	DELEGATING
S1- Defining Planning/ Prioritizing, Orienting, Teaching/showing and telling how, Checking/ monitoring, Giving feedback	S2- Exploring/asking, Explaining/clarifying, Redirecting, Sharing feedback, Encouraging, Praising	S3- Asking/listening, Reassuring, Facilitating self-reliant problem solving, Collaborating, encouraging feedback, Appreciating	S4- Allowing/trusting, Confirming, Empowering, Affirming, Acknowledging, Challenging
Characteristics:	Characteristics:	Characteristics:	Characteristics:
High Directive and Low Supportive Behavior	High Directive and High Supportive Behavior	Low Directive and High Supportive Behavior	Low Directive and Low Supportive Behavior
Development of Individual			
D1	D2	D3	D4
Low Competence	Low to some Competence	Moderate to High Competence	High Competence
High Commitment	Low Commitment	Variable Commitment	High Commitment

Figure 10.7. Hersey and Blanchard's Situational Leadership
Source. Adapted from Blanchard (1985).

communication occurring with the leader providing support, encouragement and influencing the employee to buy into the process or task. The S3 Participating style has a shared decision-making model between the leader and the employee. In this style, the leader provides less information on the process or task but maintains a high relationship focus. The S4 Delegating style has limited leader involvement. The leader does not provide input on how to accomplish processes or tasks, but instead passes those responsibilities to the employees. The leaders involvement generally revolves around monitoring and evaluating.

However, the lack of an empirical foundation raises theoretical considerations regarding the validity of the approach. Additional research is required to determine how commitment and competence are conceptualized for each developmental level, as the conceptualization of commitment itself is very unclear. Also, studies fail to support basic prescriptions of situational leadership model. It does not account for how particular demographics influence the leader-subordinate prescriptions of the model and fails to adequately address the issue of one-to-one versus group leadership in an organizational setting.

THE CHARISMATIC APPROACH

Charisma is defined as a certain quality of an individual personality by virtue of which he or she is set apart from ordinary people and treated as endowed with supernatural, superhuman, or at least specifically exceptional powers or qualities. These are not accessible to the ordinary person and are regarded as of divine origin or as exemplary, and on the basis of them the individual concerned is treated as a leader.

The first researcher to consider charismatic leadership in terms of organizational behavior was Robert House. According to House's **charismatic leadership theory**, followers attribute heroic or extraordinary leadership abilities when they observe certain behaviors.

A number of studies have attempted to identify the characteristics of a charismatic leader:

- **Vision and articulation:** The leader has a vision and expresses it as an idealized goal that proposes a future better than the status quo, and is able to emphasize the importance of the vision in terms that are understandable to others.
- **Personal risk:** Willing to take on high personal risk, incur high costs, and engage in self-sacrifice to achieve the vision.
- **Sensitivity to follower needs:** Perceptive of others' abilities and responsive to their needs and feelings.
- **Unconventional behavior:** Engages in behaviors that are perceived as novel and counter to norms.

How do charismatic leaders actually influence followers? Research has shown that it is a four-step process. It begins with articulating an appealing vision and a long-term strategy for attaining a goal by linking the present with a better future for the organization.

Second, a vision statement is required to formally articulate for the organization the overarching goals and purpose. They then communicate high performance expectations and express confidence that followers can attain them. This enhances follower self-esteem and self-confidence.

Third, the leader conveys a new set of values and sets an example for followers to imitate. Charismatic leaders also set a tone of cooperation and mutual support.

Finally, the charismatic leader engages in emotion-inducing and often unconventional behavior, to demonstrate courage and conviction about the vision. Followers "catch" the emotions their leader is conveying.

TRANSFORMATIONAL LEADERSHIP

Leadership researcher Bernard Bass proposed a theory that suggests how leaders can sometimes dramatically affect and change the behaviors of their followers and organizations, and literally transform them in ways that lead to dramatic increases in performance. According to Bass, **transformational leadership** occurs when a leader transforms, or changes, his or her followers in three important ways that together result in followers trusting the leader, performing behavior that contributes to the achievement of organizational goals, and being motivated to perform at high levels (Figure 10.8).

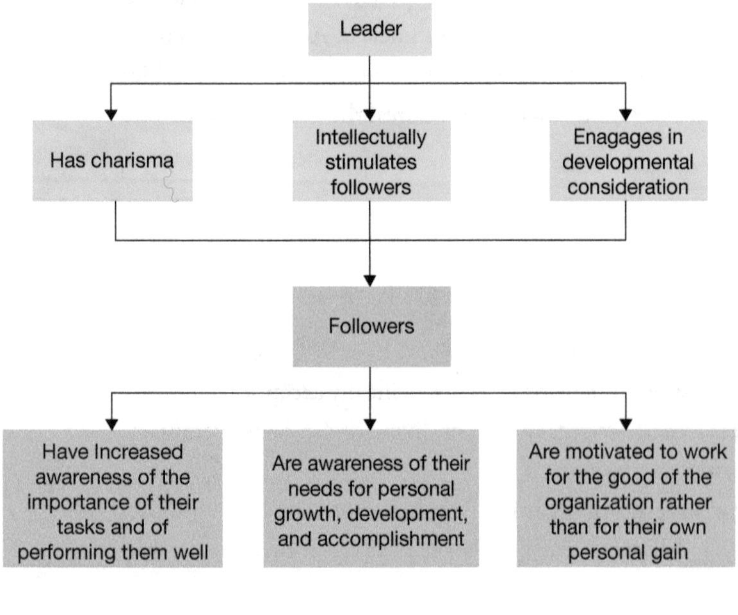

1. Transformational leaders increase subordinates' awareness of the importance of their tasks and the importance of performing them well.

2. Transformational leaders make subordinates aware of their needs for personal growth, development, and accomplishment.

3. Transformational leaders motivate their subordinates to work for the good of the organization rather than exclusively for their own personal gain or benefit.

Transformational leadership has been widely researched, including a large body of qualitative research centering on prominent leaders and CEOs in major firms. People are attracted to transformational leadership because it makes

Figure 10.8. Transformational Leadership

sense to them and treats leadership as a process occurring between followers and leaders. It provides a broader view of leadership that augments other leadership models and emphasizes followers' needs, values, and morals. Research supports that transformational leadership is an effective form of leadership.

However, critics argue that it lacks conceptual clarity in that the dimensions are not clearly defined and the parameters of transformational leadership overlap with similar conceptualizations of leadership, as some transformational factors are not unique solely to the transformational model.

Also, transformational leadership treats leadership more as a personality trait or a predisposition than a behavior that can be taught. Some say it is elitist and antidemocratic, suffers from heroic leadership bias, and has the potential for abuse. Furthermore, research on transformational leadership is based primarily on qualitative data and the measurement of transformational leadership has been questioned.

AUTHENTIC LEADERSHIP

Authentic leaders know who they are, know what they believe in and value, and act on those values and beliefs openly and candidly. Followers of authentic leaders consider them to be ethical, trustworthy, and open. The primary quality produced by authentic leadership therefore is trust. Authentic leaders share information, encourage open communication, and stick to their ideals. As a result, followers have faith in their leadership.

Because the concept of authentic leadership is relatively new, there has been little research on it. However, it is a promising way to think about ethics and trust in leadership because it focuses on the moral aspects of being a leader. Transformational or charismatic leaders can have a vision and communicate it persuasively, but sometimes the vision is wrong (Hitler), or the leader is more concerned with his or her own needs or pleasures (Kozlowski, Tyco, Skilling, and Enron).

THE ETHICAL LEADERSHIP APPROACH

This approach is concerned with the kinds of values and morals an individual or society ascribes as desirable or appropriate, and focuses on the virtuousness of individuals and their motives. Ethical leaders treat other people's values and decisions with respect, allow others to be themselves with creative wants and desires, approach others with a sense of unconditional worth, and value individual differences.

The issue of establishing trust between leaders and subordinates is a central concept in ethical leadership. Trust is the willingness of one person or group to have faith or confidence in the goodwill of another person, even though this puts them at risk because the other person might act in a deceitful way. Trust is also vital to establish good working relationships in groups and teams, so that process gains can be achieved only if team members believe other team members will also behave in ethical ways. When ethical leadership helps to establish trust, all parties' work toward a common goal and the performance can improve.

This approach provides a body of timely research on ethical issues and provides direction on how to think about ethical leadership and how to practice it. It also suggests that leadership is not an amoral phenomenon and that ethics should be considered as integral to the broader domain of leadership. Furthermore, it highlights principles and virtues that are important in ethical leadership development.

However, the theory lacks a strong body of traditional research to substantiate the theoretical foundation. It also relies heavily on the writings of just a few individuals that are primarily descriptive and anecdotal in nature, and are strongly influenced by personal opinion and a particular worldview.

SUMMARY OF CHAPTER

1. There are a variety of approaches to leadership, and no one theory or model can describe all of the elements essential to effective leadership behavior. Each approach has its strengths and limitations, and some theories have stronger research to support their assumptions than others.

2. Leadership is a multifaceted concept and leadership theory continues to evolve as new understandings of the phenomena are discovered.

3. Leadership is the exercise of influence by one member of a group or organization over other members to help the group or organization achieve its goals. Formal leaders have formal authority to influence others by virtue of their job responsibilities. Informal leaders lack formal authority but influence others by virtue of their special skills or talents.

4. The trait approach to leadership has found that good leaders tend to be intelligent, dominant, self-confident, energetic, able to withstand stress, honest, mature, and knowledgeable. Possessing these traits does not guarantee that a leader will be effective, nor does the failure to have one or more of these traits mean that the leader will be ineffective.

5. Fiedler's contingency theory proposes that leader effectiveness depends on both leadership style and situational characteristics. Leaders have either a relationship-oriented style or a task-oriented style. Situational characteristics, including leader-member relations, task structure, and position power, determine how favorable a situation is for leading.

6. Path-goal theory suggests that effective leaders motivate their followers by giving them outcomes they desire when they perform at a high level or achieve their work goals.

7. Leader–member exchange theory focuses on the leader–follower dyad and suggests that leaders do not treat each of their followers the same, but rather develop different kinds of relationships with different subordinates. Some leader–follower dyads have high-quality relationships. Subordinates in these dyads are members of the ingroup. Other leader–follower dyads have low-quality relationships. Subordinates in these dyads form the outgroup.

8. It is important for leaders to assess themselves, their followers, and the dynamics of each situation to have a better understanding of what is best in order to achieve organizational purposes. As the complexity of the world and work environments increases, the need for effective leadership grows exponentially.

9. Transformational leaders increase their followers' awareness of the importance of their jobs and the followers' own needs for personal growth and accomplishment, and motivate followers to work for the good of the organization.

10. Leaders transform their followers by being charismatic, intellectually stimulating their followers, and engaging in developmental consideration.

DISCUSSION QUESTIONS

1. Are Fiedler's contingency model and the trait approaches consistent with one another, or inconsistent? Explain.

2. Can organizations create substitutes for leadership to cut down on the number of managers they need to employ? Why or why not?

3. When might having a charismatic leader be dysfunctional for an organization?

4. Do organizations always need transformational leaders, or are they needed only some of the time?

DO I LEAD ETHICALLY?

INSTRUCTIONS

Indicate how likely you are to do each statement, when in a leadership position. Use the following scale:
1: Highly unlikely | 2: Unlikely | 3: More unlikely than likely | 4: Neutral | 5: More likely than not | 6: Likely | 7: Highly likely

1. I will be an example of ethical work for others.
2. My personal life will be conducted in the same ethical manner as my professional life.
3. I will try not to be selfish in my goals.
4. I will be trustworthy.
5. I will speak up when I know something is not following ethical standards.
6. I will make decisions that are best and equal for all.
7. I will consider the "right thing to do" when making decisions.
8. I will listen to what others have to say.
9. I will not only hold myself to high ethical standards, but will do the same with others.
10. I will place an importance on both the output of work and how they got there.

SCORING KEY:

Add up your scores from all questions.

ANALYSIS:

Ethical leaders lead with respect for the values and morals of others and they allow people to express their differences. Trust is an important aspect of the relationships between an ethical leader and their subordinates. There are no ranges of being an ethical leader, as it is on a continuum. However, the higher your score, the more ethical a leader you are. Typically, ethical leaders are sought by companies as they are perceived to be better and their follows will want to act in the same ways they do. The good news is that if you scored low, you can improve how ethically you lead others.

Adapted from: Robbins, S. P. (2009). IV.E.4: Am I an ethical leader? Self-assessment library (122-123). Upper Saddle River, NJ: Pearson Education Inc.

Original Source: Brown. M.E, Trevino, L. K. & Harrison, D. A. (2005). Ethical leadership: A social learning perspective for construct development and testing, Organizational Behavior and Human Decisions Processes, 97. p. 117-134.

CHAPTER 10 REFERENCES

Bass, B. M. (1985). *Leadership and performance beyond expectations.* New York: Free Press.

Blanchard, K. (1985). *Leadership and the one minute manager: Increasing effectiveness through situational leadership.* New York: William Morrow.

Blake, R., & Mouton, J. (1964). The managerial grid: The key to leadership excellence. Houston, TX: Gulf Publishing Co.

Blake, R.; Mouton, J. (1985). The Managerial Grid III: The Key to Leadership Excellence. Houston: Gulf Publishing Co.

Blake, R., R., McCanse, A., A. (1991). The Leadership Grid® figure from Leadership Dilemmas – Grid Solutions by Robert R. Blake and Anne Adams McCanse (Formerly the Managerial Grid by Robert R. Blake and Jane S. Mouton). Houston: Gulf Publishing Company, Grid International, Inc.

Bowers, D. G., Seashore, S. E. (1966). Predicting Organizational Effectiveness With a Four-Factor Theory of Leadership, *Administrative Science Quarterly, 11*(2), 238–263.

Conger, J. A., & Kanungo, R. N. (1988). Behavioral dimensions of charismatic leadership. In J. A. Conger, R. N. Kanungo, & associates (Eds.), *Charismatic leadership.* San Francisco: Jossey Bass.

Dvir, T., Eden, E., Avolio, B., & Shamir, B. (2002). Impact of transformational leadership on follower development and performance: A field experiment. *Academy of Management Journal, 45*(4), 735–745.

Fiedler, F. E. (1967). *A theory of leadership effectiveness.* New York: McGraw-Hill.

Fiedler, F. E. (1978). The contingency model and the dynamics of the leadership process. In L. Berkowitz (Ed.), *Advances in experimental social psychology.* New York: Academic Press.

Fleishman, E. A. (1953). The description of supervisory behavior. *Personal Psychology, 37*(1), 1–6.

Fleishman, E. A. (1967). Performance assessment based on an empirically derived task taxonomy. *Human Factors, 9*(4), 349–366.

Gardner, W. L., & Avolio, B. J. (1998). The charismatic relationship: A dramaturgical perspective. *Academy of Management Journal, 23*(1), 32–58.

Halpin, A. W., & Winer, B. J. (1957). A factorial study of the leader behavior descriptions. In R. M. Stogdill & A. E. Coons (Eds.), *Leader behavior: Its descriptions and measurements.* Columbus, OH: Bureau of Business Research, Ohio State University.

Hersey, P. (1985). *The situational leader.* New York, NY: Warner Books.

Hersey, P. and Blanchard, K. H. (1969). "Life cycle theory of leadership". *Training and Development Journal, 23*(5): 26–34.

Hersey, P. and Blanchard, K. H. (1969). *Management of Organizational Behavior – Utilizing Human Resources*. Englewood Cliffs, New Jersey: Prentice Hall.

Hersey, P. and Blanchard, K. H. (1977). *Management of Organizational Behavior 3rd Edition– Utilizing Human Resources*. Englewood Cliffs, New Jersey: Prentice Hall.

Hersey, P., & Blanchard, K. (1982). *Management of organizational behavior: Utilizing human resources.* Upper Saddle River, NJ: Prentice Hall.

Hemphill, J. K. (1050). *Leader Behavior Description*. Columbus, Ohio: Ohio State University Press.

House, Robert J. (1996). "Path-goal theory of leadership: Lessons, legacy, and a reformulated theory." *Leadership Quarterly, 7(3), 323–352.*

Jung, D. I., & Avolio, B. J. (1999). Effects of leadership style and follower's cultural orientation on performance in group and individual task conditions. *Academy of Management Journal, 42*(2), 208–219.

Jung, D. I., & Avolio, B. J. (2000). Opening the black box: An experimental investigation of the mediating effects of trust and value congruence on transformational and transactional leadership. *Journal of Organizational Behavior, 21*(8), 949–964.

Katz, R. L. (1955). Skills of an effective administrator. *Harvard Business Review*, 33(1), 33–42.

Likert, R. (1958). Effective Supervision: An Adaptive and Relative Process, *Personnel Psychology*, 11(3), 317–332.

Mumford, M. D., & Connelly, M. S. (1991). Leaders as creators: Leader performance and problem solving in ill-defined domains. *Leadership Quarterly, 2*(4), 289–315.

Mumford, M. D., Zaccaro, S. J., Connelly, M. S., & Marks, M. A. (2000). Leadership skills: Conclusions and future directions. *Leadership Quarterly, 11*(1), 155–170.

Kotter, J. P. (1988). The Leadership Factor. New York: Free Press.

Kotter, J. P. (1985). Power and Influence. New York: Free Press.

Northouse, P. (2013). *Leadership: Theory and Practice* (6th ed.). Thousand Oaks, CA: Sage Publications.

Stogdill, R. M. (1950). Leadership, membership and organization. *Psychological Bulletin*, 47(1), 1–14.

Stogdill, R. M. (1963). Manual for the Leader Behavior Description Questionnaire, Form XII.

Columbus, OH: Bureau of Business Research, Ohio State University.

Stogdill, R. M., & Shartle, C. L. (1956). Methods in the study of administrative leadership (Research Monograph No. 80). Columbus, OH: Bureau of Business Research.

Waldman, D. A. (1999). CEO charismatic leadership: Level of management and levels of analysis effects. *Academy of Management Journal, 24*(2), 266–285.

Waldman, D. A., Ramirez, G. G., House, R. J., & Puranam, P. (2001). Does leadership matter? CEO leadership attributes and profitability under conditions of perceived environmental uncertainty. *Academy of Management Journal, 44*(1), 134–144.

Wofford, J. C., & Liska, L. Z. (1993). Path-goal theories of leadership: A meta-analysis. *Journal of Management, 19*(4), 857–876.

Vroom, V. H., & Yetton, P. W. (1973). *Leadership and decision-making.* Pittsburgh, PA: University of Pittsburgh Press.

Yuki, G. (1989). Managerial leadership: A review of theory and research. *Journal of Management, 15*(2), 251–289.

INNOVATION, CHANGE, AND CONFLICT

11

CHAPTER LEARNING OBJECTIVES

After reading this chapter, you should have a good understanding of
- the definition of innovation and creativity and why they're critical to business today;
- the similarities and differences between organizational development and organizational change;
- the relative importance of change and stability to an organization and what kinds of changes should be made within an organization;
- the importance of learning to fail;
- how to evaluate change and the importance of considering the effects of change on people within the organization;
- the importance of learning how to maximize change drivers and minimize change resisters; and
- how organizational change and stress is related and techniques to handle conflict as a factor of organizational change.

"The secret of change is to focus all of your energy, not on fighting the old, but on building the new."

- SOCRATES

THE IMPORTANCE OF INNOVATION

We begin this chapter with the definitions of organizational innovation and renewal. **Organizational innovation** is the implementation of a new organizational method in the undertaking's business practices, workplace organization, or external relations. A dynamic process, organizational innovation results in new processes, products, or services. **Innovation** is defined as changing or creating more effective processes, products, services, or ways of doing things. **Creativity** is the production of novel and useful ideas and is a form of organizational innovation. Often times, innovation and creativity lead to new inventions.

Competing in today's rapidly changing business environment, organizations must be able to successfully transform themselves to meet the demands of a global marketplace. The need for businesses to continually adapt to their environments forces an ongoing process of innovation and change. **Organizational renewal**, one such ongoing process, is characterized by a progression in which innovation and adaptation are important outcomes. The ultimate goal of organizational renewal is to prevent organizational entropy. Derived from physics, **organizational entropy** is the disorder, decay, or randomness that occurs when an organization is not properly maintained.

Without renewal organizations fail to change and adapt to their environment and often face failure. Without renewal management cannot maintain a competitive advantage and excellence in their products or services. However, before these terms became popular, many organizations engaged in systematic, planned change by applying the techniques of organizational development.

Organizational development, a philosophy of planned change and growth, encompasses a broad range of strategies and implementation techniques designed to improve efficiency and effectiveness. Generally, organizations that exercise organizational development also practice continuous improvement in tandem, as part of the strategies and implementation techniques. An ongoing and continuous effort, organizational development usually involves and results in improvement to products, services, or processes. Organizational development, as well as continuous improvement efforts, seeks incremental improvement over time and also leap forward improvements.

Two basic assumptions provide the foundation for organizational innovation, renewal, and development. First, employee motivation and engagement is key to organizational improvement. Second, employees are capable of contributing ideas, from improving productivity on the floor to improving product design or service offerings. Although these basic assumptions sound simple, change is difficult to lead and manage. Because employees are often asked to change their behaviors and work patterns, change can result in upheavals and dissatisfaction. Consequently, organizations are increasingly fine tuning their ability to manage change and acknowledging the importance of creating a culture that is flexible and adaptable. The second part of this chapter will deal with change, stress, conflict, and strategies to minimize resistance to change.

CREATING A CLIMATE OF INNOVATION AND CREATIVITY

The primary key for an innovative work environment is the creation of a climate that fosters innovation and creativity. It is impossible for companies to command their employees to be more creative; however, managers can assist innovation by building a creative work environment, one where workers realize that creative thoughts and ideas are not only welcomed but valued. Managing innovation is to manage where the ideas come from. A strong creative work environment has six components that encourage and drive creativity: challenging work, an organization that is encouraging, supervisors that are encouraging, work groups that are encouraging, freedom, and few organizational obstacles (Figure 11.1).

- **Challenging work**: Challenging work requires effort, demands attention and focus, and is recognized as important to others in the organization. A central element in creating a challenging work environment is to achieve a balance between skills and task challenge. Workers become bored when they can do more than what is required of them and apprehensive when their skills aren't sufficient to complete the task. When there is a balance between tasks and skills, creativity will occur.
- **Encouragement**: A creative work environment requires three types of encouragement: organizational, supervisory, and work group. **Organizational encouragement** occurs when management encourages employees to be risk takers who seek out new ideas, supports and evaluates new ideas from employees equally, rewards and recognizes creativity in employees, and supports and encourages the sharing of ideas throughout the entire organization. **Supervisory encouragement** supports innovation by providing clear goals, encouraging open interaction with other subordinates, and openly supporting the development

team's work and ideas. **Work group encouragement** occurs when group members have experiences, education, and backgrounds that are diverse. Innovation is further supported when the group fosters a mutual openness to ideas, maintains positive and constructive challenges to ideas, and all share a deep commitment to ideas.

- **Freedom**: Creativity thrives when management allows workers autonomy over their day-to-day work and control over their ideas.
- **Remove organizational obstacles**: To foster creativity, companies should remove impediments to the workers environment. Obstacles to creativity, such as internal conflict, power struggles, rigid management structures, and a conservative bias toward a status quo position, discourage creativity.

Figure 11.1. Creative Work Environments

Fig. 11.1: Kipley, D., Jewe, R., & Helm-Stevens, R., A Foundation in the Principles of Management, pp. 116. Copyright © 2015 by Cognella, Inc. Reprinted with permission.

GENERATING IDEAS

Brainstorming is the name given to a situation in which groups of people meet to generate new ideas and solutions around a specific area of interest through intensive and freewheeling group discussion. Using rules that remove inhibitions, participants are able to think more freely and move into new areas of thought, and as such create numerous new ideas and solutions. The participants shout out as many ideas as possible, no matter how outlandish they may seem. Participants then build on the ideas raised by others. All the ideas are recorded and are not criticized. Only when the brainstorming session is over are the ideas analyzed, discussed, and evaluated.

Electronic brainstorming is an alternative approach to brainstorming where the group members use computers to communicate and generate alternative solutions. This approach overcomes two major disadvantages associated with face-to-face brainstorming. First, electronic brainstorming overcomes **production blocking**, which occurs when you have an idea but have to wait to share it because someone else is already presenting an idea to the group. During these times of delay, the group member may forget their idea or decide that it really wasn't worth sharing. Production blocking is avoided in electronic brainstorming, as all members are at their computers and can type in their thoughts whenever they occur. The second disadvantage that electronic brainstorming overcomes is **evaluation apprehension**, or what everyone else may think of your idea. With electronic brainstorming, all ideas are anonymous. When you type in your idea and submit, group members only see the idea, not the member from whom it was submitted. Some software randomizes the submissions, adding an additional level of anonymity for the group member.

Studies have shown that in a 12-person group, electronic brainstorming produces 200% more ideas than that of traditional face-to-face brainstorming.

Nominal group technique is a more controlled version of brainstorming that encourages creative thinking. This method puts the power of voting to work while still giving individuals a chance to voice their own opinion. Each member of the group writes down his or her ideas, which are then discussed and prioritized by the group. It works by allowing each voter to use tally marks to place their first, second, and third choices. For decisions that must be made quickly and in a large group, this approach allows individuals to state their opinions without lengthy discussion. The nominal group technique is commonly used in market research studies or internal brainstorming sessions. The nominal group technique should be used when:

- some group members are much more vocal than others;
- some group members think better in silence;
- there is concern about some members not participating;
- the group does not easily generate quantities of ideas;
- all or some group members are new to the team; or
- the issue is controversial or there is heated conflict.

LEADING INNOVATION AND CREATIVITY

Managers help set the stage for innovation to foster among their employees. Yet, organizational development, innovation, and renewal has to start at the top – with the leaders. So how can leadership drive organizational improvement? Following are seven approaches that leaders can make use of to deliberately create an organizational climate for innovation and change.

1. *Create a climate for change* that embraces innovation.
2. *Be a champion* by modeling the attributes that it takes, individually and collectively, for the organization to focus on renewal and become more innovative.
3. *Communicate challenging strategic issues* clearly and with transparency throughout the organization.
4. *Form highly diverse teams* to address strategic issues, promote collaboration, and listen to different opinions.
5. *Support people and provide access* by empowering employees to partake in creative experiences and creative methods.
6. *Design and build systems* to nurture organizational development, innovation, and renewal. Provide organizational resources to build and test new processes or prototypes quickly so employees can learn from mistakes.
7. *Provide incentives and rewards* to high-contributing and high-performing employees and teams.

Yet, leaders and managers commonly face challenges in fostering innovation. Certainly, leaders must be mindful of the three major categories that create obstacles: mindset, skillset, and toolset. The many and most common pitfalls leaders must overcome when attempting to foster innovative thinking are outlined in Figure 11.2, Innovative Thinking.

LEARNING TO FAIL

Self-made billionaire and inventor of Spanx, Sara Blakely, credits failure as her secret to success. In a 2007 interview, Sara said that, as a kid, she was advised to fail and learn from those failures and that her father often asked

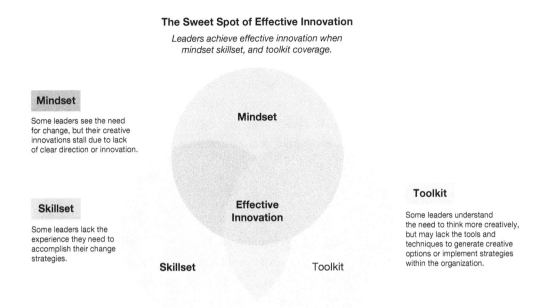

The Sweet Spot of Effective Innovation

Leaders achieve effective innovation when mindset skillset, and toolkit coverage.

Mindset

Some leaders see the need for change, but their creative innovations stall due to lack of clear direction or innovation.

Skillset

Some leaders lack the experience they need to accomplish their change strategies.

Toolkit

Some leaders understand the need to think more creatively, but may lack the tools and techniques to generate creative options or implement strategies within the organization.

Mindset

Effective Innovation

Skillset   **Toolkit**

Figure 11.2. Innovative Thinking

David Magellan Horth and Jonathan Vehar, Becoming a Leader Who Fosters Innovation, pp. 11. Copyright © 2014 by Center for Creative Leadership.

her and her siblings what failures they experienced. When Sara reported that she failed at something miserably, he would reward her with a high-five.

Sara's success inspired several interviews and articles, including titles like "If You're Not Failing, You're Not Growing." Successful failure requires the creation of a learning environment. Following are the top five strategies for creating a learning environment that fosters a climate of successful failure.

1. Set realistic expectations.
2. Keep failure in perspective.
3. Encourage responsibility for failure, not finger pointing or assigning blame.
4. Help employees see failure as temporary and to learn from failure.
5. Focus on strengths and try again.

DEFINING ORGANIZATIONAL CHANGE

Organizational change is simply the shift from its present state toward a desired state, in order to increase performance and/or effectiveness. This can involve virtually any organizational segment, but typically affects the lines of organizational authority, the levels of responsibility held by various organizational members, and the established lines of organizational communication. The

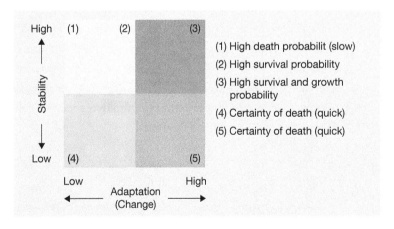

(1) High death probabilit (slow)
(2) High survival probability
(3) High survival and growth probability
(4) Certainty of death (quick)
(5) Certainty of death (quick)

Figure 11.3. Stability and Adaptation for Organizational Survival

Kipley, D., Jewe, R., & Helm-Stevens, R., "[image]: Stability/Adaptation Organizational Survival," A Foundation in the Principles of Management, pp. 118. Copyright © 2015 by Cognella, Inc. Reprinted with permission.

business environment is constantly dynamic and ever evolving—organizations must adapt to these changing events in order to survive.

In addition to organizational change, some degree of stability is required for an organization's long-term success. Figure 11.3 illustrates a model by Hellriegel and Slocum showing the relative importance of change and stability to organizational survival. The model stresses that organizational survival and growth are most probable when both stability and adaptation are high within the organization. The model also indicates that organizational survival is low when stability and adaptation to change are low.

DRIVERS OF CHANGE

Many environmental forces have an effect on the firm's performance. If managers are slow to respond to the effects of these forces, the organization's performance will degrade and will begin to lag behind its competition.

Competitive forces are a driver of change because unless the organization can match or exceed its competitors in at least one of its **functional areas**, it will not survive. Managers must continually work to achieve a competitive advantage over their rivals by performing their tasks in a more effective way.

Changing **economic, political, and global forces** affect organizations and compel them to adjust how and where they produce goods and provide services. No organization can afford to ignore the effects of the global economic and political forces on its interests. The effects of low-cost competitors and the development of new technologies erode a company's competitive advantage, forcing them to either take advantage of the low-cost inputs of labor and material from abroad or become uncompetitive.

Changing **demographic and social forces** have motivated managers to find better ways to supervise and motivate minority and female employees. Through both equity in recruitment and an affirmative promotion process, companies have had to change to accommodate the increasing diversity in the workplace. For example, companies have had to adapt to the changing needs of dual-career and single-parent families by providing employees with childcare facilities and allowing flextime work hours. Many companies have helped employees stay current with the changing technology by providing advanced education and training.

Ethical forces are driving companies to change their rules and SOPs, Standard Operating Procedures, to promote ethical behavior and to protect the interests and reputation of the organization and the people affected by unethical actions. Organizations are giving employees direct access to important decision makers and providing protection for whistle-blowers who expose ethical lapses in the organization. Additionally, firms must now consider how they are conducting business in a foreign country where bribery and sweatshops are common. Firms must take steps to impress on their employees that they should not engage in such kinds of behavior in order to protect the organization's interests.

RESISTANCE TO CHANGE

Mark Twain once said, "I'm all for progress. It's change I object to." In the last decade many of America's best-known companies, such as Chrysler, General Motors, Kodak, Circuit City, Blockbuster, and Dell, have seen their performance decline. Circuit City, Kodak, and Blockbuster have all gone bankrupt and Dell is in serious financial straits. How did such large and well-established firms (Kodak was established in 1888) lose their ability to compete in the global marketplace? The main explanation for their decline in performance is most always the inability of an organization to change with changing environmental conditions.

Logically, we understand that in order for a firm to grow and improve, the organization must adapt to changing environmental conditions. Hence, also logically, no organization can escape change. So, why do managers encounter resistance to change? Why do some levels resist more than others? How should managers use their power to influence change? These are questions that have challenged managers and will continue to challenge them for decades and decades to come.

People and organizations at all levels are prone to inertia, slow to learn, slow to adjust, and in general, do not like to change! The simple thought of change raises anxieties in people due to the fear of economic loss, inconvenience, uncertainty, and a break in normal social patterns.

Resistance to change is caused by self-interest, misunderstanding and distrust, and general intolerance for change. The amount of resistance is proportional to the degree of discontinuity in the culture and/or the power structure introduced by the change. As well, the resistance will be inversely proportional to the time that the change takes to occur (Ansoff, 1979).

Researchers have identified five common reasons why people are resistant to change:

1. **Organizational inertia** is the tendency to have the status quo remain in place. There are concerns that the company may be "throwing good money after bad decisions" despite negative performance feedback. Most often resistance is due to the lack of understanding of what is happening or why changes are taking place. Employees may simply need accurate information as to the reasons for the change.
2. There may exist **systemic barriers** to the organization's structure. An organizational structure that is highly bureaucratic, consisting of multiple layers, burdensome procedures, and rigid rules and requirements will create a "natural" barrier to change.
3. **Behavioral barriers** are those that are created by myopic managers and their inability to view issues or change unbiased. This barrier may be as a result of limited education, training, or work experience.
4. An outcropping of issue one is **political barriers**. Political barriers are those that arise from power conflicts such as vested interests, refusal to share information or resources, differences between departments or divisions, and even personal differences.
5. Gresham's law of planning states "that operational decisions will drive out the time necessary for strategic thinking and reflection." The fifth reason why people resist is **personal time constraints**, a barrier to change that stems from people not having the amount of time required for implementing strategic change.

REDUCING RESISTANCE TO CHANGE

To ensure the success of needed change, managers must be able to reduce the effects of the resistance that typically is associated with change. The following steps can improve the likelihood of a successful change implementation:

1. *Invite employee participation in the process of change*: Participation allows everyone to give opinions, to feel a part of the change process, and to identify their own self-interests regarding the recommended change. Most importantly, those individuals who will be affected by a change should be involved in the decision to make the change and in decisions about how to implement the change.
2. *Provide motivation and/or incentives to implement change*: Self-interest can be the most important motivator. Offer training and development workshops so that managers and employees can adapt to those changes.
3. *Communicate*: Effectively communicate the need for change. People can understand the purpose for the changes if the reasons are clearly stated and communicated.
4. *Provide a feedback loop*: Be transparent and open! Employees enjoy knowing how things are going and how much progress is being made.
5. *Avoid surprises*: Provide time for evaluation of the proposed change by those who will be affected by it, before management implements it. Employees will be less resistant to change if they have been given time

to absorb how the change will affect them. Whenever possible, individuals who will be affected by a change should be informed of the kind of change being considered and the likelihood that the intended change will be adopted.

6. *Reduce fear of the change*: When fear of personal loss related to a proposed change is reduced, opposition to change is also reduced. People should be given information that will help them answer questions such as:

- Will I lose my job?
- Will I be required to learn new skills?
- Am I capable of producing effectively under the new system?
- Will my power and prestige be diminished?
- Will I have to work longer or different hours?
- Will I take on greater responsibility than I can assume?

Organizations that simply react to change will find their performance lacking. Organizations must consider change as a continuous process, adapting to the shifts in their competitive environment rather than viewing change as a singular project or event. Therefore, managers must anticipate change and ideally be the creator of change.

An interesting phenomenon in resistance to change is the dilemma that the most successful and powerful managers and employees will most likely be key voices in resisting change. The more effective the manager or employee has been in the past, the less likely it is that he or she will be a champion for change. At times successful individuals feel threatened by change, since a management style that was adequate under the old conditions may not be effective under the new conditions due to different political structures. Likewise, employees who have been able to progress under the old condition may not be effective under the new condition due to the requirement of different skill sets.

LEWIN'S THREE PHASES OF PLANNED CHANGE

Psychologist Kurt Lewin describes change as a function of the forces that promote change and the opposing forces that slow or resist change. These **change forces** lead to the differences in the form, quality, or condition of an organization over time. The opposite forces, known as **resistance forces**, are those forces that support the status quo of the organization.

Managers seeking change in an organization can benefit from a simple but effective model developed by Lewin (Figure 11.4). The three phases of the Lewin model provide guidance on how to go about getting people to change: a manager will implement new processes and re-assign tasks, but change will only be effective if the people involved embrace it and help put it into practice.

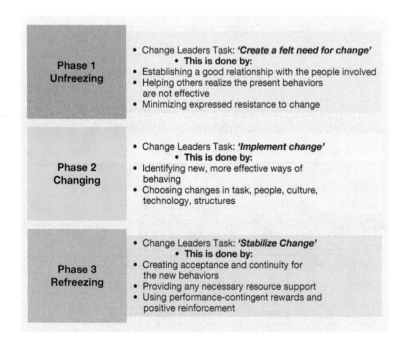

Figure 11.4. Lewin's Three Phases of Planned Organizational Change

Kipley, D., Jewe, R., & Helm-Stevens, R., A Foundation in the Principles of Management, pp. 122. Copyright © 2015 by Cognella, Inc.. Reprinted with permission.

Phase 1: **Unfreezing.** When a structure has been in place for a while, habits and routine have naturally settled in. The organization as a whole is going in the right direction, but people or processes may have strayed off course. For example, tasks that are not relevant or useful anymore are still being performed by force of habit, without anyone questioning their legitimacy. Similarly, people might have learned to do things one way, without considering other, more efficient methods. **Unfreezing** means getting people to gain perspective on their day-to-day activities, unlearn their bad habits, and open up to new ways of reaching their objectives. Basically, the current practices and processes have to be reassessed in order for the wheels of change to be set in motion.

Phase 2: **Changing.** Once the unfreezing phase has opened up the employee's minds to change, phase 2 can start. Phase 2 can be a very dynamic one and, if it is to be effective, it will probably take some time and involve a transition period. In order to gain efficiency, people will have to take on new tasks and responsibilities. This means a learning curve that will at first slow the organization down. A change process has to be viewed as an investment, both in terms of time and the allocation of resources: after the new organization and processes have been rolled out, a certain level of disorder might ensue, but that is the price to pay in order to attain enhanced effectiveness within the structure.

Phase 3: **Refreezing.** Change will only reach its full effect if it's made permanent. Once the organizational changes have been made and the structure has regained its effectiveness, every effort must be made to freeze them and make sure the new organization becomes the standard. Linking change with rewards, positive reinforcement, and resource support all helps with refreezing.

CHANGE STRATEGIES FOR MANAGERS

When it comes to actually implementing organizational change, managers have available three common change strategies: coercive change strategy, rational persuasion strategy, and shared power strategy.

Coercive change strategy involves the use of a position of power to create change by decree and formal authority, giving orders, and enforcing those orders to overcome resistance. This approach has the advantage of being fast, but it is low commitment, has high costs, can be extremely socially disruptive, and may be accompanied by high resistance.

The second method of change is **rational persuasion strategy**. Although change does not work to everyone's advantage, this approach attempts to convince individuals, through rational argument, information, and facts, that the overall benefit to change is to their personal advantage and, when successful, change can be relatively easy to accomplish.

A **shared power strategy** is a collaborative approach that empowers people in a process of participation that identifies values, assumptions, and goals from which support for change will emerge. Although a shared power strategy is slow, the process is likely to yield high commitment. The change leader works together with others as a team to develop the consensus needed to support change. This requires being comfortable and confident in allowing others to influence decisions that affect the planned change and its implementation. Figure 11.5 summarizes these three strategies.

EVALUATING CHANGE IN THE ORGANIZATION

As with any managerial action, managers should evaluate the changes they make to not only gain insight into how the change itself might be adjusted, but also to determine what steps should be taken the next time to increase overall organizational effectiveness.

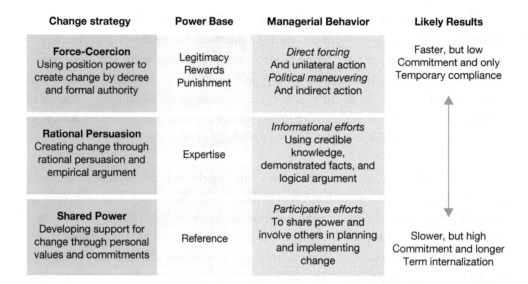

Figure 11.5. Three Change Strategies: Power, Base, and Behavior

Kipley, D., Jewe, R., & Helm-Stevens, R., A Foundation in the Principles of Management, pp. 123. Copyright © 2015 by Cognella, Inc. Reprinted with permission.

Evaluation of change often involves watching for symptoms that indicate further change is necessary. As an example, if people are reluctant to shift from past methods of task completion to the new methods, or if they have greater allegiance to departmental goals than to the overall organizational goals, further change is necessary.

A word of caution is needed at this point. Although the symptoms just provided generally indicate that further change is required, the decision to make additional change should not be made solely on that basis. Decisions for further change should include other objective information, such as increasing profitability, raising job satisfaction, increasing customer satisfaction, or contributing to the overall welfare of society.

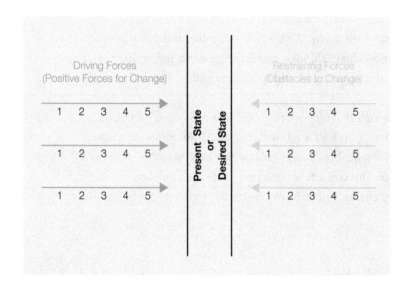

Figure 11.6. Lewin's Force Field Analysis

FORCE FIELD ANALYSIS

Lewin's cornerstone models for organizational change include a **force field analysis**—a powerful and strategic tool utilized by leaders and managers to successfully lead change. The force field analysis contains two equal but opposing forces for change—a driving force and a resisting force (Figure 11.6). Lewin proposed that when the driving forces are stronger than the resisting forces, then conditions favor change. However, when the resisting forces are more powerful than the driving forces, then the conditions to change will be unfavorable. Although there are usually driving forces that are attractive to employees and restraining forces that are unattractive, successful change will depend on the leaders' and managers' ability to minimize resistance and maximize drivers. Typically, it is less complicated to minimize resisting forces than it is to shore up or bolster driving forces.

In the first model to attempt to quantify change, Lewin proposed that each driving and resistive force be listed and assigned a relative numerical value. Once the change forces are tabulated, an informed decision can be made regarding the change. It is important to note that criticisms of Lewin's force field analysis focus on the numerical values assigned, due to the subjectivity and bias of the individual or team assigning the value. Although the model is rarely used as a numerical model for change decisions, it is extremely valuable in identifying and distinguishing factors within the situation and organization.

1. *Define the change*: In the middle, write down the objective or goal (the desired future state).
2. *Brainstorm the driving forces*: Identify those favoring change. Record them on the diagram.
3. *Brainstorm the resisting forces*: Identify those restraining or opposing change. Record them on the diagram.
4. *Assess the driving and restraining forces*: Assign a numerical value to each force. For example, use a scale from 1 (weak) to 5 (strong), and total each side.
5. *Review the forces*: Double check your assessment of both the driving and resisting forces. Do any have flexibility? Can any be influenced?
6. *Plan the change strategy*: Create a strategy designed to maximize or strengthen the driving forces and minimize or weaken the resisting forces, or both.
7. *Prioritize action steps*: Craft a plan of action designed to achieve the greatest impact, including identifying necessary resources.

CONFLICT AND CHANGE

At times, organizational change will result in conflict. **Conflict** refers to the opposing ideas and actions of different entities that result in an antagonistic state. Conflict is an inevitable part of life. Each of us possesses our own opinions, ideas, and sets of beliefs. We have our own ways of looking at things and we act according to what we think is proper. Hence, we often find ourselves in conflict in different scenarios; they may involve other individuals, groups of people, or a struggle within our own selves. Consequently, conflict influences our actions and decisions in one way or another.

Although workplace conflicts arise in many ways and at different times, the two most common categories of conflict at work are **intergroup** conflict and **personality** conflict. A critical skill in the workplace, effective conflict management is particularly important for supervisors, managers, and leaders.

INTERGROUP CONFLICT

Intergroup conflict involves two or more groups and their respective members, and generally arises within competing groups, when groups interrelate to accomplish a task, or when groups compete for resources. High levels of group cohesiveness can also contribute to intergroup conflict. Common elements leading to intergroup conflict often include the following:

- Ingroup members view themselves as unique and irreplaceable individuals but stereotype members of other groups as being identical to each other.
- Ingroup members view themselves in a positive manner and other group members negatively.

- Ingroup members view themselves as politically correct and organization minded, and view other group members as immoral and self-serving.
- Negative and/or disrespectful interactions between groups or between individual group members.
- Either group or a third party engaging in negative gossip about a group or a group member.

Intergroup conflicts impact effectiveness and efficiency and can seriously harm your organization's performance and productivity. Managers and leaders can minimize, and attempt to prevent, intergroup conflict by:

- preparing groups to work with other groups by setting norms and expectations;
- offering and providing team-building exercises designed to understand and reduce the causes of conflict;
- encouraging friendships between co-workers and fostering relationships among the different groups by having lunches or other social events; and
- swiftly and appropriately dealing with gossip as soon as it arises.

PERSONALITY CONFLICTS

Unlike intergroup conflict, personality conflicts generally involve two or more people. Personality conflicts, often referred to as personality clashes, occur when individuals disagree because of incompatible personalities, not because of an issue or incident. Their incompatibility may stem from their approach or their view. Severe symptoms of personality conflicts may include:

- incivility, such as obscene or vulgar language;
- manipulative or passive-aggressive behaviors;
- hindering workflow and work processes; or
- refusing to work with co-workers or follow orders.

Although personality conflicts can arise from something unimportant or major, if the conflict is not resolved, they often cause moral issues. Therefore, personality conflicts can also impact your organization's performance and productivity. Managers and leaders can minimize, and attempt to resolve, personality conflicts in the following ways:

- Investigate and document the conflict.
- Encourage individuals to work together to resolve their differences in a constructive and positive manner.
- Attempt informal dispute resolution.

It is important to remember not to take sides and to avoid engaging other team members, as this will only further the conflict. Lastly, if you are unable to resolve the conflict, seek help from your human resource department.

TECHNIQUES FOR HANDLING CONFLICT

Managers are fortunate to have four useful techniques for handling conflict: compromising, avoiding, forcing, and resolving (Figure 11.7).

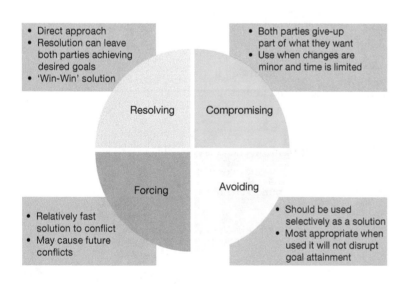

Figure 11.7. Techniques for Handling Conflict

Kipley, D., Jewe, R., & Helm-Stevens, R., A Foundation in the Principles of Management, pp. 128. Copyright © 2015 by Cognella, Inc. Reprinted with permission.

Compromising is when the two sides agree on a solution to give up some of their demands for a solution that gives each party part of what they originally wanted. Managers who choose to compromise generally feel that a solution completely acceptable to everyone would be difficult to achieve and they would rather not force someone to accept a completely disagreeable choice. Compromise is appropriate to adopt as a conflict management technique if a planned change is relatively minor and the time to make an organizational change is somewhat limited.

The second technique that managers can adopt to manage conflict is **avoiding**. As simple as it sounds, avoiding is a conflict management technique whereby managers choose to ignore the conflict. For example, if the R&D manager finds that the individuals in the production department are becoming a continual source of conflict because they are unwilling to provide any constructive feedback and resist proposed change, the manager can avoid dealing with the department. The manager can opt to propose and implement desirable change by dealing with others in the organization who may have power over the production department.

The avoiding strategy is logical if you assume that all conflict is bad. If you are successful in avoiding all conflict, the work environment could seem to be positive. However, managers often disagree and those with opposing viewpoints have important ideas that should be considered through conflict.

From an employee's viewpoint, managers who use the avoiding technique can be seen as irritating, puzzling, or unprofessional. It is important that managers give equal attention to the views of all employees, not just the views that are easily understood by the manager. Hence, to make sure that organizational change is designed and implemented most effectively and efficiently, a manager must ensure that employees know the manager wants to be aware of any employees' thoughts about how to improve organizational change.

The third technique available to managers is a more direct approach. **Forcing** is a technique for managing conflict in which managers use their authority to declare that conflict is over. In effect, this declaration ends any conflict because they have the authority to end it. As an example, a worker may complain to the manager that the recent changes are unfair because the worker has lost overtime hours. The manager can force closure on this issue by simply saying, "I make the work assignments, and your job is to do what you are told."

The advantage to forcing as a solution to conflict is that it is a relatively fast way to manage a conflict, and it may be the best approach in an emergency. The downside is that, by forcing a conclusion to the conflict, employees may become frustrated and the frustration may build to form another conflict later.

The final technique used by managers in conflict management is **resolving**. Resolving is the most direct and sometimes the most difficult solution in managing conflict. With this technique, the manager first identifies the differences between the manager and the employees, and then listens to the viewpoints of others in an honest effort to understand rather than argue. Next, both sides should identify the issues about change on which they agree and the ways they can both benefit from implementing the change that reflect the ideas on which they agree. Both sides should be honest and diligent to reach a mutually agreed-upon, change-related strategy.

Resolving is different from the other techniques, as they tend to assume managers and employees are in a **win-lose conflict**. In other words, the outcome of the conflict will be that one side achieves a desired goal (wins) and the other side does not (loses). Resolving assumes that conflict can be a **win-win conflict**, wherein the conflict resolution leaves both parties achieving a desirable outcome and, as such, helps the organization maximize organizational success.

STRESS AND CHANGE

Stress from change is a natural part of life. Unfortunately, without appropriate stress management it can have a negative effect any improvements that were anticipated from the change, not to mention the effect on workers' physical, mental, and emotional health. Therefore, understanding how change leads to stress, as well as how to manage that stress, is an important part of leading a healthier, happier life.

Stress is the body's reaction to a change that requires a physical, mental, or emotional adjustment or response. It can come from any situation or thought that makes you feel frustrated, angry, nervous, or anxious. A **stressor** is an environmental demand that causes people to feel stress. Stressors are common in situations where individuals are confronted by circumstances for which their usual behaviors are inappropriate or insufficient, and where negative consequences are associated with failure to deal properly with the situation. Organizational change characterized by continual layoffs or firings is an obvious stressor, but many other factors related to organizational policies, structure, physical conditions, and processes can act as stressors. In organizations, these stressors cause the human body to unconsciously mobilize energy when confronted with the demands of work.

STRESS AND WORK

Job stress can wear on your nerves, cause sleepless nights, and contribute to health problems such as heart disease and depression. "Chronic job stress can put both your physical and emotional health at risk," says Paul J. Rosch, MD, the president of the American Institute of Stress. Controlling stress at work is important for several reasons:

1. Stress can have a damaging effect on an employee's psychological and physiological health. It can limit their concentration and decision-making skills as well as decrease productivity. Stress is also associated with heart disease, increased psychiatric symptoms, and adverse effects on family relationships.
2. Stress is a major factor in employee absenteeism and turnover.
3. A stressed employee can affect the safety of other workers or even the public.
4. Stress is expensive to organizations. Some estimates of the cost of stress to the U.S. economy are in excess of $150 billion per year. Many organizations spend a great deal of money treating stress-related employee problems through medical programs and legal fees when handling stress-related lawsuits.

Managers often find it difficult to identify the employees in the organization who are experiencing high levels of stress. Part of this difficulty stems from the fact that people respond differently to high stress and that the signs of physiological reactions, such as high blood pressure, pounding heart, and gastrointestinal disorders are difficult to observe or monitor.

Nevertheless, managers can learn to recognize several observable symptoms of undesirably high stress levels, such as constant fatigue, low energy, moodiness, increased aggression, excessive use of alcohol, temper outbursts, compulsive eating, high levels of anxiety, and chronic worrying.

Additionally, the following list provides eight "risk of stress" employee types that managers should look for:

1. *The overworked worker:* Employees are busy from the time they get to work until the time they leave and have little freedom while at work. Employees have say over how to do the work or the types of projects they are assigned.
2. *The frustrated worker:* Employee who works his or her tail off to make the boss look good, yet receives little to no credit—or compensation for their work.
3. *The castaway worker:* Employee feels like they are all alone, and not in a good way. If they require help or guidance, the boss or supervisor won't give it to them, and when they need to vent there are no colleagues to turn to.

4. *The doormat worker*: Employees that constantly deal with demanding and verbally abusive customers yet are required to swallow any resentment they may feel and maintain a facade of professionalism, calm, and courtesy.

5. *The technology-prisoner worker*: Thanks to the smartphone, laptop, and tablet your company has so generously provided, your boss can now reach you 24/7. This worker is constantly (if virtually) connected to the office; their work and personal life now become indistinguishable.

6. *The burned-out employee*: This employee is terminally exhausted, both physically and emotionally, to the point where it becomes difficult to function. Employees at this stage feel as if they are on the verge of a breakdown.

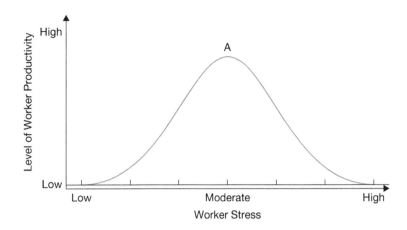

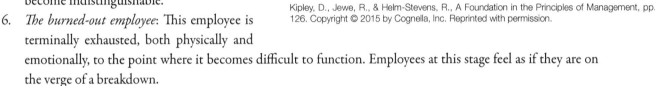

Figure 11.8. Relationship Between Stress and Performance

Kipley, D., Jewe, R., & Helm-Stevens, R., A Foundation in the Principles of Management, pp. 126. Copyright © 2015 by Cognella, Inc. Reprinted with permission.

7. *The abused employee*: This employee is a victim of the manager's insults often in front of their colleagues. Frequently given impossible deadlines to meet or assigned busywork just because the manager can.

8. *The wronged victim worker*: For this employee, work is not fair. The manager plays favorites and the decisions made by management are confusing and arbitrary. The manager treats the employees like children.

STRESS AND WORKER PERFORMANCE

To deal with stress at work, managers must understand the relationship between the amount of stress felt by an employee and the employee's performance. Figure 11.8 illustrates the relationship between stress and performance. Notice that both low and high stress have negative effects on performance, and a certain level of stress is actually good for employee performance. In sum, an appropriate amount of stress is generally considered to be advantageous for the organization because it increases productivity. However, when employees experience too little or too much stress, productivity is negatively affected.

REDUCING STRESS IN THE WORKPLACE

Stress is difficult to reduce until the stressors causing it have been dealt with satisfactorily, or eliminated from the environment. For example, if too much organizational change is creating conditions of high stress for workers, management may be able to reduce the level of stress by initiating a training program that is preparing workers for the demands of the new change, thus reducing worker anxiety. Management may also curtail additional changes until the organizational culture has first absorbed and adjusted to the current changes. The following four strategies are examples that management can adopt to mitigate the initial development of unwanted stressors in organizations:

1. *Create a climate of support for individuals*: Organizational climate clearly influences the success of an organization. Companies that utilized a progressive a human resource department focused on supporting workers made a greater impact on areas such as customer commitment, communication, empowerment, innovation,

rewards and recognition, community involvement, environmental responsibility, and teamwork than organizations with less progressive practices.

2. *Initiate courses that focus on stress management*: Research has proven that employees who participated in a stress management course that focused on stress identification, coping strategies, and stress prevention were less likely to become depressed than employees who did not participate. Clearly, the implementation of a stress management course could be beneficial for the whole workplace.

3. *Create stimulating jobs*: Jobs that are routine and mundane often do not allow employees any freedom of expression, resulting in employee stress. Managers should strive to make employees' jobs as interesting as possible to prevent the stressor stemming from a routine, boring job.

4. *Design and operate career counseling programs*: Career path development can become a stressor for employees. If employees do not know what their next steps could be in their career development, they may become discouraged and stressed. Designing and operating a career counseling program that will assist employees with their next career path steps from both a realistic and achievable approach will reduce stress levels.

SUMMARY OF CHAPTER

1. We learned the definitions of innovation and creativity why their critical to business today.
2. We examined the similarities and differences between organizational development and organizational change.
3. We explored the relative importance of change and stability to an organization and what kinds of changes should be made within an organization;
4. The importance of learning to fail and how it is tied to creating a learning organization.
5. How to evaluate change and the importance of considering the effects of change on people within the organization;
6. We learned that Lewin's three phases of planned change are unfreezing, changing, and refreezing.
7. The importance of learning how to maximize change drivers and minimize change resisters; and
8. How organizational change and stress is related and techniques to handle conflict as a factor of organizational change.
9. The different reasons for conflict, including inter-group- and personality conflicts.
10. How stress affects workplace performance and current approaches for reducing stress in the workplace.

DISCUSSION QUESTIONS

1. Provide an example of how you might use unfreezing, change, and refreezing in making specific organizational changes.
2. When is it better to pursue incremental change rather than discontinuous change?
3. What are the three phases of planned change according to Lewin?
4. What may be the benefits of learning to fail? And, how is this tied to the concept of organizational development?

DO I REACT WELL TO CHANGE IN THE WORKPLACE?

INSTRUCTIONS:

Indicate how you would react to the following features of a managerial job. Use the following scale:

1: I would not like this at all
2: I would not like that but it is manageable
3: I have no reaction to that feature one way or the other
4: I would like that most of the time
5: I would like that completely

1. I have to read about 150 pages of technical materials each week.
2. Many of my coworkers do not speak English as their first language.
3. The degree I got for this job is no longer appropriate and I should go back to get a new degree.
4. Many things I am asked to do, I do not have the authority to complete.
5. My organization and department is reorganized every couple of years or so.
6. I have to spend multiple weeks in training seminars to keep up in my job position.
7. Each month, I spend about a week out of town.
8. My job is relatively new and I am making it up as I go.
9. A promotion is not likely to happen soon.
10. I am a team member with an equal amount of power as the other members.
11. I regularly have to learn how to use the new equipment and technologies introduced to my department.
12. My department is highly interdependent on others to the point that task distinction does not matter.
13. I have plenty of ideas on how to make the organization run better, but cannot actually influence any decisions made about it.
14. My job performance is not just evaluated by my boss, but by many members of the organization.
15. There is no real pathway for my career in my organization.
16. My meetings with people whom report me include people participating by phone or electronics.
17. I work closely with people of diversity (i.e., ethnicity, gender, and nationality).
18. I have three bosses and each has an equal say in my job appraisals.
19. My effectiveness cannot be measured objectively.
20. I spend a lot of time postponing scheduled work due to emergencies.

SCORING KEY:

To find how you respond to change, add up all your responses.

ANALYSIS:

Though there are no significant cutoffs, if you scored at 60 or below, you may want to be weary of a management job in the 20th century, as the above statements come from current managers describing their jobs. Some aspects above can occur for short periods of time, others may become part of the job. You will have to decide what levels of ambiguity and change you are comfortable managing in and dealing with as you find the job that is best for you.

Adapted from: Robbins, S. P. (2009). III.C.1: How well do I respond to turbulent change?, Self-assessment library (91-93). Upper Saddle River, NJ: Pearson Education Inc.

Original Source: Vaill, P.B. (1989). Managing as a performing art: New ideas for a world of chaotic change. (p. 8-9) San Francisco: Jossey-Bass.

CHAPTER 11 REFERENCES

Abernathy, W., & Utterback, J. (1978). Patterns of industrial innovation. *Technology Review, 80*(7), 40–47.

Amabile, T. M., Conti, R., Lazenby, J., & Herron, M. (1996). Assessing the work environment for creativity. *Academy of Management Journal, 39*(5), 1154–1184.

Anderson, P., & Tushman, M. L. (1991). Managing through cycles of technological change. *Research/Technology Management, 34*(3), 26–31.

Ansoff, H. (1979). *Strategic Management*. New York: Palgrave MacMillan.

Bernholz, P., Gersbach, H. (1992). "Gresham's Law: Theory." The New Palgrave Dictionary of Money and Finance, vol. 2. Macmillan: London and Basingstoke 1992, 286-288.

Deutschman, A. (2005, May). Making change: Why is it so darn hard to change our ways? *Fast Company*, 52–62.

Duck, J. D. (1988). Managing change: The art of balancing. *Harvard Business Review on Change*, 55–81.

Dumaine, B. (1994). The trouble with teams. *Fortune*, 86–92.

Eisenhardt, K. M. (1995). Accelerating adaptive processes: Product innovation in the global computer industry. *Administrative Science Quarterly, 40*(1), 84–110.

Ettlie, J. E., & O'Keefe, R. D. (1982). Innovation attitudes, values, and intentions in organizations. *Journal of Management Studies, 19*(2), 163–182.

Gallupe, R. B., & Cooper, W. H. (1993). Brainstorming electronically. *Sloan Management Review*, 27–36.

Hellriegel, D., Slocum, J. (1972). "Systems Strategies Applied to Organizations," Business Horizons, 15, 2.

Hellriegel, D., Slocum, J. (1973). "A Contingency Approach to Organizational Design," Business Horizon, 16, 2. Reprinted in Richards and Nielander, Readings in Management, 4th ed., South-Western Publishing Company, 1978; and R. Golembiewski, F. Gibson, and G. Miller, Managerial Behavior and Organizational Demands: Management as a Linking of Levels of Interaction. New York: Peacock, 1978; and M. Richards, Readings in Management, 5th ed., South-Western Publishing Company, 1982.

Hellriegel, D., Slocum, J. (1974)."Organizational Climate: Measures, Research and Contingencies," *Academy of Management Journal, 17,* 255–280.

How Companies Overcome Resistance to Change. (1972). *Management Review, 61*(11), 17–25.

Janis, I. L. (1983). *Groupthink.* Boston: Houghton Mifflin.

Jenn, K., & Mannix, E. (2001). The dynamic nature of conflict: A longitudinal study of intragroup conflict and group performance. *Academy of Management Journal, 44*(2), 238–251.

Kahn, W. (2004). Facilitating and undermining organizational change: A case study. *Journal of Applied Behavioral Science, 40*(1), 7–30.

Kanter, R. M. (1989). The new managerial work. *Harvard Business Review,* 85–92.

Kay, G. (1994). Effective meetings through electronic brainstorming. *Management Quarterly, 35*(4), 15.

Kotter, J. P. (1995). Leading change: Why transformation efforts fail. *Harvard Business Review, 73,* 59.

Kotter, J. P., & Schlesinger, L. A. (1979). Choosing strategies for change. *Harvard Business Review,* 106–114.

Lawless, M. W., & Anderson, P. C. (1996). Generational technological change: Effects of innovation and local rivalry on performance. *Academy of Management Journal, 39*(5), 1185–1217.

Lewin, K. (1951). *Field theory in social science: Selected theoretical papers.* New York: Harper & Brothers.

Mathews, H. L., Slocum, J. (1972). "Correlates of Commercial Bank Credit Card Use," *Journal of Bank Research,* 2, 4.

Morgan, J. S. (1972). *Managing change: The strategies of making change work for you.* New York: McGraw-Hill.

Neck, C. P., & Manz, C. C. (1994). From groupthink to teamthink: Toward the creation of constructive thought patterns in self-managing work teams. *Human Relations, 47*(8), 929–952.

Robertson, W. J., Roberts, D. R., & Porras, J. I. (1993). Dynamics of planned organizational change: Assessing empirical support for a theoretical model. *Academy of Management Journal, 36*(3), 619–634.

Rothwell, W. J., Sullivan, R., & McLean, G. M. (1995). *Practicing organizational development: A guide for consultants.* San Diego, CA: Pfeiffer & Co.

Selye, H. (1956). *The stress of life.* New York: McGraw-Hill.

Slocum, J., Sheridan, J., Richards, M., and Altimus, C. (1973) "The Impact of Leadership Styles on the Job Satisfactions of Blue-Collar Workers in Different Cultures," *Quarterly Journal of Management Development,* 4.

Smereka, C. M. (1990). Outwitting, controlling stress for a healthier lifestyle. *Healthcare Financial Management, 44*(3), 70–75.

Tribus, M. (1989). Changing the corporate culture: A roadmap for the change agent. *Human Systems Management, 8*(1), 11–22.

Van de Ven, A. H., & Poole, M. S. (1995). Explaining development and change in organizations. *Academy of Management Review, 20*(3), 510–540.

Zimmerman, J. H. (1995). The principles of managing change. *HR Focus, 72,* 15–16.

ORGANIZATIONAL CULTURE AND CONTROL

12

CHAPTER LEARNING OBJECTIVES

After reading this chapter, you should have a good understanding of

- the significance of organizational culture and the major categories and components of organizational culture;
- how cultures are measured in terms of strength and the differences and similarities between strong and weak cultures;
- the four different types of culture found within organizations and their advantages and disadvantages;
- how organizational culture influences control and the types of control found in business today;
- regulatory processes and the importance of control to organizations; and
- the basic role of control and three major steps in the control process.

"Corporate culture matters. How management chooses to treat its people impacts everything—for better or for worse."

- SIMON SINEK

Defining and understanding organizational culture is important to scholars, but also pivotal to leaders is finding a way to make their organizational culture work. In 1994, William Schneider wrote a groundbreaking book, *The Reengineering Alternative: A Plan for Making Your Current Culture Work*. In his book, Schneider outlined four distinct types of organizational culture and provided a framework for assessing culture and developing culture, character, and effectiveness.

Organizational culture has wide implications. It is intimately tied to leadership, power, and order. Organizational culture establishes management practices and routines and provides consistent patterns for employees. The first section of this chapter will explore the components of organizational culture and provide a basic understanding of the differences between strong and weak cultures. The more successful the organization, the more committed the organization is to its culture. The middle section of this chapter will explore the four kinds of organizational culture as presented by William Schneider. We examine the core components of culture and the identities of the control, collaboration, competence, and cultivation cultures.

An organization's culture, mission, and vision influence the direction and measure of organizational control. The last part of this chapter will examine the relationship between organizational culture and control. A regulatory process, **control** establishes the standards necessary to achieve organizational goals. Used to measure performance standards, control begins with the establishment of clear expectations and standards, the design of systems and methods used to compare actual performance to desired performance, and strategies for taking corrective action if the actual performance does not meet desired performance. Simply, the purpose of control is to identify deviations and deficiencies in performance and take corrective action.

ORGANIZATIONAL CULTURE

Organizational culture became a topic of rigorous exploration during the early 1980s. Since then, it has been a steadily debated topic that scholars have struggled to define and understand. In 1998, a study identified 54 different definitions of organizational culture developed between 1960 and 1993. In 2005, Bruce Tharp summed up the definitions by explaining, "For some, culture is considered the 'glue' that holds an organization together and, for others, the 'compass' that provides directions."

Organizational culture has many definitions because it is complex and cumbersome to completely and fully identify. Organizational culture permeates all levels of the organization. It is thick and rich, with many cognitive layers and symbols. It has roots in company history, is constructed socially, and is affected by the environment. It is explicitly and implicitly embedded and continuously evolving.

Over the last 15 years, Edgar Schien has contributed to the field of organizational culture and behavior. His understanding of the subject has lead to categorization of where organizational culture is found. Three fundamental categories—values, underlying assumptions, and observable artifacts—divide the places where organizational culture resides (Figure 12.1).

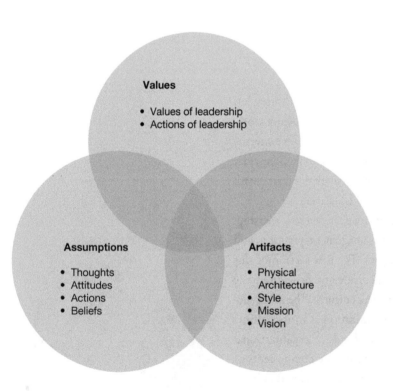

Figure 12.1. Categories of Organizational Culture

Observable artifacts include a company's beliefs, behaviors, and attitudes. This category represents the company's view—how they see things (perspective) and what they value (importance). Observable artifacts include the visible and recognizable, such as physical architecture, style, mission, and vision.

For example, Target's purpose or mission statement is as follows:

We fulfill the needs and fuel the potential of our guests. That means making Target your preferred shopping destination in all channels by delivering outstanding value, continuous innovation and exceptional experiences—consistently fulfilling our Expect More. Pay Less.® brand promise.

Underlying assumptions represent the basic thoughts, attitudes, actions, and beliefs of the organization. Although underlying assumptions are central to the culture, they are often unconscious patterns that are taken for granted. At times, employees are unaware of their influence, yet underlying assumptions serve as motivation and drivers for perception, behavior, and action.

Espoused values represent the ideals, principles, and standards championed by leaders and managers. Simply put, espoused values are those values promoted and advocated by leadership.

At times, **espoused** values do not align with **enacted** values. It is important to be able to distinguish between those values that are verbalized and those that are performed or carried out. For example, an organization may claim that it "values people," yet they pay below-average wages, rarely give raises that keep pace with cost of living increases, do not offer job security, and the policies and processes they enact make it difficult to promote. Just because the CEO claims that the company values people doesn't necessarily mean that it actually values its employees.

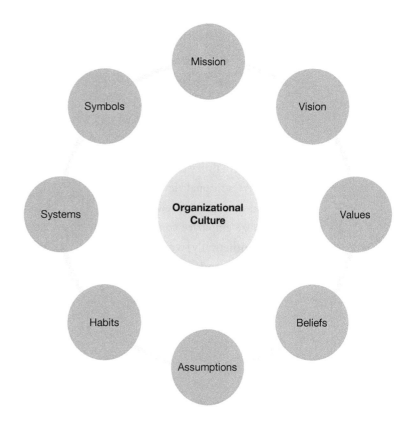

Figure 12.2. Components of Organizational Culture

Organizational culture is a system of shared values, beliefs, and assumptions that guides how employees behave in the workplace. Organizational culture includes the organization's vision and mission, along with its values, beliefs, assumptions, habits, systems, and symbols (Figure 12.2). These components have an influence on how people perform their jobs, behave, dress, and communicate at work.

Generally shaped by the company's founders, organizational culture drives consistent and observable patterns of workplace conduct, performance, behavior, and activities. Organizational culture is built and lives through a system of explicit patterns—codified materials such as policies and procedures—and implicit patterns, such as norms. Organizational culture is unique and reflects different characteristics and meanings from one company to another.

WEAK ORGANIZATIONAL CULTURES

Weak organizational cultures are distinguished by an individualistic workforce with diverse opinions and ideas. Typically, individual thoughts and contributions are encouraged and debate is not seen as an indication of dissent. Weak organizational cultures are generally quick to change due to their flexibility. Disadvantages of weak cultures may include a higher-than-average degree of conflict, inconsistent communication, and power struggles. This can lead to poor management and unmotivated employees.

STRONG ORGANIZATIONAL CULTURES

Strong organizational cultures are distinguished by workforces in which the majority of the employees hold the same values and beliefs to similar depths. Ways of doing things are deeply embedded in the company, so managers and employees understand what is required. They know who they are and what they do. Employees share the same goals, follow the same rules, and apply the same ethics in decision making. Disadvantages of a strong organizational culture can include lack of flexibility, poor decision making, and being closed-minded to new ideas. New employees are generally quickly indoctrinated into the culture, making it difficult to bring in innovation and outside expertise.

Recent research examined the relationship between the strength of an organization's culture and its performance and, interestingly, in stable economic times, organizations with strong cultures were able to deliver successful business strategies and perform well. However, in unstable economic times, strong cultures tend to lead to business failures and poor overall performance.

Two examples of very different companies that have very strong cultures and are both extremely successful are Disney and Google. Disney is more widely known for its rigidity with its rules, its strict adherence to codes and to uniforms, and its traditional views of business, whereas Google is known for being fairly free flowing and allowing employees a fair amount of freedom to express their creativity and work in a space that caters to their needs, in order to maximize employee comfort. Both of these companies have maintained their cultures for years and, if they were to hypothetically switch corporate cultures for a day, certainly their businesses would start to experience a loss in performance and general dissatisfaction.

An important note to make is that a company may have a weak or strong culture and still be a successful company. Some companies with weak cultures are able to adapt more easily to extreme changes in environment—just because they are called "weak" does not mean they are a dysfunctional company. When searching for jobs or developing a business of your own, remember to take into account the type of culture you want to create within your company or what culture already exists and consider whether it is a good match for you and for the environment.

FOUR TYPES OF ORGANIZATIONAL CULTURES

In *The Reengineering Alternative: A Plan for Making Your Current Culture Work*, William Schneider identified four different types of organizational cultures and detailed their strategic focus, leadership and management focus, structural focus, power focus, and relationship focus.

Control and **competence** cultures are impersonal, while **collaboration** and **cultivation** cultures are personal. Collaboration and control cultures focus on actuality—what is—while cultivation and competence cultures focus on possibility—what could be (Figure 12.3).

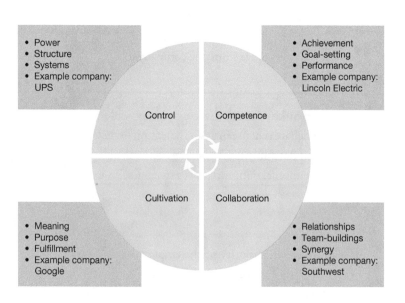

Figure 12.3. Four Types of Organizational Cultures

The first type of organizational culture, control culture, has its roots in military models and prototypes. **Control cultures** are power-based, rich in policies and procedures, utilize detailed tracking systems, and exert significant influence over employees and situations. Order, predictability, and compliance are valued. These organizations prize structured environments, status quo is foremost, and change is resisted. Information is closely guarded, plans and objectives are highly structured, and decision making is routine, methodical, and systematic. Control cultures are typically focused on domination of their market or industry, and customers and clients must learn to adapt to the organization.

Control cultures are motivated by power. Leaders in control cultures are typically conservative and cautious, and focus on rules and regulations. Leaders in control cultures are usually authoritative and directive, and command respect. Control cultures typically employ hierarchical structures, titles and positions are important, and the chain of command is always followed.

Collaborative cultures, on the other hand, have their roots in sports team models and prototypes. Modeling family and team, **collaboration cultures** value building relationships, developing people, and teamwork. Collaboration cultures seek to achieve synergy and harmony between their employees and teams by sharing resources and knowledge. Collaboration cultures value diversity and unique contributions. They care about their employees, empower their employees, and trust them to utilize resources effectively.

Figure 12.4. Southwest Airlines

Copyright © Southwest Airlines (CC BY-SA 2.5) at https://commons.wikimedia.org/wiki/File:Classic_Colors_Southwest_Airlines_N648SW_Boeing_737-3H4_SJC.jpg.

Since collaborative cultures value relationship building and affiliation, they dislike "lone wolves" and grandstanding. Considerable emphasis is placed on group accomplishments and achievements. Employees are generally dedicated and loyal to the company. Decision making is highly participatory, with creativity, innovation, and different perspectives being prized and responsibility for decision making shared. At times, customers and clients of collaborative cultures feel a part of the family. An example of a company with a collaborative culture is Southwest Airlines (Figure 12.4).

Collaborative cultures are motivated by affiliation. Leaders in collaborative cultures are typically team oriented and attempt to create balance between cooperation and coordination for an integrative focus. Leaders value relationship building and foster building trust, commitment, and loyalty. They respect individual opinions and contributions. Leaders, managers, and employees often make personal sacrifices for the team or the company.

Competence cultures are rooted in achievement and competition. The need to achieve by doing more and doing better than before or better than others drives competence cultures. Fueled by the desire to compete against a standard of excellence, competence cultures are built upon encouraging intellectual ability and capability. In competence cultures, objectives are generally set as stretch goals, employees take personal responsibility for achieving their goals, and they value feedback. Employees participate by offering innovative ideas, looking for opportunities for improvement, and trying new things. Generally based on projects and productivity, relationships between employees are fluid and flexible. Valuing conceptual systematization, the competence culture defines success as improvement and the pursuit of excellence. Competence cultures operate as meritocracies—they recognize and reward innovation, process improvement, superior performance, and results.

Competence cultures are motivated by achievement. Leaders in competence cultures emphasize doing things well and being the best. Leaders are usually long-term focused and strategy oriented, and utilize ideas and concepts to motivate people. Leaders and managers typically dispense incentives along with monetary rewards. Competence culture leaders is invest in continuous improvement and are frequently dissatisfied with the status quo.

Cultivation cultures are rooted in faith, beliefs, and mission. These organizations are dedicated to the human spirit and their purpose. Values and ethics form the foundation of their philosophy and provide the platform for their business systems and processes. Business objectives and goals guide progress towards worthwhile accomplishments. A shared commitment to individual and collective fulfillment of worthwhile pursuits and valuable purposes fuels employee motivation. Typically, cultivation cultures provide energetic work environments, employees are encouraged to participate, and opportunities for growth are provided. Operating under a system of continuous improvement, cultivation cultures invest in their workers and harvest their energy and ideas.

Leadership in a cultivation culture is purpose focused and mission and vision oriented. Generally, leaders employ a democratic style, encourage participation, and cultivate innovative and diverse ideas and contributions. Leaders emphasize trust and commitment. Organizations are generally structured in wheel-like fashions, with most activities and functions decentralized. Employees are allowed and encouraged to ask questions and seek answers from different departments or areas of expertise. Employees frequently receive training and participate in growth opportunities, such as job rotation. Feedback is given often and valued when received.

ORGANIZATIONAL CONTROL

An organization's culture, mission, and vision determine the direction and measure of control. Driven by the mission, vision, and strategic plans of the company, organizational control frameworks keep business functions, processes, and tasks on track. Control processes help managers review and evaluate workplace activities and determine if those activities are on target to help the company meet its goals.

Strategic plans are translated into departmental goals and objectives with specific performance measures. Throughout the process, managers monitor and evaluate their department's strategy, structure, and workplace activities to determine if they are working as intended. If performance does not meet standards, then managers are responsible for correcting the deficiency and, if standards are met, then managers are responsible for improving processes and procedures. Organizational control also focuses on challenges facing the company, anticipating future events, and working to take advantage of strategic opportunities.

TYPES OF CONTROL

Management controls refer to the processes and systems managers utilize to foster, promote, and restrict the actions of groups and individuals in order to achieve departmental objectives and organizational goals. In the workplace, management control encompasses two broad and different categories of control: normative and regulative.

NORMATIVE

Normative control refers to governing employee behavior through accepted patterns of behavior, including team norms and organizational culture. Normative controls represent shared forms of control, since they govern workplace behavior through norms—accepted patterns of behavior and action. Typically, normative controls are implicit, as they evolve from company-wide values and beliefs. In other words, normative controls are not written or codified. Rather, they are implied and accepted guidelines for employee behavior and action (Table 12.1).

Companies create normative controls in three ways. First, organizations create normative control through the hiring process. Typically, normatively controlled companies will screen and select applicants based on their attitudes and values. Second, organizations create normative control by sharing organizational stories, values, and beliefs in new employee orientation. Third, organizations create normative control through team norms and organizational culture. In normatively controlled companies, employees observe others in the workplace and learn what they should and should not do. Both team norms and organizational culture are covered in detail in previous chapters.

Table 12.1. Types of Normative Control

Kipley, D., Jewe, R., & Helm-Stevens, R., A Foundation in the Principles of Management, pp. 276. Copyright © 2015 by Cognella, Inc. Reprinted with permission.

Type of Normative Control	Description	Possible Advantages	Possible Disadvantages
Team Norms	Informal and implicit team rules and responsibilities.	1. Common goals lead to great employee involvement. 2. Collective power allows for group synergy.	1. Self-preservation may lead to group mobilization. 2. Teams are susceptible to groupthink.
Organizational Culture	Shared organizational beliefs, values, and traditions.	1. Organizational commitment may lead to better employee loyalty. 2. Company may be able to build strong culture without being rule-bound.	1. Overpowering cultures can be invasive to employees. 2. Disenfranchised employees may not find work meaningful or lose faith in the company.

For example, Nordstrom sees customer service as a strategic competitive advantage. Nordstrom's website let's everyone know their one goal:

> Make customers feel good. We work hard every day with the goal of making customers feel good. The customer is tops in our book.

By uprooting the traditional structure and placing the customer at the top of the corporate pyramid, Nordstrom embeds customer service into the organizational culture, instead of acting as if customer service is a separate function or department. To achieve a culture of customer service, Nordstrom ensures that policies and procedures support organizational culture and norms. Their efforts focus on creating alignment throughout the organization. As an example, for many years, Nordstrom had a one-paragraph employee handbook:

> We're glad to have you with our Company. Our number-one goal is to provide outstanding customer service. Set both your personal and professional goals high. We have great confidence in your ability to achieve them. Nordstrom Rules: Rule #1: Use your good judgment in all situations. There will be no additional rules.

REGULATIVE

The opposite of normative controls, **regulative controls** refer to the process of governing employee behavior by establishing bureaucratic controls, financial controls, and quality controls. Regulative controls are driven from the top down and find their roots in long-standing policies and procedures. Commonly referred to as standard operating procedures, these processes and procedures tend to be rigid and inflexible. Contemporary organizations are becoming more flexible, flattening their hierarchical structures, and empowering their employees to provide great customer service and improve the bottom line (Table 12.2). Nonetheless, both large and small organizations rely heavily on regulative controls to ensure standards are met and company goals are achieved.

Table 12.2. Types of Regulative Control

Type of Regulative Control	Description	Possible Advantages	Possible Disadvantages
Bureaucratic Control (stems from authority and chain of command)	Generally codified in the form of standard operating policies and procedures. Formal and explicit.	1. Standardization ensures that outcomes are predictable. 2. Allows for efficiency in routine problems and situations. 3. Lower training costs.	1. Rules are difficult to dismantle. 2. Companies may become rigid, inflexible, and slow to respond to customers or market changes. 3. Tendency to be punishment focused.
Financial Control	Management and control of key financial targets.	1. Proven methods to assess the strength of the company. 2. Investors and analysts can gain insight into the company's financial performance. For example, economic value added helps managers assess whether they are performing well enough to pay the cost of the capital needed to run the business.	1. Financial measures are past oriented. 2. Linking rewards to key financial targets may lead to short-term decision making. 3. Managers may be tempted to focus internally and miss external factors, such as customer satisfaction.
Quality Control	Acceptable levels of variations in product or process.	1. Products defects are uncovered and reported prior to distribution. 2. Increased likelihood of a quality product reduces risk of recalls, etc.	1. Visual inspection relies on the competence and integrity of the employee. 2. Requires collection and sifting of data by knowledgeable personnel.

Organizational control processes provide managers with the mechanisms to help regulate the quantity and quality of goods and services produced. Regulatory control systems allow managers to systematically assess the organization's efficiency and effectiveness in producing and distributing goods and services. Without a control process, managers would not have an orderly method to understand the performance of their department or division. Without a good understanding of performance, managers would have no idea how to improve workplace activities.

Throughout the control process, managers monitor and regulate the effectiveness and efficiency of their department, division, and work group. Managers play a significant role in the control process and it is their responsibility to ensure that activities under their direction support the achievement of organizational goals and objectives. Effective managers consistently monitor the performance of their department and find ways to improve performance.

BUREAUCRATIC CONTROL

When managerial control is discussed at the workplace, managers and employees generally think of bureaucratic control. Similar to all regulatory control types, bureaucratic control is driven from the top levels of the organization and information generally flows from the top down. **Bureaucratic control** refers to the system of rules and standard operating procedures that regulate workplace activities and behaviors. Simply put, bureaucratic control is the use of formalized policies and procedures to influence employee behavior. Policies are procedures are in written form, such as an employee manual.

Generally, bureaucratic organizational structures have numerous layers of management and foster a company culture of rules and regulations with closely controlled operational processes, procedures, and tasks. Standardization ensures that workplace activities are accomplished in an effective and efficient manner. In an effort to improve productivity, bureaucratic organizations will often benchmark and adopt best practices. On the other hand, bureaucratic structures must be cautious not to discourage innovation and creativity. Bureaucratically controlled companies rigid in their policy-driven decision making may become resistant to change. If the organization becomes inflexible, then it may be slow to respond to customers or competitors, or unable to adapt to changing conditions in the marketplace or environment. Additionally, managers in bureaucratically controlled organizations must be cautious to balance punishment with reward. The lack of balance between reward and punishment will cause poor employee morale.

THE CONTROL PROCESS

Control processes center on ensuring that performance does not deviate from established standards. The **control process** consists of three essential steps: establishing performance standards, comparing actual performance against performance standards, and taking corrective action if necessary. Yet, the control process is not a one-time workplace management activity. Instead, it is a continuous, dynamic process that reoccurs over time. In order to set, maintain, and improve performance levels, managers repeat and refine the entire process daily, weekly, and monthly.

To varying degrees, managers at all levels in the organization engage in the managerial function of control. So, it is important for managers to differentiate between the managerial functions of control and behavioral control. The managerial function of control is primarily concerned with ensuring that work activities are contributing to and in alignment with organizational goals and departmental objectives. Managers ensure that subordinates' work performance meets pre-established standards. The control function does not suggest that managers attempt to control an employee's personality. Control is achieved when the employee's workplace behavior and actions conform to company standards, processes, and procedures. The overreaching aim of the managerial function of control is to ensure company objectives and goals are accomplished.

Control is achieved when behavior and work procedures conform to established standards and organizational or departmental goals are accomplished. By contrast, **control loss** occurs when workplace behavior and procedures do not conform to established standards. Typically, control loss prevents the accomplishment of goals. When control losses occur, managers need to analyze and identify what corrective actions can be taken to prevent these mistakes from occurring again in the future.

ESTABLISHING STANDARDS

The control process starts when managers begin the task of setting goals and establishing standards. **Standards** are defined as a basis of comparison for measuring the degree to which workplace performance is satisfactory or unsatisfactory. Designing and establishing effective standards begins with a plan. In order to accomplish this task, managers must understand the internal environment (who is doing what and how well) and be able to scan and understand the external environment (what are others doing and how well). This is generally accomplished by monitoring. In Chapter 2, you learned about the different managerial roles as identified by Henry Mintzberg. A subcategory of the information managerial roles, **monitoring** is defined as actively seeking and obtaining a wide variety of information, both internal and external, to develop a thorough understanding of the organization and its environment.

INTERNAL STANDARDS

Internal standards refer to the process of setting and monitoring systematic performance standards, in an effort to ensure workplace tasks and activities are conducted in an effective and efficient manner. There are three common techniques and types of internal standards: standardization of work skills, standardization of outputs, and standardization of work processes.

- **Standardization of work skills** involves hiring employees who possess the necessary skills, knowledge, and abilities to perform the tasks required by the job and make necessary decisions regarding those tasks. For example, most firms consider engineers and doctors as self-controlling.
- **Standardization of outputs** involves providing employees with precise product, quality, and performance specifications. The goal is to maintain control by gauging outputs against performance specifications.
- **Standardization of work processes** involves reducing or eliminating an employee's discretion to deviate from the set standards by developing rules, regulations, and operating procedures. All approaches to internal standards focus on developing systematic performance standards designed to monitor workplace tasks and activities.

EXTERNAL STANDARDS

External standards refer to the process of systematically scanning the environment and identifying best practices. The concept of **best practices** implies that the organization or industry executes methods, processes, or techniques that accomplish desired outcomes in the most effective and efficient manner. Simply put, best practices are methods and techniques that consistently demonstrate superior results. **Industry-wide best practices** define guidelines (such as ethics) and methods (techniques and processes) that represent the most efficient or prudent course of action for a commercial or professional procedure or process. Typically, organizations identify and use the best practices of other companies in benchmarking.

BENCHMARKING

Benchmarking refers to the process of comparing a set of product or customer metrics, measurements, and performance of one company to those of another company. The goal of benchmarking is to set appropriate performance metrics and measurement for your organization based on the performance metrics of similar companies and similar processes.

Also referred to as best practices, benchmarking is a strategic management process that allows organizations to evaluate critical aspects of their functions in relation to other organizations. Generally, managers select both peer and aspirant organizations as comparisons. A **peer** organization is defined as an organization in the same industry equal or similar in scope and size. An **aspirant** organization is defined as an organization in the same industry but in a better competitive position or larger in scope and size—a leader in the field. Identifying peer and aspirant organizations allows managers to plan improvements and develop future-oriented strategies.

Utilizing benchmarking as a process improvement methodology has many advantages. First, benchmarking can be applied to any business function or process. Second, it has the flexibility to be low cost, and low technology for small businesses, or more robust with software for technical and product benchmarking. The most common costs are site visit costs (to visit peer or aspirant companies), time costs (researching, traveling), and technology and database costs (these costs have been reduced dramatically due to the Internet). Third, benchmarking can be applied internally (comparing performance among departments, divisions, and teams within the organization) and externally (comparing performance to that of other companies in a specific industry or across industries).

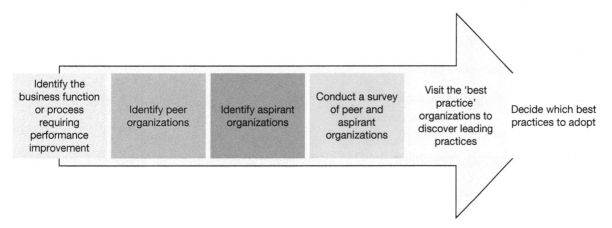

Figure 12.5. The Process of Benchmarking

The wide appeal of benchmarking has led to the emergence of various benchmarking methodologies. Within these broad methodologies there are three specific types of benchmarking categories: process, performance, and strategic benchmarking. The typical benchmarking methodology contains six processes (Figure 12.5).

In all benchmarking methodologies, the goal is to learn how well the selected comparison organizations perform, and, more importantly, the business processes that enable those organizations to perform more effectively and efficiently. Simply put, it is looking at companies that perform the same business functions more successfully and finding out why.

SETTING CONTROL STANDARDS

Setting control standards requires formal target setting. **Standards of performance** are set as performance targets against which actual performance will be measured. Standards vary from company to company. However, common performance standards include quality, efficiency, innovation, safety, and responsiveness to customers.

After top executives set the organization's overall strategy and goals, performance goals are set for departments and divisions to help the organization achieve its larger goals. Department and division managers develop business unit performance standards and goals, while functional managers develop specific performance targets and standards for different functions under their responsibility.

Typically, organizations require that standards of performance be aligned to organizational goals and objectives, since performance goals and targets set at one level affect those at other levels. **Alignment of performance standards** refers to the harmony of goals at each level. Throughout the organization, performance standards should support and be congruent with the organizational strategy and goals. This requires the coordination and collaboration of managers at all levels of the organization.

Performance standards, also referred to as performance targets, should be measurable, clear, and specific, and set realistically achievable outcomes. Performance targets are derived from core business functions, processes, and tasks. They do not represent difficult outcomes, innovative projects, or long-term goals. Simply, performance standards help employees understand what is expected of them.

STRETCH GOALS

Stretch goals have different roles than performance goals and targets. Many organizations utilize the concept of stretch goals to promote organizational effectiveness and achieve objectives. **Stretch goals** are defined as goals that are a little more difficult. These are goals that you may not know how to immediately reach, as they are sufficiently beyond current levels of achievement. Managers and employees may lack a clear idea of how to reach them. There are two major purposes of stretch goals:

1. Improvement of organizational effectiveness
2. Personal growth and professional development

Today, organizations utilize stretch goals to force innovation and creativity. Faced with stretch goals, managers and their staff must utilize collaboration, cooperation, and innovation as they acknowledge that existing methods and systems are insufficient and explore new ideas and avenues.

COMPARING STANDARDS

The previous phase of establishing standards laid the foundation for the second step in the control process—comparing actual performance against desired performance. This next step is the active principle of the control process. **Comparing standards** is defined as the process of identifying and analyzing performance deviations. Managers utilize different methods to compare actual performance to desired performance, such as walking around the plant or obtaining computer-generated company reports measuring results.

GAP ANALYSIS

A contemporary management technique, the gap analysis helps managers compare a department's actual performance against established performance goals and standards. Simply put, the term **gap analysis** refers to the comparison of *actual* performance against *desired* performance. Gap analysis methodology consists of identifying present levels of performance or competencies, measuring them against desired or established levels, and identifying the gap or distance between the two. Common gap analysis techniques consist of three steps:

1. Current state: identifying and listing current/actual performance levels
2. Future state: listing defined and established/desired standards
3. Highlighting gaps: identifying the distance between what is and what should be

Highlighting gaps includes identifying and recording all elements and components between the current state and the future state. Gap elements should be specific and descriptive. Once gap elements are determined and defined, then managers can begin the task of conducting a root cause analysis to determine the factors contributing to gap elements.

Root cause analysis is a method of problem solving that identifies the preliminary cause of a discrepancy or deviation. Managers should list the contributing factors in relevant, objective, and specific terms. For example, 15 delayed orders shipped could be attributable due to different factors, such as five wrong zip codes, seven incorrect postage calculations, and three back orders. Each of these different factors may require different remedies, such as training. Additionally, each of these different factors could stem from different departments or positions. For example, the customer service department may take the zip code information with the order, while the distribution center operates the postage meter.

The gap analysis is an effective tool in helping managers analyze and understand performance discrepancies. Additionally, the gap analysis is particularly helpful in new business settings, changes to production or operation functions, and in prioritizing and allocating resources (Figure 12.6).

Gap Performance Analysis Example				
Key Outputs	**Key Goals**	**Key Tasks**	**Performance Gaps**	**Root Cause**
• 15 Orders To Be Shipped	• Ship 100% of orders within two days	• Package Product • Prepare to Ship • Send Shipment to Customer	• Product was not finished • Shipment was late	• 5 wrong zip codes • 7 incorrect postage codes • 3 back orders

Figure 12.6. Gap Performance Analysis Example

Kipley, D., Jewe, R., & Helm-Stevens, R., A Foundation in the Principles of Management, pp. 283. Copyright © 2015 by Cognella, Inc. Reprinted with permission.

CORRECTIVE ACTION

The last step in the control process, correcting the deficiency, is perhaps the most difficult for new managers. After identification of performance deficiency and analysis of performance deviation, managers need to identify all possible remedies and chart a course of action. **Corrective action** refers to the process of identifying and implementing remedies to repair deficiencies. Remedies should directly address the responsible factors that were identified in the comparing standards stage.

Once the deviation from the established standards has been identified and analyzed, the manager develops and implements solutions to correct them. Solutions can take many forms, such as training employees, revising processes, and creating new procedures.

Corrective action should occur as close as possible in time to the employee's poor performance or mistake. Addressing issues in a timely manner allows managers to help employees make quick adjustments in their effort and direction. Utilizing feedback skills, managers are responsible for helping their employees understand why their performance is deficient, how it can be improved, and the expectations of future performance, behavior, or actions.

When possible, managers attempt to prevent deviations before they occur. Whether preventative or after the fact, however, corrective action means addressing and correcting problems when discovered.

FEEDBACK MECHANISMS

Typically, organizations utilize three basic types of control feedback mechanisms: feedback control, concurrent control, and feed-forward control.

Feedback control refers to mechanisms that gather information about performance deficiencies after they occur. Feedback control focuses on outcomes and results. Although the manager is notified after the occurrence, this information is used to address, correct, or prevent future performance deficiencies. Research has clearly demonstrated that effective feedback improves organizational performance and employee performance. Effective feedback is beneficial in helping the employee correct the deficiency, prevent future occurrences, and improve performance.

Concurrent control refers to mechanisms that gather information about performance deficiencies as they occur. Concurrent control also focuses on outcomes and results, but is an improvement over feedback due to immediate notification. Concurrent control attempts to eliminate or reduce the delay that occurs in feedback control. By eliminating or reducing the delay between performance and feedback about the deficiency, the occurrence

Figure 12.7A and 12.7B. Home Depot Core Values
© 2000-2015 Homer TLC, Inc.

is still vivid for the employee. Employees are more likely to recall specifics and, therefore, contribute to finding possible solutions.

Feed-forward control refers to mechanisms that gather information about performance deficiencies before they occur. Feed-forward control provides information to the manager about performance deficiencies by monitoring inputs, not outcomes or results. The primary advantage of feed-forward control is the proactive attempt to prevent or minimize performance deficiencies before they occur.

For example, Home Depot utilizes a variety of control mechanism to ensure employees' performance is aligned with organizational values. One of Home Depot's eight core values is excellent customer service (Figure 12.7). Using feedback control, Home Depot tracks the customer service experience by printing a web survey link on each receipt.

The survey begins by asking customers to enter information from their receipt and continues through a series of customer experience questions. Associates who provide exceptional customer service are recognized and awarded a Home Depot Values badge that can be worn on their smocks. Badges are awarded as symbols of excellence.

The Home Depot Value of Excellent Customer Service: "Along with our quality products, service, price and selection, we must go the extra mile to give customers knowledgeable advice about merchandise and to help them use those products to their maximum benefit."

CONTINUOUS IMPROVEMENT

Since control is an ongoing and dynamic process, corrective action is not a one-time achievement or result. Managers repeat the entire control process over time. However, most contemporary companies have adopted a culture of continuous improvement to help them identify opportunities for improvement and integrate those improvements into daily routines, tasks, and processes (Figure 12.8). This type of commitment to continuous improvement is aimed at increasing effectiveness and efficiency, reducing waste, and cutting costs by finding opportunities to improve workplace activities.

The **continuous improvement process** is an ongoing and dynamic effort to improve products, services, processes and tasks. Its goal is to improve organizational efficiency, effectiveness, and flexibility by continually identifying opportunities for workplace improvement and continuously working towards incremental improvement of goods, services, or processes. A

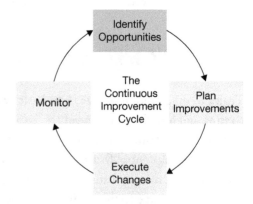

Figure 12.8. The Continuous Improvement Cycle

Kipley, D., Jewe, R., & Helm-Stevens, R., A Foundation in the Principles of Management, pp. 285. Copyright © 2015 by Cognella, Inc. Reprinted with permission.

continual improvement process, continuous improvement should be part of the organizations system. In many successful companies, feedback from employees and customers are constantly evaluated against organizational goals.

A pioneer in the field, W. Edward Deming considered continuous improvement as part of the management system. The basic cycle of the continuous improvement process contains four steps:

1. Identify opportunities for improvement in process or procedure.
2. Plan how to improve the workplace process or procedure.
3. Execute the change.
4. Review how the change is working.

Continuous improvement processes can be either formal or informal. Today, most companies utilize one or more types of continuous improvement processes, as many organizations are working to constantly cut costs, reduce waste, and improve efficiency and effectiveness.

SUMMARY OF CHAPTER

1. This chapter discussed the importance of organizational culture and the basic categories and components that build and shape culture.
2. We explored the two major types of normative control and the three major types of the regulatory control process.
3. We learned about establishing standards and looked at the differences between internal and external control.
4. We looked at the differences between normative, regulative, and bureaucratic control.
5. We examined the contemporary trends of benchmarking and best practices, and how managers can utilize these methods to increase effectiveness and efficiency.
6. This chapter discussed the importance of comparing standards and how managers can use a gap analysis to compare actual performance to desired or established performance.
7. We learned that corrective action, if needed, is necessary to repair performance deficiencies, and examined the three basic methods of feedback control, concurrent control, and feed-forward control.

DISCUSSION QUESTIONS

1. Explain why the control process must begin with the establishment of clear performance standards. Discuss the corrective action process and how it is used to repair performance deficiencies.
2. Outline the steps involved in comparing actual performance to desired performance. Identify the differences between feedback, concurrent, and feed-forward control methods.
3. How can "controlling" help a manager reach department goals and achieve more efficiency and effectiveness in departmental functions?
4. How should managers obtain control? How do managers need to be careful when attempting to obtain control?

WHAT ORGANIZATIONAL CULTURE DO I THRIVE IN?

INSTRUCTIONS

Circle the following adjectives that describe the type of leadership and management styles you prefer.

1. Cautious
2. Humanistic
3. Participative
4. Personal
5. Assertive
6. Challenging
7. Driven by policy and procedure
8. Diverse
9. Fosters self-expression
10. Empowering
11. Leaders call the shots
12. Objective
13. Formal and impersonal
14. Adaptive
15. Leaders set the standards
16. Authoritative
17. Leaders inspire workers
18. Leaders are seen as coaches
19. Analytical
20. Committed

SCORING KEY:

To find which organizational culture is best for you, add up how many words you have selected from the following groups.

Control: Items 1, 7, 11, 12, 16
Collaboration: Items 3, 4, 8, 14, 18
Competence: Items 5, 6, 13, 15, 19
Cultivation: Items 2, 9, 10, 17, 20

ANALYSIS:

Every organizational culture is different, but they can be placed into one of four types of culture: control, collaboration, competence, and cultivation. Whichever culture has the most points (adjectives you circled) is where you thrive best.

Control cultures focus on power structures and policies; they do not like change. Collaboration cultures focus on relationships and harmony; there is a lot of teamwork in these organizations. Competence cultures focus on achievement and competition. Cultivation cultures focus on their values, mission, and accomplishments.

Everyone works best in certain ways and organizations. Keep these in mind as you look for jobs and places to volunteer. Try to find a job that you like, with the right organizational culture for you.

Adapted from: Schneider, W. (1994). The reengineering alternative: A plan for making your current culture work, McGraw-Hill Education.

CHAPTER 12 REFERENCES

"A Change of Pace: Refreshing Continuous Improvement and Developing Leaders at Pace." *Training Journal* (December 2004): 50–52.

Camp, Robert C. (1989). *Benchmarking, The Search for Industry Best Practices That Lead to Superior Performance.* Portland, OR: ASQC Quality Press.

de Jager, B., et al. (2004). "Enabling Continuous Improvement: A Case Study of Implementation." *Journal of Manufacturing Technology Management, 15*(4), 315–324.

Deal, T. E., & Kennedy, A. A. (1982). *Corporate cultures: The rites and rituals of corporate life.* Reading, MA: Addison-Wesley. (See especially p. 4.)

Deming, W. E., (1986). *Out of the Crisis.* Cambridge, MA: MIT Press. *ISBN 0-911379-01-0. OCLC 13126265.*

Deming, W. E., (2000). *The New Economics for Industry, Government, Education (2nd ed.).* Cambridge, MA: MIT Press. *ISBN 0-262-54116-5. OCLC 44162616.*

Deming, W. E., (1966). *Some Theory of Sampling.* New York: Dover Publications. *ISBN 0-486-64684-X. OCLC 166526.*

Dessinger, J. and Moseley, J.L. *Confirmative Evaluation: Practical Strategies for Valuing Continuous Improvement.* San Francisco, CA: Pfeiffer, 2004.

Etienne-Hamilton, E.C. (1994). *Operations Strategies for Competitive Advantage: Text and Cases.* Fort Worth, TX: The Dryden Press.

Flint, Perry. (2004). "Rewired for Success." *Air Transport World, 41*(9), 38–39. Retrieved from: http://www.referenceforbusiness.com/management/Comp-De/Continuous-Improvement.html#ixzz42ZGVz66h

Franklin, M. (2006). Performance gap analysis: human performance improvement. InfoLine, Alexandria, VA: ASTD Press.

Hofstede, G. (1980). *Culture's consequences: International differences in work-related values*. Beverly Hills, CA: Sage. (See especially p. 25.)

Kouzes, J. M., Caldwell, D. F., & Posner, B. Z. (1983). Organizational culture: How it is created, maintained, and changed. Presentation at OD Network National Conference, Los Angeles, October 9.

McNair, C. J., Leibfriend, K. H. J. (1993). Benchmarking: A Tool for Continuous Improvement (Coopers & Lybrand Performance Solutions Series) John Wiley and Sons, New York, New York.

O'Reilly, C. (1983). Corporations, cults, and organizational culture: Lessons from Silicon Valley firms. Paper presented at the Annual Meeting of the Academy of Management, Dallas, Texas.

Ouchi, W. G. (1981). *Theory Z: How American business can meet the Japanese challenge*. Reading, MA: Addison-Wesley. (See especially p. 41.)

Peters, T. J., & Waterman Jr., R. H. (1982). *In search of excellence: Lessons from America's best-run companies.* New York: Harper & Row. (See especially p. 103.)

Schein, E. H. (1983). The role of the founder in creating organizational cultures. *Organizational Dynamics, 12*(1), 13–28.

Schein, E. H. (1992). *Organizational culture and leadership: A dynamic view* (2nd ed.). San Francisco: Jossey-Bass. (See especially p. 9.)

Sandmeyer, L. (2009). "Creating a Culture for Innovation and Improvement: Lessons Learned," Innovation Insights Series Number 22, The Pennsylvania State University. http://www.psu.edu/president/pia/innovation/

Schneider, W. E. (1994). *The reengineering alternative: A plan for making your current culture work*. Burr Ridge, IL: Irwin Professional Pub.

Shojania KG, Ranji SR, Shaw LK, Charo LN, Lai JC, Rushakoff RJ, McDonald KM, Owens DK. Diabetes Mellitus Care. Vol. 2 of: Shojania KG, McDonald KM, Wachter RM, Owens DK. Closing The Quality Gap: A Critical Analysis of Quality Improvement Strategies. Technical Review 9 (Contract No. 290-02-0017 to the Stanford University-UCSF Evidence-based Practice Center). AHRQ Publication No. 04-0051-2. Rockville, MD: Agency for Healthcare Research and Quality. September 2004.

Spender, J. C. (1983). Myths, recipes and knowledge-bases in organizational analysis (Unpublished manuscript). Graduate School of Management, University of California at Los Angeles. (See especially p. 2.)

Tharp, B. M. (2005). *Defining culture and organizational culture: From anthropology to the office*. Hawthorne Publishers. (See especially p. 2.)

Van Maanen, J., & Barley, S. R. (1983). Cultural organization: Fragments of a theory. Paper presented at the Annual Meeting of the Academy of Management, Dallas, Texas. (See especially p. 7.)

Walsh, J., McDonald, K. M., Shojania K. G. (2004). *Closing the Quality Gap: A Critical Analysis of Quality Improvement Strategies*, Rockville, MD: Agency for Healthcare Research and Quality.

Watson, Gregory H. 1992. *The Benchmarking Workbook: Adapting Best Practices for Performance Improvement*. Portland, OR: Productivity Press.

GLOSSARY

Ability an acquired or natural capacity or talent that enables an individual to perform a particular job or task successfully (Chapter 3)

Abraham Maslow a practicing psychologist, he developed one of the most widely recognized need theories, the hierarchy of needs (Chapter 1)

Absolute comparisons each criterion is compared with a standard or ranked on its own merits (Chapter 8)

Active listening the process of participating in giving the speaker nonjudgmental feedback that demonstrates you accurately heard the speaker's message (Chapter 7)

Adjourning occurs after the completion of the project or task, involves closing the project and reviewing successes and failures (Chapter 9)

Affective commitment a feeling that is the likely result of increased job satisfaction (Chapter 4)

Alignment of performance standards refers to the harmony of goals at each performance level (Chapter 12)

Analytic style a high tolerance for ambiguity in decision making (Chapter 8)

Aspirant an organization in a better competitive position, or larger in scope and size, than another organization—a leader in the field (Chapter 12)

Attitudes a set of complex beliefs and feelings that people have about specific ideas, people, or situations (Chapter 4)

Attribution theory suggests that we attribute causes to behavior based on our observations of certain internal or external characteristics of that behavior (Chapter 4)

Authentic leaders people who know who they are, know what they believe in and value, and act on those values and beliefs openly and candidly (Chapter 10)

Authoritarianism the extent to which a person believes that power and status differences are appropriate within hierarchical social systems, such as an organization (Chapter 3)

Autonomy the degree to which workers have the independence and authority to utilize resources, access information, and decide how and when to accomplish their tasks (Chapter 9)

Avoiding the conflict management technique where managers choose to ignore the conflict (Chapter 11)

Award programs can be an effective means of motivation in which employees receive awards for everything from seniority to perfect attendance, from zero defects to cost reduction suggestions (Chapter 6)

Baird decision making framework examines ethical situations through four lenses: the rights lens, the relationship lens, the results lens, and the reputation lens (Chapter 8)

Bank Wiring Observation Room Experiment an experiment conducted by Mayo and F.J. Roethlisberger focusing on whether piecework incentives would increase productivity (Chapter 1)

Base pay the most important reward for work is the pay a worker receives (Chapter 6)

Behavioral barriers created by myopic managers and their inability to view issues or change unbiased (Chapter 11)

Behaviors the actions we take with regard to a particular object or entity (Chapter 4)

Beliefs represent what we have learned or come to know through experience—as such, they are either true or represent what we think is true (Chapter 4)

Belongingness (need) primarily concerned with social needs, such as the need for love and affection and the need to be accepted by peers (Chapter 5)

Benchmarking the process of comparing a set of products or customer metrics, measurements, and performance of one company to those of another company (Chapter 12)

Best practices implies the organization or industry executes methods, processes, or techniques that accomplish desired outcomes in the most effective and efficient manner (Chapter 12)

Big Five Model a widely accepted model that supports the theory that five basic dimensions underlie all others and encompass most of the significant variations in human personality (Chapter 3)

Board representatives employees who sit on a company's board of directors and represent the interests of the firm's employees (Chapter 6)

Bonus systems provide managers with lump-sum payments from a special fund based on the financial performance of the organization or a unit (Chapter 6)

Brainstorming a situation in which groups of people meet to generate new ideas and solutions around a specific area of interest through intensive and freewheeling group discussion (Chapter 11)

Bureaucracy impersonal, objective form of organization (Chapter 1)

Bureaucratic control the system of rules and standard operating procedures that regulate workplace activities and behaviors (Chapter 12)

Business ethics a form of applied or professional ethics that examines ethical principles and moral or ethical problems that arise in a business environment (Chapter 8)

Centralized networks when information is funneled through a limited number of employees within the organization (Chapter 7)

Challenging mental models members routinely challenge the way business is done, setting aside of old ways of thinking (Chapter 1)

Change forces lead to differences in the form, quality, or condition of an organization over time (Chapter 11)

Change-related activities aimed at modifying organizational components, such as proposing new strategies and visions, encouraging innovation, and taking risks, to promote needed change (Chapter 2)

Charisma a quality of an individual personality by virtue of which he or she is set apart from ordinary people and treated as being endowed with supernatural, superhuman, or at least specifically exceptional powers or qualities (Chapter 10)

Charismatic leadership theory followers attribute heroic or extraordinary leadership abilities when they observe certain behaviors (Chapter 10)

Clarifying asking the sender to explain or provide more details, to help the receiver understand confusing or ambiguous statements (Chapter 7)

Classical conditioning developed by Ivan Pavlov, it is a simple form of learning in which a conditioned response is linked with an unconditioned stimulus (Chapter 5)

Classical organizational approach unlike the scientific management approach, it focuses on the total organization and the importance of the development of managerial principles versus the productivity and study of work methods of individuals (Chapter 1)

Classical view an approach to management best illustrated by Robert Katz, who described three skills that are essential for administrative work: technical, human, and conceptual (Chapter 2)

Closed system not influenced by and does not interact with its environment, it is mainly mechanical and has predetermined motions or activities that must be performed, regardless of the environment (Chapter 1)

Closure the tendency to fill in the gaps when information is missing (Chapter 7)

Coercive change strategy involves the use of a position of power to create change by decree and formal authority, giving orders, and enforcing those orders to overcome resistance (Chapter 11)

Cognition bits of knowledge that can pertain to any variety of thoughts, values, facts, or emotions (Chapter 4)

Cognitive abilities brain-based skills that are needed to carry out any task, from the simplest to the most complex (Chapter 3)

Cognitive dissonance theory when two sets of cognitions or perceptions are contradictory or incongruent, a person experiences a level of conflict and anxiety (Chapter 4)

Cohesiveness a critical characteristic of successful work teams, it is the extent to which team members are attracted to a team and motivated to stay as a part of the team (Chapter 9)

Collaboration cultures cultures that value building relationships, developing people, and teamwork (Chapter 12)

Communication channel used to describe the means through which employees send and receive information (Chapter 7)

Communication network composed of a group of employees sharing regular lines of communication (Chapter 7)

Communication process the exchange of information between two or more people (Chapter 7)

Comparing standards the process of identifying and analyzing performance deviations (Chapter 12)

Comparison-other it might be a person in the same work group, someone in another part of the organization, or even a composite of several people scattered throughout the organization (Chapter 5)

Competence cultures rooted in achievement and competition (Chapter 12)

Competitive forces a driver of change, because if an organization cannot match or exceed its competitors in at least one of its functional areas, it will not survive (Chapter 11)

Compromising when two sides agree to give up some of their demands for a solution that gives each party part of what they originally wanted (Chapter 11)

Concentration of effect the inverse function of the number of people affected by a decision (Chapter 8)

Conceptual skills the ability to see the organization holistically and understand how the different parts of the company affect each other, and the skill to develop ideas and concepts and implement strategies (Chapter 2)

Conceptual style individuals with a conceptual style of decision making are usually broad in their approach and prefer to consider all options and alternatives (Chapter 8)

Concurrent control refers to mechanisms that gather information about performance deficiencies as they occur (Chapter 12)

Conflict pertains to the opposing ideas and actions of different entities, thus resulting in an antagonistic state (Chapter 11)

Consideration the extent to which a person's work relationships are characterized by mutual trust, respect for employees' ideas, and regard for their feelings (Chapter 10)

Consistency the observation of a person's actions over time (Chapter 4)

Constructive feedback addresses areas of improvement, with the intention to be helpful or corrective (Chapter 7)

Contemporary view a more modern view on management skills, listing what activities managers should perform and what skills they require (Chapter 2)

Contingency approach a management approach that can be summarized as an "it all depends" approach, in which decisions depend on circumstances; flexible management (Chapter 1)

Continuance commitment when an individual weighs the pros and cons of leaving an organization, they are more likely to feel this if they have an established, successful role, or have had several promotions at that organization (Chapter 4)

Continuous improvement process an ongoing and dynamic effort to improve products, services, processes, and tasks (Chapter 12)

Contrast effect a form of bias that results from the perceptions one has of the target person becoming distorted by the perceiver's perception of others in the same situation (Chapter 4)

Control establishes the standards necessary to achieve organizational goals (Chapter 12)

Control cultures power based, rich in policies and procedures, utilize detailed tracking systems, and exert significant influence over employees and situations (Chapter 12)

Controlling an ongoing process that provides a means to validate if the tasks assigned are being performed on time and according to the standards set by management (Chapter 2)

Control loss occurs when workplace behavior and procedures do not conform to established standards (Chapter 12)

Control process consists of three essential steps: establishing performance standards, comparing actual performance against performance standards, and taking corrective action if necessary (Chapter 12)

Corrective action the process of identifying and implementing remedies to repair deficiencies (Chapter 12)

Creativity the production of novel and useful ideas and a form of organizational innovation (Chapter 11)

Cross-functional teams intentionally composed of employees at about the same hierarchical level but from different functional areas of the organization (Chapter 9)

Cultivation cultures rooted in faith, beliefs, and mission (Chapter 12)

Decentralized networks when information is broadly shared and flows through many individuals within the organization (Chapter 7)

Decision making the process of choosing a solution from available alternatives (Chapter 8)

Decision rule a standard sequence or automated responses that organizational members follow routinely whenever they encounter a specific type of problem or opportunity (Chapter 8)

Decoding the process by which the receiver interprets the communication, and will translate the message using their knowledge, background, and experience (Chapter 7)

Deforming characterized by team member isolation (Chapter 9)

Delphi technique a series of questionnaires, surveys, and so on, are sent to a selected panel of experts (the Delphi group) through a facilitator, who oversees their responses (Chapter 9)

Demographic and social forces motivate managers to find better ways to supervise and motivate minority and female employees (Chapter 11)

De-norming characterized by the deterioration of team performance (Chapter 9)

De-storming distinguished by a decrease in group cohesiveness (Chapter 9)

Destructive feedback tends to occur in the form of generalized or subjective comments, is critical and disapproving without any intention of being helpful (Chapter 7)

Deviant behavior are deliberate or intentional behaviors of a broad syndrome, such as theft of company property, with the desire to cause harm to the organization(Chapter 4)

Directive style individuals with this style are efficient, rational, and logical; they tend to have a low tolerance for ambiguity (Chapter 8)

Distinctiveness the extent to which a specific action engaged in by an individual is unusual or uncommon for that particular individual (Chapter 4)

Distributive justice deals with the fairness of pay, promotions, and desirable working conditions, and the assignment of employees without respect to ethnicity, race, age, or gender (Chapters 5 and 8)

Distributive norm the standard of behavior that is required, desired, or designated as normal within a particular group (Chapter 8)

Disturbance handler responsible for corrective action when an organization faces important or unexpected disturbances (Chapter 2)

Douglas McGregor wrote *The Human Side of Enterprise* (1960), in which he identified Theory X and Theory Y (Chapter 1)

Downward communication the communication that flows from upper to lower levels in an organization (Chapter 7)

Dual roles individuals equally comfortable contributing to either the task or the socio-emotional role (Chapter 9)

Economic, political, and global forces affect organizations and compel them to adjust how and where they produce goods and provide services (Chapter 11)

Effort-to-performance (expectancy) a person's perception of the probability that effort will lead to successful performance (Chapter 5)

Electronic brainstorming an alternative approach to brainstorming in which the group members use computers to communicate and generate alternative solutions (Chapter 11)

Empathetic listening the ability to understand by paying attention to another person's feelings, concerns, or emotional state (Chapter 7)

Employee involvement creating an environment where people have an impact on decisions and actions that affect their jobs (Chapter 6)

Employee-oriented leader (relationship-oriented style) emphasizes interpersonal relationships by taking a personal interest in the needs of employees and accepting individual differences among them (Chapter 10)

Employee stock option plans set aside stock in the company for employees to purchase at a reduced rate (Chapter 6)

Empowerment the process of enabling workers to set their own work goals, make decisions, and solve problems within their spheres of responsibility and authority (Chapter 5)

Encoding selecting a form for the message, such as written or verbal, that can be recognized and acknowledged by the receiver (Chapter 7)

Entrepreneur this type of manager searches both within the organization and its environment and initiates improvement projects to bring about change (Chapter 2)

Equitable rewards when policies are perceived as just and fair there is likely to be greater job satisfaction (Chapter 4)

Equity theory of motivation based on the simple premise that people in organizations want to be treated fairly (Chapter 5)

ERG theory of motivation created by Clayton Alderfer to explain motivation after seeing Maslow's hierarchy and deciding that Maslow's model poorly reflected the true complexity of human motivation (Chapter 5)

Espoused values represent the ideals, principles, and standards championed by leaders and managers (Chapter 12)

Esteem needs the first of the higher order needs, it encompasses both the needs for positive self-image and self-respect and the need to be respected by others (Chapters 1 and 5)

Ethical behavior used to describe what we accept as right or wrong, or good or bad (Chapter 8)

Ethical decision making a decision that is both legally and morally acceptable to the larger community, utilizing all ethical perspectives and models to inform and influence the decision making to produce the best possible outcomes for all stakeholders (Chapter 8)

Ethical forces drive companies to change their rules and Standard Operating Procedures (SOP's) to promote ethical behavior and to protect the interests and reputation of the organization and the people affected by unethical actions (Chapter 11)

Ethical intensity the degree of moral importance given to an issue (Chapter 8)

Ethical leadership treating other people's values and decisions with respect, allowing others to be themselves with creative wants and desires, approaching others with a sense of unconditional worth, and valuing individual differences (Chapter 10)

Ethical perspectives provide a philosophical basis for evaluating behavior and decision making (Chapter 8)

Ethics the code of moral principles that sets standards of good or bad, right or wrong, in our conduct (Chapter 8)

Ethics training prepares employees for facing ethical dilemmas in the workplace (Chapter 8)

Evaluation apprehension in electronic brainstorming, what everyone else may think of your idea (Chapter 11)

Expectancy theory motivation depends on how much we want something and how likely we think we are to get it (Chapter 5)

Extended work scheduling refers to work schedules having longer than normal workdays; some consider it to be between 8 and 12 hours, while others think it is over 12 hours (Chapter 6)

External locus of control individuals with this tend to believe that outside forces beyond their control are mainly responsible for their fate and see little connection between their own actions and what happens to them (Chapter 3)

External noise is related to the environment, literal sounds or an interruption in technology (Chapter 7)

External standards the process of systematically scanning the environment and identifying the best practices (Chapter 12)

Extinction decreases the frequency of behavior, especially behavior that was previously rewarded (Chapter 5)

Extrinsically motivated work behavior behavior performed to acquire material or social rewards, or to avoid punishment (Chapter 5)

Feedback a return message from the receiver to the sender, indicating the receiver's translation and understanding of the message (Chapter 7)

Feedback control mechanisms that gather information about performance deficiencies after they occur (Chapter 12)

Feedback signal the interpretation of the message by the receiver, oftentimes influenced by experience, background, or emotional state (Chapter 7)

Feed-forward control mechanisms that gather information about performance deficiencies before they occur (Chapter 12)

Ferrell ethical decision making framework considers four factors when evaluating ethical dilemmas: ethical issue intensity, individual factors, organizational factors, and opportunity (Chapter 8)

Fiedler's theory acknowledges that personal characteristics influence the effectiveness of leaders; he was particularly interested in styles of leadership or how a person approaches the task of leadership (Chapter 10)

Figurehead when this is a manager's position of the company, the manager performs a number of routine duties of a legal or social nature, such as greeting company visitors, speaking at the openings of new facilities, or representing the company at community functions (Chapter 2)

Flexible work arrangements generally intended to enhance employee motivation and performance by giving workers more flexibility in how and when they work (Chapters 5 and 6)

Flexible work scheduling (flextime) has become extremely popular with both employees and their employers, with approximately 43% of the U.S. full-time workforce having flexible daily arrival and departure times (Chapter 6)

Force field analysis a powerful and strategic tool utilized by leaders and managers to successfully lead change (Chapter 11)

Formal communication channels the system of official organizational channels that carry approved information and messages (Chapter 7)

Formal leaders managers who are given legal authority to influence other members in the organization to achieve its goals (Chapter 10)

Forming characterized as the meet-and-greet stage; when team members first meet each other, they are polite and try to avoid controversy and conflict (Chapter 9)

Frank and Lillian Gilbreth a pioneering team in work and motion studies, they focused on worker efficiency and a help to worker welfare; they created the first motion study on brick layers, noting which motions were necessary and which could be cut out (Chapter 1)

Frederick Taylor often called the "father of scientific management," he thought that organizations should study tasks and then create precise procedures to accomplish those tasks (Chapter 1)

Frontline managers responsible for a work group to a higher level of management, they oversee a company's primary production activities and must generate efficient productivity and control costs (Chapter 2)

Functional manager a person who has management authority over an organizational unit, such as a department within a business, company, or other organization (Chapter 2)

Functional roles assist the team to successfully and productively attain their goal, including task, socio-emotional, and dual roles (Chapter 9)

Gain-sharing programs grant additional earnings to employees or work groups for cost-reduction ideas (Chapter 6)

Gap analysis the comparison of actual performance against desired performance (Chapter 12)

General managers refers to any executive who has responsibility for the day-to-day operations of a business (Chapter 2)

Goal specificity the clarity and precision of the goal (Chapter 5)

Grapevine the most common informal communication channel, the grapevine is a network of employee-to-employee messages that occur outside of formal communication channels (Chapter 7)

Group two or more people interacting to achieve their goal (Chapter 1)

Group decision making a type of participatory process in which multiple individuals, acting collectively, analyze problems or situations, consider and evaluate alternative courses of action, and select from among the alternatives a solution or solutions (Chapter 9)

Group polarization a potential disadvantage of group decision making, it is the tendency of the group to converge on more extreme solutions to a problem (Chapter 9)

Groupthink occurs when the desire for harmony or conformity among group members results in illogical, irrational, or unscientific decision making (Chapter 9)

Halo effect when our general overall impression of a person influences or distorts how we feel and think about their character (Chapter 4)

Harshness, leniency, and average tendency bias the set of biases that occur when a supervisor rates a subordinate's performance; all of these can be problematic because 1) the supervisor is not correctly perceiving the subordinates, and 2) it makes it difficult to compare subordinates under different supervisors (Chapter 4)

Hawthorne studies a series of experiments that rigorously applied classical management theory, only to reveal its shortcomings; consisted of two studies at the Hawthorne Works of Western Electrical Company between 1924 and 1932 (Chapter 1)

Hearing involuntary and uncontrollable, involves receiving and perceiving sounds (Chapter 7)

Henri Fayol generally regarded as the pioneer of classical administrative theory, he created the 14 principles of management, which include planning, organizing, commanding, coordinating, and controlling (Chapter 1)

Henry Gantt an American engineer and famous management consultant who was best known for his planning methodology, the Gantt chart, a bar graph that measures planned and completed work along each stage of production (Chapter 2, Figure 2.3)

High authoritarians may accept directives or orders from someone who is the boss (Chapter 3)

High-functioning team generally regarded as a tight-knit team, aligned with and committed to a common goal, capable of achieving a high level of collaboration and innovation (Chapter 9)

High need for achievement people with this require challenging, but not impossible tasks; they thrive when solving difficult problems (Chapter 5)

High need for affiliation concerned with establishing and maintaining good relations with other people; people with this work best in groups (Chapter 5)

High need for power people with this have a strong desire to exert emotional and behavioral control or influence over others; they work best when they are in positions of power (Chapter 5)

High self-efficacy people that possess this believe that they can perform well on a specific task (Chapter 3)

High self-esteem people that have this are more likely to seek higher-status jobs, set higher goals for themselves, be more confident in their ability to achieve higher levels of performance, and derive greater intrinsic satisfaction from their accomplishments (Chapter 3)

High self-monitors want their behavior to be socially acceptable and are attuned to any social cues that signal appropriate or inappropriate behavior, perform well in jobs with lots of interaction with people (Chapter 3)

Hindering roles include individual actions that impede the team's progress, often delay or obstruct the team's progress (Chapter 9)

Human motivation theory states that every person has one of three main driving motivators: the needs for achievement, affiliation, or power (Chapter 5)

Human relations movement refers to the researchers of organizational development who studied the interactions of people in organizations; the objective was to enhance organizational success by building appropriate relationships with workers (Chapter 1)

Human skills the ability to motivate and interact well with others (Chapter 2)

Hygiene factors certain factors that cause job dissatisfaction, such as pay, working conditions, supervisors, and job security (Chapter 5)

Incentive systems plans in which employees can earn additional compensation in return for certain types of performance (Chapter 6)

Indirect compensation commonly referred to as the employee benefits plan, it includes social security contributions, unemployment compensation, and so on (Chapter 6)

Individual differences personal attributes that vary from one person to another (Chapter 4)

Individual factors the notion that people base their ethical decisions on their own values and principles of right or wrong (Chapter 8)

Individualism-collectivism the degree to which individuals are integrated into groups, defined as the degree of believing one should be self-sufficient and that loyalty to one's self is more important than loyalty to one's team or company (Chapter 9)

Individualism view focuses on the long-term advancement of self-interest in the context of ethical behavior (Chapter 8)

Individualists put their welfare and interest and those of their immediate family first, and generally prefer independent tasks; they may prefer to work alone (Chapter 9)

Individual level at this level, organizational behavior involves the study of learning, perception, creativity, motivation, personality, turnover, task performance, cooperative behavior, deviant behavior, ethics, and cognition (Chapter 1)

Industry-wide best practices define guidelines (such as ethics) and methods (techniques and processes) that represent the most efficient or prudent course of action for a commercial or professional procedure or process (Chapter 12)

Informal communication channels occur outside of the organization's established channels, generally arise from a lack of information or truthfulness from the formal communication channel, as well as the increased ease of use, as informal channels are unregulated (Chapter 7)

Informal leaders have no legal authority to influence other employees, but their personal skills and qualities give them the ability to exert influence in an organization, sometimes as much influence as formal leaders (Chapter 10)

Informational justice the perception that the employees have about the extent to which the manager is explaining their decisions and the procedures used to arrive at them (Chapter 5)

Informational roles based around gathering and disseminating information through and with employees (Chapter 2)

Initiating structure the extent to which a leader is likely to define and structure his or her role and those of employees in the search for goal attainment (Chapter 10)

Innovation changing or creating more effective processes, products, services, or ways of doing things (Chapter 11)

Inputs an individual's contributions to the organization, including such factors as education, experience, effort, and loyalty (Chapter 5)

Instrumental values concern the means for accomplishing these ends, are core values, and as such are permanent in nature, comprising personal characteristics and character traits (Chapter 8)

Interactional justice focuses on the interpersonal treatment of others with dignity and respect when procedures are implemented (Chapter 8)

Intergroup conflict involves two or more groups and their respective members; it generally arises within competing groups, when groups interrelate to accomplish a task, or when groups compete for resources (Chapter 11)

Internal locus of control people with this believe that their own actions and behaviors have an impact on what happens to them (Chapter 3)

Internal noise is generally semantic or psychological; examples include grammatical errors and acronyms (Chapter 7)

Internal standards the process of setting and monitoring systematic performance standards in an effort to ensure workplace tasks and activities are conducted in an effective and efficient manner (Chapter 12)

Interpersonal justice the perceived fairness of the interpersonal treatment employees receive from the distributors of outcomes (typically managers) (Chapter 5)

Interpersonal roles involve constantly working and interacting with people, very people intensive (Chapter 2)

Job characteristic model developed by Hackman and Oldman (1976), a contemporary job design theory; similar to job rotation, job enlargement, and job enrichment, the job characteristic model (JCM) attempts to overcome the deficiencies of job specialization (Chapter 6)

Job design a critical component of how organizations design jobs; it is the number, kind, and variety of tasks performed by an individual employee (Chapter 5 and 6)

Job enlargement a method of job redesign aimed at motivating employees, it increases the number of different tasks assigned to an employee (Chapter 6)

Job enrichment based on the dual-structure theory of motivation, this theory contends that employees can be motivated by positive job-related experiences, such as feelings of achievement, responsibility, and recognition (Chapter 6)

Job involvement employees with a high level of involvement strongly identify with and care about the kind of work they do (Chapter 4)

Job rotation a method of job redesign aimed at motivating employees by introducing variety into an employee's workday (Chapter 6)

Job sharing a form of regular part-time work in which two people split a traditional 40-hour-a-week job (Chapter 6)

Job specialization the first widespread model of how individual work should be designed (Chapters 5 and 6)

Justice view considers the behavior ethical when people are treated impartially and fairly, according to legal rules and standards, in the context of moral reasoning (Chapter 8)

Kinesics involves facial and body movements; examples include facial expressions, eye contact, and hand gestures, such as tapping fingers or jingling keys (Chapter 7)

Knowledge-of-predictor bias occurs when a manager or even a professor knows a person's standing on a predictor of performance; the information may bias their perceptions of that person (Chapter 4)

Leader someone who is responsible for the motivation, training, and encouragement of subordinates to accomplish organizational objectives (Chapter 2)

Leader-member exchange theory (LMX) works in two ways: it describes leadership and it prescribes leadership; the central concept is the dyadic relationship between leaders and their subordinates (Chapter 10)

Leadership the ability to influence a group toward the achievement of a vision or a set of goals (Chapter 10)

Leading guiding the activities of organization members in the direction that helps the organization move towards the fulfillment of the goals (Chapter 2)

Learning organization approach all employees systematically participate in identifying and solving organizational problems that will enable continuous change and improvement, increasing the organization's capacity to grow, learn, and achieve its purpose (Chapter 1)

Learning reinforcement theory also known as "operant conditioning," it is generally associated with the work of B.F. Skinner; in its simplest form, reinforcement theory suggests that behavior is a function of its consequences (Chapter 5)

Least preferred coworker (LPC) questionnaire used to identify style by measuring whether a person is task or relationship oriented; it asks respondents to think of all the coworkers they have ever had and describe the one person they least enjoyed working with by rating that person on a scale of 1 to 8 for each of 16 sets of contrasting adjectives (Chapter 10)

Liaison a person who networks by connecting people inside the company as well as externally (Chapter 2)

Listening requires attention, as it is a conscious effort to hear and understand (Chapter 7)

Long-term compensation gives managers additional income based on stock price performance, earnings per share, or return on equity (Chapter 6)

Low authoritarians people who are more likely to question things and express disagreement with their leader (Chapter 3)

Low need of affiliation individuals with this can be part of a more independent personality; people with this are often seen as loners (Chapter 5)

Low self-efficacy individuals with this tend to doubt their ability to perform a specific task (Chapter 3)

Low self-esteem if someone possesses this, they may be content to remain in lower-level jobs, question their self-worth, be apprehensive about their ability to succeed in different endeavors, and focus more on extrinsic rewards (Chapter 3)

Low self-monitors more likely to be frank with their response and say what they think is true or correct; not concerned about how others will react to them (Chapter 3)

Machiavellianism named after Niccolo Machiavelli, a 16th-century author famous for his book *The Prince*, which describes how to gain power and control others (Chapter 3)

Magnitude of consequences the harm or benefits accruing to individuals affected by a decision or behavior (Chapter 8)

Management science approach also called the operations research approach, it was first developed during World War II to find solutions to warfare issues, such as which gun sight would best stop German attacks on the British mainland; also known at the quantitative approach because it uses mathematical models to solve problems by analyzing a mix of variables, constraints, and costs to enable management to make optimal decisions (Chapter 1)

Manager a person responsible for controlling or administering all or part of a company or similar organization (Chapter 1)

Managerial effectiveness management's use of organizational resources in meeting organizational goals (Chapter 2)

Managerial efficiency the proportion of total organizational resources that contribute to productivity during the manufacturing process (Chapter 2)

Managerial skills skills that are necessary to make business decisions to reach the organization's goals by leading and working with people and utilizing other organizational resources within a company (Chapter 2)

Mary Parker Follett stressed the interactions of management with workers and the importance of an organization establishing common goals for its employees; she also stressed the importance of employees being involved in decision making (Chapter 1)

Max Weber considered to be the father of bureaucratic management, he felt organizations should be managed impersonally and that they should follow a formal organizational structure wherein specific rules are followed (Chapter 1)

Mentally challenging work jobs with too little challenge are deemed boring, frustrating, and can produce feelings of failure (Chapter 4)

Merit pay a plan in which base pay raises based on the employee's performance (Chapter 6)

Mid-level managers the intermediate management of a hierarchical organization, being subordinate to the top-level management but above the lowest levels of operational staff (Chapter 2)

Monitoring involves actively seeking and obtaining a wide variety of information, both internal and external, to develop a thorough understanding of the organization and its environment (Chapters 2 and 12)

Moral rights approach asserts that human beings have fundamental rights and liberties that cannot be taken away by an individual's decision (Chapter 8)

Motivation the process of arousing and sustaining goal-directed behavior (Chapter 5)

Motivation factors things such as achievement and recognition are often cited by people as primary causes of satisfaction and motivation (Chapter 5)

Myers–Briggs Type Indicator (MBTI) the most widely used personality assessment tool in the world, it is used to measure psychological preferences of people based on how they feel about a certain situation (Chapter 3)

Nature the part of your personality characterized by its biological heritage (Chapter 3)

Need for achievement arises from an individual's desire to accomplish a goal or task more effectively than in the past (Chapter 5)

Need theory a motivational model that attempts to explain how the needs for achievement, power, and affiliation affect the actions of people from a managerial context (Chapter 1)

Negative reinforcement also known as avoidance, it is a means of increasing the frequency of desirable behavior (Chapter 5)

Negotiator responsible for representing the organization at major negotiations, including schedules, projects, goals, outcomes, resources, and employee raises (Chapter 2)

Noise interference with the transmission of the intended message (Chapter 7)

Nominal group technique a controlled version of brainstorming that encourages creative thinking (Chapter 11)

Non-functional roles detract from the team and hinder performance (Chapter 9)

Non-participative roles refer to the actions of individuals that are absent either physically or mentally (Chapter 9)

Non-programmed decisions occur in unusual situations that have not been addressed often (Chapter 8)

Nonverbal communication includes gestures and facial expressions, any communication that does not involve words (Chapter 7)

Normative control governing employee behavior through accepted patterns of behavior, including team norms and organizational culture (Chapter 12)

Norming the third stage of team development; having resolved differences, team members can begin the process of learning to work together productively (Chapter 9)

Nurture the argument that a person's environment or life experiences shape their personality (Chapter 3)

Observable artifacts a company's beliefs, behaviors, and attitudes (Chapter 12)

Omniscience when people believe they know everything and lack awareness of what they do not know (Chapter 4)

Open system a system that is continuously interacting with its environment (Chapter 1)

Opportunity the conditions within an organization that limit or permit ethical or unethical behavior (Chapter 8)

Organization a collection of people who work together and coordinate their activities to meet a need or to pursue a common goal or goals (Chapter 1)

Organizational behavior not the study of how organizations behave, but rather the study of individual behavior within an organizational setting (Chapter 1)

Organizational change the shift from the present state toward a desired state to increase performance and/ or effectiveness (Chapter 11)

Organizational commitment when an employee identifies strongly with the employing organization (Chapter 4)

Organizational culture a system of shared values, beliefs, and assumptions that guides how employees behave in the workplace (Chapter 12)

Organizational development a philosophy of planned change and growth, it encompasses a broad range of strategies and implementation techniques designed to improve efficiency and effectiveness (Chapter 11)

Organizational effectiveness the ability of an organization to achieve its goals (Chapter 1)

Organizational entropy the disorder, decay, or randomness that occurs when an organization is not properly maintained (Chapter 11)

Organizational factors refers to the consideration that organizational culture can have a stronger influence on employees than an individual's values (Chapter 8)

Organizational inertia the tendency to have the status quo remain in place (Chapter 11)

Organizational innovation the implementation of a new organizational method in the undertaking's business practices, workplace organization, or external relations (Chapter 11)

Organizational justice an employee's perception of their organization's overall fairness (Chapter 5)

Organizational justice theory proposes that employees will not be motivated to contribute their inputs unless they perceive fair procedures will be used to distribute outcomes in the organization and that they will be treated fairly by managers (Chapter 5)

Organizational renewal an ongoing process, characterized by a progression in which innovation and adaptation are important outcomes; the ultimate goal of organizational renewal is to prevent organizational entropy (Chapter 11)

Organization level a level of organizational behavior that involves the study of issues such as organizational culture, organizational structure, cultural diversity, inter-organizational cooperation and conflict, change, technology, and external environmental forces (Chapter 1)

Organizing assigning the tasks developed in the planning stages to various individuals or groups within the organization (Chapter 2)

Outcomes what a person receives in return for their efforts, such as pay, recognition, social relationships, intrinsic rewards, and such similar things (Chapter 5)

Paralanguage involves vocal characterizers and qualifiers (Chapter 7)

Paraphrasing restating what was said to you in your own words, it helps the receiver understand and provides the opportunity for the sender to further expand upon the message (Chapter 7)

Participative management employees at all levels are encouraged to contribute ideas towards identifying and setting organizational goals, problem solving, and other decisions that may directly affect them (Chapters 5 and 6)

Path-goal theory describes how leaders can motivate their followers to achieve group and organizational goals, and the kinds of behaviors they can engage in to accomplish that (Chapter 10)

People-related activities focus on managing people within the organization and giving support, encouragement, and recognition (Chapter 2)

Perception a subjective, active, and creative process, it is defined as the process of experiencing the world around us (Chapters 4 and 7)

Performance feedback a return of information about a workplace activity, process, or result; there are several types of performance feedback in the workplace (Chapter 7)

Performance-to-outcome (instrumentality) a person's perception of the probability that performance will lead to certain other outcomes (Chapter 5)

Performing distinguished by performance; the team has become a well-oiled machine—an effective and efficient, fully functioning team (Chapter 9)

Perquisites special privileges awarded to selected members of an organization, usually top managers (Chapter 6)

Personal ethics guides for our behavior, helping us make moral choices among alternative courses of action (Chapter 8)

Personal mastery members are committed to gaining deeper self-awareness and the ability to remain open to others (Chapter 1)

Personal time constraints a barrier to change that stems from people not having the amount of time required for implementing strategic change (Chapter 11)

Person-job fit theory a match between an employee's abilities, needs, and values and the organizational demands, rewards, and values (Chapter 4)

Peter Senge author of the popular book *The Fifth Discipline*, which identifies the following ingredients of learning organizations: challenging of mental models, personal mastery, systems thinking, shared vision, and team learning (Chapter 1)

Physiological needs the lowest needs on Maslow's hierarchy of needs; the most basic of all human needs are in this category, such as food, water, and physical well-being (Chapter 1)

Piecework programs that tie a worker's earnings to the number of units produced (Chapter 6)

Planning involves choosing tasks that must be performed to attain organizational goals, outlining how the tasks must be performed, and indicating when they should be performed (Chapter 2)

Political barriers arise from power conflicts, such as vested interests, refusal to share information or resources, differences between departments or divisions, and even personal differences (Chapter 11)

Positive feedback used to reinforce desired behavior, it includes giving information or input to a staff member about a job well done (Chapter 7)

Positive reinforcement a reward or other desirable consequence that follows behavior (Chapter 5)

Primacy effect the tendency for the first items presented in a series to be remembered better, more easily, or for them to be more influential than those presented later in the series (Chapter 4)

Probability of effect the likelihood that, if a decision is implemented, it will lead to the harm or benefit predicted (Chapter 8)

Problem-solving teams designed for specific issues, they help to solve organizational problems by offering suggestions and advice to management (Chapter 9)

Procedural justice refers to the idea of fairness and transparency in the processes that resolve disputes and allocate resources (Chapters 5 and 8)

Production blocking occurs when you have an idea but have to wait to share it because someone else is already presenting an idea to the group (Chapter 11)

Production-oriented leader (task-orientated style) emphasizes the technical or task aspects of the job, focusing concerns on the accomplishment of the group's tasks (Chapter 10)

Profit sharing plans that distribute a portion of the firm's profits to all employees at a predetermined rate (Chapter 6)

Programmed decisions involve situations that have occurred before, and for which policies and processes already exist on how to handle the decision; they are routine and almost automatic (Chapter 8)

Proximity of effect the sense of closeness (social, cultural, psychological, or physical) that the decision maker has for victims or beneficiaries of the decision (Chapter 8)

Punishment an unpleasant, or aversive, consequence of a behavior (Chapter 5)

Rational decision making a systematic process in which managers define problems, evaluate alternatives, and choose the optimal solution that provides the maximum benefits to their organization (Chapter 8)

Rational persuasion strategy this approach attempts to convince individuals, through rational argument, information, and facts, that the overall benefit to change is to their personal advantage; when successful, change can be relatively easy to accomplish (Chapter 11)

Receiver receives message, decodes message, interprets message, and may provide feedback (Chapter 7)

Reflecting feelings involves indicating that you understand the sender's emotions (Chapter 7)

Regulative controls the process of governing employee behavior by establishing bureaucratic controls, financial controls, and quality controls (Chapter 12)

Relative comparisons each of the listed criteria is compared directly with every other criterion (Chapter 8)

Representative participation the most widely legislated form of employee involvement around the world (Chapter 6)

Resistance forces forces that support the status quo of the organization; they do not want change (Chapter 11)

Resistance to change caused by self-interest, misunderstanding and distrust, and general intolerance for change (Chapter 11)

Resolving the most direct and sometimes the most difficult solution in managing conflict; with this technique, the manager identifies the differences between the manager and the employees, and then listens to the viewpoints of others in an honest effort to understand, rather than argue; next, both sides identify the issues about change on which they agree, and the ways they can both benefit from implementing the change to reflect the ideas on which they agree (Chapter 11)

Resource allocator responsible for the allocation of the organization's resources (Chapter 2)

Reward constitutes many of the inducements that organizations provide to employees as their part of the psychological contract (Chapter 6)

Reward system consists of all organizational components, including people, processes, rules and procedures, and decision-making activities involved in allocating compensation and benefits to employees, in exchange for their contributions to the organization (Chapter 6)

Risk propensity the degree to which a person is willing to take chances and to make risky decisions with a higher probability of failure, given that there is a worthwhile reward in the chance of success (Chapter 3)

Robert Owens a British industrialist, he strove to better the conditions for industrial workers; he improved working conditions, increased minimum age for child workers, introduced meals for employees, and shortened the workday (Chapter 1)

Role a set of behaviors or tasks a person is expected to perform because of the position they hold in a group or organization (Chapter 2)

Root cause analysis a method of problem solving that identifies the preliminary cause of a discrepancy or deviation (Chapter 12)

Safety needs the second level of Maslow's hierarchy of needs; these needs include the need for basic security, stability, protection, and freedom from fear (Chapter 1)

Satisfice when managers don't maximize, choosing the alternative that is simply "good enough" (Chapter 8)

Scientific management era arose in the early 1900s because of the need to increase productivity and efficiency; the emphasis then was on trying to find the best way to get the most work done by examining how the work process was actually accomplished (Chapter 1)

Selective perception the tendency to notice and accept stimuli consistent with our experiences, values, beliefs, and expectations, while discounting or ignoring stimuli that is inconsistent with our beliefs (Chapters 4 and 7)

Self-actualization needs the highest level of needs, they involve a person realizing his or her full potential and becoming all that he or she can be (Chapters 1 and 5)

Self-efficacy a person's belief about their capabilities to perform a task (Chapter 3)

Self-esteem the extent to which a person believes that he or she is a worthwhile and deserving individual (Chapter 3)

Self-fulfilling prophecy a knowledge-of-predictor bias results in a self-fulfilling prophecy, where an individual gets more attention due to bias that has been placed upon them (Chapter 4)

Self-managed teams the greatest degree of autonomy that can be awarded, as they generally take on supervisory responsibilities (Chapter 9)

Self-monitoring the extent to which people try to control the way they present themselves to others (Chapter 3)

Self-serving bias occurs when individuals and organizations tend to attribute their own success to internal factors, such as ability and effort, while placing the blame for failure on external factors, such as bad luck or unproductive coworkers (Chapter 4)

Shared power strategy a collaborative approach that empowers people in a process of participation that identifies values, assumptions, and goals from which support for change will emerge (Chapter 11)

Shared vision members have a common purpose of the organization and a sincere commitment to accomplish said purpose (Chapter 1)

Similar-to-me effect the fact of life that people tend to like others similar to themselves (Chapter 4)

Social consensus the amount of public agreement that a proposed decision is bad or good (Chapter 8)

Social needs after the physical and safety needs are satisfied and are no longer motivators, the need for belonging, affection, and love emerges as a primary motivator (Chapter 1)

Socio-emotional roles include individual actions that help communication, participation, and preserve team relationships (Chapter 9)

Spokesman a role where managers share the information (plans, policies, results, etc.) within and outside of the organization, and may also serve as experts on the organization's industry (Chapter 2)

Standardization of outputs involves providing employees with precise product, quality, and performance specifications (Chapter 12)

Standardization of work processes involves reducing or eliminating an employee's discretion to deviate from the set standards by developing rules, regulations, and operating procedures (Chapter 12)

Standardization of work skills involves hiring employees who possess the necessary skills, knowledge, and abilities to perform the tasks required by the job and make necessary decisions regarding those tasks (Chapter 12)

Standards a basis of comparison for measuring the degree to which workplace performance is satisfactory or unsatisfactory (Chapter 12)

Standards of performance set as performance targets against which actual performance will be measured (Chapter 12)

Stepladder technique a simple and effective tool to improve group decision making by determining how and when people enter the decision-making process (Chapter 9)

Stereotyping categorizing or labeling people on the basis of a single attribute; while typically negative, it can be a benefit (Chapter 4)

Storming often distinguished by disagreements and conflicts (Chapter 9)

Stress the body's reaction to a change that requires a physical, mental, or emotional adjustment or response (Chapter 11)

Stressor an environmental demand that causes people to feel stress (Chapter 11)

Stretch goals goals that are a little more difficult to achieve (Chapter 12)

Subsystems support the work of the larger system (Chapter 1)

Summarizing involves providing a review of the sender's main points or emotions (Chapter 7)

Supportive colleagues the opportunity for social interaction with friendly coworkers and supervisors adds greatly to the dimension of job satisfaction (Chapter 4)

Supportive working conditions the working environment is very important in terms of safety, health, and wellness of employees (Chapter 4)

System a number of interdependent parts functioning as a whole for some purpose (Chapter 1)

Systemic barrier an organizational structure that is highly bureaucratic, consisting of multiple layers, burdensome procedures, and rigid rules and requirements that will create a "natural" barrier to change (Chapter 11)

Systems approach based on the general systems theory proposed in the 1940s by biologist Ludwig von Bertalanffy, the main premise is that to understand the operations of an entity, the entity must be viewed as a system (Chapter 1)

Systems thinking every organizational member understands his or her own job and how the jobs fit together to provide final products to the customer (Chapter 1)

Task-related activities the critical management-related activities, such as short-term planning, clarifying objectives of jobs in organizations, and monitoring operations and performance (Chapter 2)

Task roles include individual actions that help the project stay on task and move forward (Chapter 9)

Team groups in which members work together to achieve a common group goal, intra- and intergroup conflict and cohesion, leadership, power, norms, interpersonal communication, networks, and roles (Chapter 1)

Team leaders a relatively new role in management that is the result of companies shifting to more self-managed teams (Chapter 2)

Team learning members work together, develop new solutions to new problems together, and apply solutions together to accomplish the plan of action (Chapter 1)

Team member diversity refers to individualism, such as variance in level of ability, experience, personality, education, and background (Chapter 9)

Team norms implicit agreed-on standards that regulate team behavior (Chapter 9)

Technical skills knowledge and proficiency in the trade required to get a job done (Chapter 2)

Telecommuting as close as it gets to the ideal job for many people, provides the benefits of flexible hours, freedom to come and go as you please, few interruptions from coworkers, and no commuting (Chapter 6)

Temporal immediacy the length of time that elapses between making a decision and when the consequences of that decision are known (Chapter 8)

Terminal values the goals that we work towards and view as most desirable (Chapter 8)

Theory X manager a manager with a negative view of employees, who assumes that they generally dislike work, lack ambition, act irresponsibly, resist change, and are untrustworthy and incapable of assuming responsibility (Chapter 1)

Theory Y manager this group of managers assumes that employees are trustworthy and capable of assuming responsibility, and also have high levels of motivation, creativity, and willingness to work (Chapter 1)

Theory Z also known as the Japanese management style, it was proposed by Dr. William Ouchi, who disliked Theory X and Theory Y and created a blend of the two, focusing on long-term employment, job security, informal control, and the happiness and overall well-being of employees (Chapter 1)

Top-level managers include boards of directors, presidents, vice presidents, CEOs, general managers, and senior managers (Chapter 2)

Total quality management encompasses organization-wide efforts aimed at installing and embedding an organizational climate of continuous improvement in the delivery of goods and services to customers (Chapter 1)

Transformational leadership when a leader transforms, or changes, his or her followers in three important ways that together result in followers trusting the leader, performing behavior that contributes to the achievement of organizational goals, and being motivated to perform at high levels (Chapter 10)

Type A behavior when a person who is aggressively involved in a chronic, incessant struggle to achieve more in less time and, if required to do so, against the opposing efforts of other things or people (Chapter 3)

Type B behavior Type B people never suffer from a sense of time urgency with its accompanying impatience, and can relax without guilt (Chapter 3)

Underlying assumptions represent the basic thoughts, attitudes, actions, and beliefs of the organization (Chapter 12)

Understanding feelings the receiver's desire to understand and reflect the sender's feelings (Chapter 7)

Unfreezing getting people to gain perspective on their day-to-day activities, unlearn their bad habits, and open up to new ways of reaching their objectives (Chapter 11)

Unrealistic optimism the tendency for people to believe that they are so smart they can do whatever they want and not worry about the consequences (Chapter 4)

Upward communication includes the communication that flows from lower levels to upper levels in an organization (Chapter 7)

Utilitarian view considers that ethical decisions should be resolved by delivering the greatest good to the greatest number of people, as long as the majority of those involved are helped and a minimum number are harmed (Chapter 8)

Values the underlying beliefs and judgments regarding what is right or desirable that influence individual attitudes and behaviors (Chapter 8)

Variable pay programs base a portion of an employee's pay on some individual and/or organizational measure of performance (Chapter 6)

Variable work schedules a variation on the traditional 9-to-5, Monday-to-Friday workweek, the two most popular are a compressed workweek and staggered work hours (Chapter 6)

Virtual teams composed of geographically and/or organizationally dispersed employees who use technology to meet and accomplish assigned tasks (Chapter 9)

Work group a collection of individuals operating towards a business goal with little or no collaboration between the members of the group (Chapter 9)

Work team a collaborative group of individuals with complementary talents and skills, joined together to accomplish a common organizational objective or goal (Chapter 9)

Works council a nominated or elected group of employees that represents a company's workers for the purpose of receiving information from and consulting with the company's management on decisions that affect employees (Chapter 6)

CPSIA information can be obtained
at www.ICGtesting.com
Printed in the USA
BVHW091241120919
558275BV00010B/187/P